C000049532

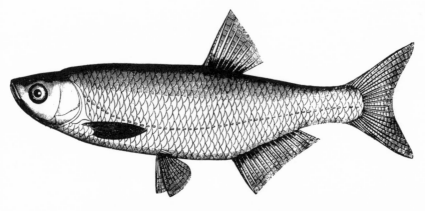

*Notes on Fishing*

NORTHWESTERN UNIVERSITY PRESS

*Studies in Russian Literature and Theory*

*Founding Editor*

Gary Saul Morson

*General Editor*

Caryl Emerson

*Consulting Editors*

Carol Avins

Robert Belknap

Robert Louis Jackson

Elliott Mossman

Alfred Rieber

William Mills Todd III

Alexander Zholkovsky

# Notes on Fishing

## and Selected Fishing Prose and Poetry

### Sergei Aksakov

TRANSLATED, INTRODUCED, AND ANNOTATED

BY THOMAS P. HODGE

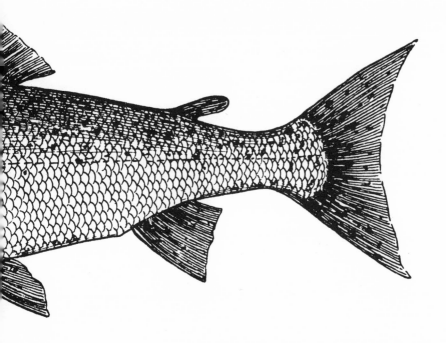

Northwestern University Press    Evanston, Illinois

Northwestern University Press
Evanston, Illinois 60208-4210

Copyright © 1997 by Northwestern University Press.
Published 1997. All rights reserved.
Printed in the United States of America
ISBN 0-8101-1366-X
Library of Congress Cataloging-in-Publication Data
Aksakov, S. T. (Sergeĭ Timofeevich), 1791–1859.
[Zapiski ob uzhen'e ryby. English]
Notes on fishing : and selected fishing prose and poetry
/ Sergei Aksakov ; translated, introduced, and annotated by
Thomas P. Hodge.
p. cm. — (Studies in Russian literature and theory)
Includes bibliographical references.
ISBN 0-8101-1366-X (cloth : alk. paper)
1. Fishing—Russia. 2. Fishes—Russia. I. Hodge, Thomas P.
II. Title. III. Series.
SH633.A5713 1997
799.1—dc21                                        97-14128
                                                     CIP

The paper used in this publication meets the minimum
requirements of the American National Standard for
Information Sciences—Permanence of Paper for Printed
Library Materials, ANSI Z39.48-1984.

Cover: Vasily Polenov, *The Abandoned Pond* (1879).
Tretyakov Gallery, Moscow, Russia.
Credit: Scala/Art Resource, NY

# CONTENTS

# ACKNOWLEDGMENTS

I offer my sincere thanks to those who took the time to critique the manuscript: Andrew Durkin, Rachel May, Adam Weiner, David James Duncan, Michael Katz, John Kolsti, Michael McNally, Grant Hiroshima, and Mel Hodge. For their advice on specific problems, I thank Ekaterina Lazareva, Konstantin Polivanov, Omry Ronen, Joyce Toomre, Karsten Hartel, Victor G. Springer, Julia Friedman, Elena Semeka-Pankratov, Nina Kochergin, and Fils. For their early encouragement of this project, I am grateful to Aleksandr Il′in-Tomich, Andrew Wachtel, Elizabeth Lieberman, Thomas Cushman, Susan Harris, Caryl Emerson, Gary Saul Morson, and Konstantin Polivanov. Hilary Teplitz and Lynn Stromski provided excellent editorial assistance. I also wish to thank the Kathryn W. and Shelby Cullom Davis Center for Russian Studies at Harvard University for its support, and the Davis Fund for Russian Area Studies at Wellesley College for funding a research trip to Moscow. I am likewise indebted to the staff of the Russian State Library and Book Museum in Moscow, and of the Widener and Houghton Libraries at Harvard University.

The people who advised me on this translation have only improved it; responsibility for the book's deficiencies is mine alone.

For her gift to my life and this work, my deepest thanks go to Caroline Johnson, who prompts a quotation from Walton: "Lord, what music hast thou provided for the saints in heaven, when thou affordest bad men such music on Earth?"

This translation is gratefully dedicated to Mel and Jane Hodge, who taught me to fish.

# TRANSLATOR'S INTRODUCTION
## Aksakov's *Notes on Fishing* in Russian Context

*Angling or float fishing I can only compare to a stick and a string,*
*with a worm at one end and a fool at the other.*

Attributed to Samuel Johnson

Sergei Timofeevich Aksakov is revered outside Russia for his great autobiographical trilogy: *A Family Chronicle, Childhood Years of a Bagrov Grandson*, and *Memoirs*. When these works arrived on the literary scene in the middle of the nineteenth century, they caused a sensation, but this was neither Aksakov's first triumph as a writer nor his first trilogy. Those distinctions go to the cycle we may conveniently call his "sporting trilogy": *Notes on Fishing, Notes of an Orenburg-Province Hunter*, and *A Sportsman's Stories and Memoirs on Various Kinds of Sport*. These writings, little known in the West, appeared first, and they achieved a level of literary fame their author had scarcely dreamed possible.

As the first and most painstakingly revised part of the sporting trilogy, *Notes on Fishing* deserves pride of place. It was Aksakov's first book, and his first major success as a writer, but its significance transcends Aksakov's own oeuvre and the borders of his native Russia. *Notes on Fishing* is a literary achievement that merits mention alongside such works as Juliana Berners's *Treatise of Fishing with an Angle*, Walton's *The Compleat Angler*, Gilbert White's *Natural History of Selborne*, Thoreau's *Walden*, Hemingway's *The Old Man and the Sea*, and Norman Maclean's *A River Runs Through It*. In short, it belongs among the Western classics of fishing literature and nature writing.

Sergei Aksakov (1791–1859) probably began work on *Notes on Fishing* in 1845, some seven years after his retirement from government service, and just after he had started to go blind. Family letters written in the autumn of that year mention that he was occupied with "a little book on angling." This was the commencement of Aksakov's most ambitious literary project after the short piece of fictionalized family history he had written in 1840 (the seed that would eventually grow into *A Family Chronicle*). The most informative early description of *Notes on Fishing* dates from November 1845, when Aksakov himself told his friend, the renowned Nikolai Gogol, of his goals for the work:

> I undertook to write a little book about angling not only in relation to its technical side, but in relation to nature in general: my passionate fisherman loves natural beauty just as passionately. In a word, I fell in love with my work, and I hope this little book will prove pleasant not only to the angling sportsman, but also to anyone whose heart is open to the impressions of early morning, late evening, luxurious noontide, etc. The wondrous natural world of the Orenburg region, as I came to know it forty-five years ago, will play its part. This project has enlivened and reinvigorated me.[1]

Aksakov finished his book by the end of 1846. After receiving approval from the censorship on 5 February 1847, it was published in Moscow in 1847 under the title *Notes on Angling*, and ran to 163 pages. The dedication read, "To my brothers and friends, N. T. and A. T. A—." Encouraged by the success of *Notes on Angling*, Aksakov finally published the second component of the sporting trilogy, *Notes of an Orenburg-Province Hunter*, in 1852, less than a month after Gogol, who passionately championed that work, had died. Aksakov dedicated that book to his brothers as well.

Aksakov's "considerably enlarged" edition of his first book, now called *Notes on Fishing* (literally, Notes on the angling of fish), came out in 1854. This edition passed the censor on 6 November 1853, and sported the verse epigraph from his "Epistle to M. A. Dmitriev" that Aksakov had unsuccessfully attempted to publish the previous year in the front matter of the second edition of *Orenburg-Province Hunter*. The Moscow censorship, nervous after foolishly allowing Turgenev to publish his supposedly subversive eulogy of Gogol in *Moscow Gazette*, had rejected Aksakov's proposed epigraph because the lines "I venture into nature's world, / The world of serenity and freedom" were deemed too libertarian. Fortunately, that opinion had softened enough a year later to allow the verse epigraph to appear, but only with the offending phrase "and freedom" ellided.

Now 274 pages long, the second edition of *Notes on Fishing* contained two entirely new chapters—"On Fish in General" and "Crayfish"—as well as a host of new material both inserted into the text and added in the form of footnotes. Aksakov's preface remained virtually unchanged, while "The Hook," "Bait," and "On Fishing Skill" were significantly supplemented; "Selecting a Swim" doubled in size, and "Boulters and Trimmers" tripled. To the chapters on individual fish species, Aksakov added short comments on spawning and biting habits, regional names, and favorable swims. "Gudgeon," "Ide," "Crucian Carp," "Perch," "Pike," "Taimen," "Trout," and "Grayling" were considerably expanded, usually with new paragraphs appended to chapter-ends.

In the early 1850s, Aksakov planned to publish a periodical he would call *The Sportsman's Miscellany,* but his proposal was rejected by the censorship. He gathered the material he had intended for that series and published it in book form. Aksakov's *A Sportsman's Stories and Memoirs on Various Kinds of Sport, with an Appended Article on Nightingales by I. S. Turgenev* thus became the third and final component of the sporting trilogy; its first edition appeared in 1855, the second in 1856. Turgenev, a literary sportsman even more famous than Aksakov, had befriended the aging nobleman in December 1850, and the two writers quickly developed a warm relationship based on mutual respect in matters both literary and sporting. Turgenev opened his contribution to Aksakov's *Sportsman's Stories and Memoirs* with a laudatory salutation: "I send you, dear and most esteemed S[ergei] T[imofeevich], a lover of and expert in all forms of sport, the following story about nightingales, their singing, their keeping, their capture, etc., transcribed by me from the words of an old and experienced hunter from among the house serfs."[2]

The third edition of *Notes on Fishing* (the last to appear in Aksakov's lifetime) passed the censor on 20 July 1856, with the scandalous word "freedom" at last restored to the verse epigraph. Aksakov added very little new material to this edition, as he noted at the end of his preface. The main change in this version of *Notes on Fishing* was the inclusion of illustrations and notes. Aksakov was now seeking to make his sporting books more scientifically rigorous and to open them further—in the spirit of the ill-fated *Sportsman's Miscellany*—to contributions by others. For these reasons he arranged a collaboration with the distinguished biologist Karl Frantsevich Rul′e (1814–58), a pioneer in evolutionary paleontology and zoology, who found engraved illustrations of the fish species, added taxonomic footnotes, and provided a concluding article entitled "The Fish's Upstream Journey." Unfortunately, Rul′e found it difficult to identify positively all the species Aksakov described, which resulted in some rather confusing footnotes and a dearth of illustrations: only eighteen of the twenty-five fish species had a portrait, and the engravings that did appear were of uneven quality and inconsistent provenance. Though Rul′e's scholarly afterword contained interesting generalized speculation on the origin of spawning-migration impulses in fish, its style and content were only tenuously linked to Aksakov's text.[3] Rul′e likewise added scientific footnotes to the third edition of *Orenburg-Province Hunter,* which was published in 1857, the last appearance of a component of the sporting trilogy before Aksakov's death in 1859.

The third edition of *Notes on Fishing* was reprinted, with Rul′e's material included, as a "fourth edition" in 1871, but it was not until 1886, with the publication of Aksakov's *Complete Works,* that the work received its first satisfactory annotation. Though the confusing Rul′e notes were reprinted, these were corrected and explained by ichthyologist N. A. Varpakhovskii, who also furnished new supplemental notes as well as an excellent scientific afterword, "A Short Description of the Fish Species Mentioned in S. T. Aksakov's *Notes on Fishing.*"[4] Here Varpakhovskii provided a classification key, detailed measurements of body parts, up-to-date scientific names, and even invited readers to send preserved specimens—postage paid—to the Academy of Sciences for identification: "If only one amateur fisherman sends fish from his locality to the museum—either as a gift to the museum or for classification—I will count myself rewarded in full for the effort I have expended in compiling the present article" (191). At last, Aksakov's *loshók* was properly identified as a minnow

(Phoxinus phoxinus), though Varpakhovskii believed—mistakenly, in my view—that Aksakov's *lokh* (*krasúlia*) was a form of trout rather than a taimen. Finally, Varpakhovskii initiated the tradition of replacing the unsatisfactory illustrations that had accompanied the third edition with engravings from Heckel and Kner's ichthyological classic, *Die Süsswasserfische der ostreichischen Monarchie* (Leipzig, 1858). These beautiful engravings, almost contemporaneous with the third edition of *Notes on Fishing*, were matched with all twenty-five of Aksakov's species, and have been reproduced in the best Aksakov editions ever since.

In the twentieth century, Aksakov's *Notes on Fishing* has been reprinted at least a dozen times, including many editions during the Soviet period. The finest modern edition appeared in volume 4 of Aksakov's *Collected Works* (Moscow, 1956), exactly a century after the definitive text of the third edition. S. I. Mashinskii, Aksakov's chief Russian exponent in the twentieth century, provided fine literary (as opposed to ichthyological) notes for that edition, drawing extensively on valuable archival material. Numerous mass-produced editions of *Notes on Fishing* continue to appear in Russia, and the affection that greeted "the little book on angling" Aksakov wrote a century and a half ago, as he went blind and old age ravaged his health, seems only to have grown deeper with the passage of time.

———

Though Aksakov clearly had serious literary intentions for *Notes on Fishing,* the book's enthusiastic reception in 1847 took him by surprise. When M. A. Dmitriev received a copy from Aksakov, he replied, "Your talent as a writer is such that even this subject becomes literary in your hands."[5] One of the first published notices appeared in Ivan Panaev and Nikolai Nekrasov's *The Contemporary*, the leading literary journal of mid-nineteenth-century Russia. "Lovers of 'quiet delight' will find in this brochure reliable instruction on the successful execution of their undertaking," wrote the anonymous reviewer. "The naturalist will glean from the author's descriptions fascinating details of our ordinary fishes' way of life."[6] *Notes of the Fatherland,* from which Nekrasov and Panaev had just defected, published a similarly laudatory review: "A sensible book which will be read with pleasure and utility by angling sportsmen. The author knows and passionately loves his subject."[7] The *Finnish Herald* made bolder claims for *Notes on Fishing*, calling it "a book that can be read, at leisure, with pleasure not only by sportsmen keen on angling, but also by any educated person."[8] The only negative review of the first edition appeared in *Library for Reading*, whose anonymous critic parodied what he or she perceived as Aksakov's snobbish approach: "There are people who sit down to angle only in order to catch fish; these people do not know how to fish. . . . Such fishermen only dishonor a noble profession whose proper goal is reflection, not a plate of fish. How sweet is the lofty, poetic dream of drowsy angling with a cast outfit in your hand, on a bankside rock. . . . These pleasures are accessible only to fishermen-philosophers. . . . The uninitiated mob does not understand them."[9]

The critical praise soon accorded *Notes of an Orenburg-Province Hunter* in 1852 helped earn redoubled critical enthusiasm for the second, enlarged edition of *Notes on Fishing* in 1854. "We now hasten to gladden our readers," wrote the *Moscow Gazette* in a review devoted mainly to *Orenburg-Province Hunter*, "with news of the imminent publication of the second edition of a previous work by the same author: *On Fishing* [*sic*]. This new edition is no mere repetition of the previous one; the small booklet has grown into quite a large one; its contents have increased by a whole third over the previous edition. Among new additions, the large chapter on fish in general is especially interesting."[10] Another reviewer wrote, "Five years before this one the first edition of this little book—useful and diverting in the highest degree—appeared, and indeed it is now so *enlarged* that . . . it is a superb manual—the only one in Russian—on the proper angling of fish, whose physiology the author has researched in the finest detail. . . . And all this is set forth as pleasantly and as captivatingly as is characteristic of the author of *Notes of an Orenburg-Province Hunter*."[11] Still higher praise came from Panaev, who reviewed the second edition of *Notes on Fishing* for *The Contemporary*:

There is so much simplicity and truth [in *Notes on Fishing*] that one could confidently trade it for dozens of the so-called novels, stories, and dramas that have enjoyed particularly noteworthy success in Russia of late. There is more poetry in this little booklet than you will find in whole volumes of the assorted poems and epics that have found favor and actually do possess certain poetic merits. *Notes on Fishing*, perhaps, has more significance for artists and *littérateurs* than it does for specialists, for sportfishermen.[12]

When the third edition of Aksakov's book came out, *Notes of the Fatherland* and *The Contemporary* published very favorable reviews yet again.[13]

The full acceptance of Aksakov's *Notes on Fishing*—and of his sporting trilogy in general—was also due in large part to the brilliant review of *Notes of an Orenburg-Province Hunter* that Ivan Turgenev published in *The Contemporary* in 1853. This essay is certainly one of the most insightful appraisals of Aksakov's art yet written. Turgenev had recently earned fame (and infamy) for his early masterpiece, *Notes of a Hunter*, a cycle of stories that had begun to appear in *The Contemporary* in 1847, and that were then gathered and published in book form in 1852. Turgenev's frank depiction of the pitiable lot of Russian serfs in *Notes of a Hunter* made his book a cause célèbre for liberals, and, along with his Gogol eulogy, landed him first in jail and then in exile on his country estate of Spasskoe. The magnificent natural descriptions suffusing Turgenev's book both supported his abolitionist agenda and established him as one of nineteenth-century Russia's most gifted prosaists.

The details of hunting and the hunter's quarry yield to descriptive art and political suggestion in Turgenev's *Notes of a Hunter*, and this seems to have made him especially grateful to Aksakov for writing in concrete terms about the sport itself—for leaving Russia's social ills out of the picture:

He looks upon nature (both animate and inanimate) not from some sort of exclusive point of view, but as one should look at her: clearly, simply, and with complete concern; he does not act the sage, use cunning or add extraneous motives and goals: he observes intelligently, conscientiously and keenly; he only wants to learn, to see. And before such scrutiny, nature opens up and allows him to "peep in" at her. You will laugh at this, but I assure you that when I read, for example, the chapter on the black grouse, it actually seemed to me that it would be impossible to live better than a black grouse. . . . I am extraordinarily fond of the style. This is real Russian speech: genial and direct, supple and deft. There is nothing precious and nothing extraneous, nothing strained and nothing sluggish—freedom and precision of expression are equally noteworthy.[14]

Turgenev was an avid hunter, but, as Aksakov himself declared in *A Sportsman's Stories and Memoirs on Various Kinds of Sport*, Turgenev detested fishing and therefore left no direct commentary on *Notes on Fishing*. His assessment of Aksakov's style in *Orenburg-Province Hunter*, however, is perfectly applicable to *Notes on Fishing*, in which Aksakov adopts precisely the same approach. Turgenev goes on to discuss overobservant, overrefined writers who seek to describe the hidden details of nature, and expresses relief that Aksakov is not one of them: "He does not act the sage, does not notice anything unusual, anything 'the few' strive for; but what he sees, he sees clearly, and, with a firm hand and forceful brushstrokes, paints a broad, well-balanced picture."[15] Then—in what might strike us today as outrageous hyperbole had it not been confirmed by subsequent generations of Russian critics—Turgenev likens Aksakov's style to that of Pushkin, Gogol, and even Shakespeare, at least in Edgar's description of the seacoast to blind Gloucester in *King Lear*. In late January 1853, Aksakov responded in a blushing letter that he "expected less praise,"[16] and inserted in the second edition of *Notes on Fishing* a subtle dig at Turgenev by including the phrase "slyly play the sage" dressed in italics.[17] It is clear in his review that Turgenev aims much of the critique at himself, suggesting that he lacks the Aksakovian virtue of shunning political subtexts.[18] Turgenev was the Westernizer par excellence, while Aksakov was patriarch of Russia's most illustrious Slavophile family. The two men, who were ideological foes, found common ground in their love of outdoor sport and literary art.

A few years later, however, Aleksei Khomiakov—the formidable Slavophile poet and theoretician—subtly claimed Sergei Aksakov for the Slavophile aesthetic camp. Khomiakov's obituary article on Aksakov offers a superb analysis of Aksakov's authorial heritage and strategy:

The simplicity of Pushkin's forms in the stories, and especially those by his good friend Gogol, influenced him [Aksakov]; all this could have been the case, and all this was the case; but there is no doubt that it never entered his mind—it could not enter his mind—to choose fishing lessons, even serious ones, as the subject for a work of art. The concept of art was removed: he freed himself of it entirely. A passionate fisherman deprived of his accustomed enjoyment by the vagaries of life, he wanted to recall years gone by, former quiet joys, and, owing to a temperament that was sociable in the highest degree, he wanted to communicate them, explain them to others—and a book was written, a book the author never dreamed would earn him literary fame. And the reader took it just as good-naturedly, without the expectation of artistic enjoyment, but simply in hopes of learning something about the art of fishing . . . and then, as he got a grasp of the text, with a strange sense of astonishment he noticed that the subject became more and more absorbing, that the whims of the water's currents and the floods of lakes and ponds became more and more alluring and beautiful; the fish themselves, from the common gudgeon to the rare taimen, grew more lovable. There were some people who guessed that there was art concealed here—true art; but the majority of simple readers—lovers of fishing—felt only a deep sense of gratitude to the author for his useful information and especially for his love of the sport they had in common. Their letters of thanks breathed this sense of simple-hearted gratefulness; but S. T. Aksakov had already acquired his literary fame, which surprised even him. They listened to him, and they listened with pleasure, with animation; he himself gave rein to his reminiscences, he himself began to be animated by them more and more, feeling that he had before him, so to speak, not merely cold, unseen, unknown readers, but sympathetic friends. The relatively narrow circle of the fisherman's reminiscences gave way to the reminiscences of a hunter. In them, Russia's natural world was spread out in wondrous beauty, and the Russian written language took a step forward, even after Pushkin and Gogol. Sergei Timofeevich's reputation was ensured and confirmed for good. Afterward, other subjects drew his attention, but he never lost what he had acquired. This infinitely important acquisition was freedom from artistic premeditation.[19]

Khomiakov's Slavophile reading of Aksakov offers as much insight as Turgenev's appraisal, and, in at least one important way, it offers the *same* insight: that Aksakov achieved art by abandoning art. Turgenev's "not acting the sage" and Khomiakov's "freedom from artistic premeditation" point to the same literary quality: the guilelessness of Aksakov's choice of a subject as "stupid" as fishing and the simplicity of its verbal description. "After the doctor's departure," wrote Lev Tolstoy of the most important intellectual in *Anna Karenina*, "Koznyshëv wished to ride to the river with his fishing gear. He loved angling and seemed proud that he could love such a stupid activity." Unlike Tolstoy's Koznyshëv, however, Aksakov is a master at concealing his "premeditation."

Khomiakov, like Turgenev, has a great deal to say about Aksakovian language:

But what are the basic elements of Aksakov's art? The first is language, in which he scarcely has a rival for correctness and precision of expression and for turns of phrase that are entirely Russian and alive . . . it was unbearable for Sergei Timofeevich to use an incorrect word or an adjective inappropriate to the subject he was discussing and which failed to express it. He felt incorrectness of expression as a kind of insult to the subject itself, as a kind of untruth in relation to his own impression, and he would rest easy only when he found the right word. It stands to reason that he found it easily, because this very demand arose from clarity of feeling and awareness of linguistic wealth. This strictness toward his own language, and consequently toward his own thought, gave all his stories and all his descriptions matchless clarity and simplicity, while it imparted to the descriptions of nature a truthfulness of color and distinctness of outline that you will not find in anyone else. Gogol was nearly the first to recognize this quality and he admired it when he listened to Sergei Timofeevich's first, still unpublished sporting reminiscences.[20]

Khomiakov's tribute to Aksakov's language hinges on his faith in the intrinsic greatness of the Russian language—another opinion he shared with Turgenev the Westernizer—and once again the Slavophile program is subtly advanced.

Linguistic precision is a hallmark of Aksakov's style in both the autobiographical and sporting trilogies; the passion of his search for the *mot juste* is evident on virtually every page of his prose. In 1847, one of Aksakov's first reviewers had noted the attention he paid to provincial vocabulary in *Notes on Fishing*: "Comparative lexicography will be indebted to *Notes* for pointing out many of the folk terms used for the same fish in various regions of Russia."[21] Writing in the 1880s, the prodigious literary historian Semën Vengerov also called particular attention to Aksakov's precise use of rich, concrete language:

> The Academy of Sciences is at present undertaking the publication of dictionaries of the language of our classic writers, beginning with Lomonosov. We have no doubt that if some day Sergei Aksakov has his turn, the dictionary of his language will be one of the fullest, one of the richest in subtle and various shades of meaning. And, of course, this dictionary will be rich and abundant not in abstract words, but in concrete terms necessary for the description of real qualities and traits. In a word, this will be the dictionary of a true artist who speaks not in allegories and tropes, but in images and pictures.[22]

This dictionary was never compiled, but *Notes on Fishing* is filled with specialized, local, technical, and folk terms that have indeed proved useful to general lexicographers: the Academy of Sciences *Dictionary of the Modern Russian Literary Language*—Russia's monumental equivalent of the *Oxford English Dictionary*—actually employs excerpts from *Notes on Fishing* as the first or only illustrative quotations for dozens of Russian terms.

Khomiakov is correct in pointing out that Gogol, who in his later years was strongly influenced by Slavophilism, admired Aksakov's sporting works. "Regarding your little book," Aksakov's daughter wrote to him in 1848 of Gogol's reaction to *Notes on Fishing*, "he said that although he has no interest at all in the subject, he nonetheless read the whole thing from cover to cover with great pleasure."[23] In 1851, Gogol wrote to Aksakov that his only wish was that his own characters in volume 2 of *Dead Souls* "might be as alive as your birds" in *Notes of an Orenburg-Province Hunter*.[24] After "invention," Khomiakov gives the third "basic element of Aksakov's art" as his natural ability to inject himself into seemingly objective narratives—to animate the inanimate world: "S. T. Aksakov lives in his works: if he is discussing a sunny day, you feel his joyous smile in reply to the smiling natural world. . . . He was the first of our writers to look upon our life with a positive, rather than negative, point of view. This is true, but it could not have been otherwise."[25]

---

Sergei Aksakov was born on 20 September 1791 in Ufa, Orenburg Province, a town founded in the late sixteenth century in the steppe country at the confluence of the Belaia and Dëma rivers. Ufa, one thousand miles east of Moscow, was at the center of Bashkiria—since 1992 the Republic of Bashkortostan—homeland of the Bashkirs, a nomadic Muslim people who speak a Turkic language similar to Tatar. The Aksakovs were an old gentry family of modest means, and Sergei's paternal grandfather had been lured to Orenburg Province from the Simbirsk region by the prospect of inexpensive, fertile land where crops and livestock would thrive.

Aksakov spent his early childhood in Ufa and his boyhood in the wild country 160 miles southwest, at Novo-Aksakovo, the estate his grandfather had founded. The settlement was located on the banks of the Great Buguruslanka River, some nineteen miles downstream from the headwaters and sixteen miles north of the town of Buguruslan. It was here that Sergei spent most of his time between the ages of five and ten, before entering the Kazan' Gymnasium in 1801.

Though it is somewhat fictionalized, Aksakov's autobiographical trilogy is generally thought to be accurate on the details of its author's early life and family relationships. In that trilogy, fishing is constantly mentioned,[26] and, significantly, "Bagrov"—the pseudonym that replaces "Aksakov"—is derived from *bagór*, the Russian word for "gaff." In *A Family Chronicle*, the account of Aksakov's father's generation, Sergei Aksakov writes that the Great Buguruslanka "seethed with all the species of fish that could bear its freezing water: pike, perch, chub, ide, even grayling and taimen were found there in abundance; there was an incredible multitude of every kind of beast in both forest and steppe; in a word, this was—and still is—a little piece of the Promised Land."[27] In this wilderness at the edge of European Russia, Aksakov spent so much time fishing and hunting with his father and his servant, Efrem Evseich, that it hampered his early studies. In *Childhood Years of a Bagrov Grandson*, Aksakov explains that the women of his father's family—most notably his Aunt Tat'iana—were also excellent anglers; in *Memoirs*, we learn that Tat'iana eventually marries a fellow angler and moves to an estate with fine trout-fishing. Aksakov's mother, however, openly hated fishing and could never understand her husband's appetite for the sport. According to *Childhood Years*, she felt jealous of the time he and Sergei spent outdoors, and often forbade the frail and excitable boy to go fishing. Young Aksakov therefore struggled constantly with the choice between the two loves of his boyhood—his mother and his fishing—and this tension made its way into *Notes on Fishing*: on the first page of his preface, Aksakov defended angling against precisely the imprecations he had constantly heard from his mother as he grew up.[28]

After leaving the Kazan' Gymnasium, Aksakov attended the just-opened Kazan' University from 1805 to 1807, but did not finish his degree. His schooling had left him as passionate about amateur theatricals as he was about outdoor pursuits, and in 1808 he moved to Saint Petersburg, where he worked as a translator in the civil service and plunged himself into the literary-theatrical whirl of the capital. There Aksakov became acquainted with the greatest poet of the time, Gavriil Derzhavin, and with the conservative arbiter of Russian language and literature, Admiral A. S. Shishkov, whom he later credited as an early pioneer of Slavophilism. Aksakov moved to Moscow in 1811, where he would become close to such renowned figures as the actors Ia. E. Shusherin and F. F. Kokoshkin, the novelist M. N. Zagoskin, the dramatists A. A. Shakhovskoi and A. I. Pisarev, and the composer A. N. Verstovskii. Even in this talented company, Aksakov gained a considerable reputation as a declaimer and storyteller. After enlisting in the Moscow militia to fight Napoleon's forces in 1812, Aksakov returned to Orenburg Province during the occupation of Moscow, then came back to Saint Petersburg in 1814.

In 1816, Aksakov married Ol'ga Semënovna Zaplatina, the daughter of a landowner in Kursk Province, and the young couple moved to Novo-Aksakovo, where their son Konstantin, the future Slavophile leader, was born in 1817. In 1821, Aksakov lived in Moscow, but in 1822 he moved the family to another family estate, Nadëzhdino (where his second son, Ivan, was born in 1823), but his attempts to succeed as a gentleman-farmer came to naught, and in 1826 he returned to Moscow and began working as a censor there in 1827. Aksakov was fired in 1832 for accidentally passing a veiled satire of the Moscow police; he then worked for the Konstantinovskii Surveying Institute until his retirement in 1838.

From the late 1820s through the 1840s, Aksakov and his wife hosted one of Moscow's most famous salons. It was at one of the Aksakovs' "Saturdays" in 1832 that Sergei met Gogol, who would become his close friend and literary hero. The Aksakov salon's regular visitors included some of the most important writers and thinkers of the day, and the chief topic of debate in their circle was the conflict between the liberal Westernizers, who felt Russia should turn to Europe for enlightenment, and the most conservative Slavophiles, who held that the native culture of Russia held all that was necessary. Among members of the former group who visited the Aksakovs were such luminaries as N. V. Stankevich, A. I. Gertsen (Herzen), M. A. Bakunin, V. G. Belinskii, T. N. Granovskii, and P. Ia. Chaadaev. In the Slavophile camp were Aksakov, his sons Ivan and Konstantin, M. P. Pogodin, S. P. Shevyrëv, Verstovskii, M. A. Dmitriev, Khomiakov, the Kireevskii brothers, and Iu. F. Samarin.

In 1843, Aksakov purchased Abramtsevo, a lovely estate northeast of Moscow with excellent fishing. As Aksakov's blindness and ill health grew worse toward the end of the 1840s, his late-blooming literary career gathered momentum. He wrote intensively at Abramtsevo, dictating his work to members of his family. The oral transmission of Aksakov's works resulted in a natural, clear, informal Russian liberally spiced with arcane, but precise and apposite vocabulary. In the 1850s, Aksakov continued his friendship with Gogol, cultivated his tie with Turgenev, and by 1856 was also receiving the young Lev Tolstoy. In the autumn of 1858, ill health prompted Aksakov to vacate his beloved Abramtsevo, and he died in Moscow on 30 April 1859.

Forced to give up hunting because of his failing eyesight, Aksakov had nonetheless gratefully continued to fish through the 1840s and 1850s, systematically recording and evaluating his own techniques, and comparing his angling experiences around Moscow with his halcyon days on the waters of Orenburg Province. The incredibly productive fishing of his boyhood and early manhood combined with the more scientific approach he adopted in his later suburban angling to produce a mixture of poignant nostalgia and clear-eyed technical expertise. That mastery—what Aksakov always referred to as "fishing skill"—is clearly evinced by his fishing success in later years; the author's fishing records for the summer of 1843 (17 June through 6 October), for example, tell us that he landed 375 perch, 733 crucian carp, 5 pike, 13 gudgeon, 53 roach, 55 dace, 7 ide, 1 chub, 48 bleak, and 11 tench, for a total of 1,301 fish.[29]

Aksakov wrote a good deal of poetry during the 1820s and 1830s, as well as numerous theater reviews. His only significant literary success prior to the creative explosion of his retirement, however, was "The Snowstorm" (1834), a critically acclaimed sketch depicting the effects of a blizzard near Orenburg; Pushkin drew on the story for a crucial snowstorm scene in his historical novel, *The Captain's Daughter*.[30] As we have seen, the popular sporting trilogy's components appeared from 1847 to 1855. *A Family Chronicle* and *Memoirs* were first published in 1856, followed by *Childhood Years of a Bagrov Grand-*

*son* in 1858. Throughout the 1850s, Aksakov also published important biographical, critical, and memoiristic sketches.

After Khomiakov, Aksakov's most perceptive nineteenth-century critic was Vengerov, who keenly understood the intermingling of Aksakov's personal experience and his art. Aksakov, Vengerov asserted, had two passions: "sport in all its forms—from collecting butterflies and catching fish to fox- and wolf-hunting—and the theater. . . . With regard to his passion for sport, one could say that it was this that made Aksakov a real writer."[31] Vengerov, who consistently contrasted the technique of Aksakov's sporting works with Turgenev's in *Notes of a Hunter*, had nothing but praise for Aksakov's disciplined artistic response to his literary success:

> Any other person in his position would probably have been carried away, would not have held firm within the humble boundaries of various technical instructions and suggestions on sport. But Sergei Timofeevich did not give in to temptation and, even though he knew, for example, that he had a masterly talent for writing natural descriptions, he did not abuse this talent and provided them in exactly the quantity required by the progress of his exposition. And that is why his second sporting book retained the chief attraction of the first: simplicity, directness, and freshness. . . . Any other writer in Aksakov's position, if he had wanted to interest the reader in sandpipers and gudgeon, would probably have resorted either to stories of some sort of unusual sporting occurrences, or to the comparison and similarity of the psychology of animals and people, as even very good writers do. . . . Sergei Timofeevich did not lay out for the reader all the details known to him. As an artist of great merit, he took only details that were absolutely characteristic, only those details that delineated the individuality of each bird, fish, or beast he described, and because of this his characterizations are so vivid and clear, because of this his sporting notes are not a collection of remarks by an idle sportsman, but a truly splendid gallery of animal *portraits*.[32]

Eventually, Aksakov did indulge himself by relating "unusual sporting occurrences" in some of the fishing literature he wrote after completing *Notes on Fishing*. These more conventionally entertaining works, which offer rich material in the vein of traditional "fish stories," are gathered together in Appendix 1 of the present volume.

––––––

Vengerov also captured the excitement that readers of Aksakov's *Notes on Fishing* and *Notes of an Orenburg-Province Hunter* must have felt in the middle of the nineteenth century:

> The sporting "notes" of Aksakov must doubtless be recognized as wonderful literary works in which a great talent for painting vivid pictures with words brilliantly manifested itself. For the reader of those years [the late 1840s and early 1850s] who approached both of these books in hopes of learning something about gudgeon or sandpipers and suddenly stumbled on first-class descriptions of nature, on characterizations of representatives of the animal kingdom expounded in wondrous language and sketched vividly, distinctly—for such a reader Sergei Timofeevich's sporting books were a valuable literary acquisition and could afford a great deal of artistic pleasure.[33]

*Notes on Fishing*, as Ivan Aksakov told his father in 1854, also possessed enough scientific validity to enter an ichthyological debate at Khar'kov University: "Tomorrow a certain Master's student's thesis defense is scheduled on some sort of fish fry, and [botany professor V. M.] Cherniaev, with your book in hand, intends to refute him or demonstrate that this fish is identical to the toppie or bluelet you described."[34] But Vladimir Nabokov, who was a distinguished lepidopterist, hinted in his novel *The Gift* that Aksakov lacked scientific rigor; near the end of chapter 1, Godunov-Cherdyntsev tells Koncheev: "My father used to find all kinds of howlers in Turgenev's and Tolstoy's hunting scenes and descriptions of nature, and as for the wretched Aksakov, let's not even discuss his disgraceful blunders in that field." The context suggests that Nabokov himself might have agreed with this pronouncement, even though Aksakov made very few outright "mistakes" in *Notes on Fishing*, such as his belief that zander and grayling are kinds of trout, and his apparent acceptance of exaggerated longevity claims for carp. On the contrary, Aksakov only ventures opinions verified by his own observations, and is always suspicious of fishermen's exaggerations. Though he lacked formal training in ichthyology, Aksakov's general approach—that of a learned country gentleman—could be informally described as scientific.

Vengerov's point on the pleasant surprise that awaited readers of *Notes on Fishing* is certainly valid: before Aksakov, Russia's homegrown sporting works were few and of poor quality, for the most part consisting of anonymous, short, clumsily written or translated instructions on various aspects of fishing or hunting.[35] "As far as I know," Aksakov boldly asserted in his preface to *Notes on Fishing*, "not a single line has thus far been printed in Russian about fishing in general or angling in particular that was written by a literate sportsman who knew his subject intimately." This statement is a deliberate swipe at the only important Russian fishing writer who antedated Aksakov: Vasilii Alekseevich Lëvshin (1746–1826).[36] Though the prolific Lëvshin frequently dabbled in belles lettres, he is chiefly remembered today—if he is remembered at all—as an old-fashioned writer of agricultural handbooks. In *Eugene Onegin* (canto 7, stanza 4), Pushkin jocularly mentions Lëvshin as a mentor to "Priams of the countryside." In the first edition of *Notes on Fishing*, Aksakov alluded comically to Lëvshin's *The Perfect Huntsman* (1779), and, in the second edition, twice mocked the doubtful ichthyological assertions Lëvshin had made in *A Book for Sportsmen* (1819).

Nowhere, however, does Aksakov acknowledge the most significant Russian precursor of his *Notes on Fishing*: volume 4, chapters 5 and 6 of Lëvshin's *Universal and Complete Art of Housekeeping* (1795). Lëvshin translated and adapted most of his handbooks from French or German, and this hefty work—a Russian adaptation of Louis Liger's *La nouvelle maison rustique*—was no exception.[37] In it, Lëvshin offers 49 pages of advice on fish culture (chapter 5), and another 48 on fishing techniques and fish species (chapter 6).[38] This latter section resembles Aksakov's work in scope and structure, but sorely lacks the depth and literary quality of *Notes on Fishing*. In his preface, Aksakov alluded to his knowledge of foreign fishing treatises ("In French and English we find many whole books on the topic and even more small booklets strictly about angling"), but claimed they had never been translated into Russian, which suggests he simply had no knowledge of Lëvshin's 1795 translation. Nonetheless, with his series of anonymous, translated fishing articles in Nikolai Novikov's *Economic Magazine* in the 1780s, Lëvshin at least earned the honor of being the first Russian writer to publish serious piscatory works in Russian.[39]

After Aksakov, Leonid Pavlovich Sabaneev (1844–98) produced the next most popular Russian fishing works of the nineteenth century in his frequently reprinted *Fishes of Russia* and *Fishing Calendar*, which first appeared in 1875 and 1885. These lengthy books were much closer to ichthyological and fisheries manuals than Aksakov's literary *Notes on Fishing*, but Sabaneev's writings too have become Russian classics. In his essay entitled "Clear Spring-water," the prominent "village prose" writer Vladimir Soloukhin (b. 1924) offers a modern appraisal of Aksakov and Sabaneev:

In the cultural life of nineteenth-century Russia, two books have had an amazing and enviable fate: Sergei Timofeevich Aksakov's *Notes on Fishing* and Leonid Pavlovich Sabaneev's *Fishes of Russia*. Neither book is a novel, fascinating topical narrative, or even belles lettres, but both books are nonetheless read with keen interest by generation after generation of Russians; they do not grow old, do not lose their significance, and, I daresay, their charm.

There are several reasons for this, it seems to me. Let's dwell on one of them.

First of all (though this is not the most important thing for this kind of literary success), there is thorough grounding in and knowledge of the subject. . . .

But not only by knowledge of the subject, or, to put it more forcefully, by the author's learning and the work's erudition, can the book's success be explained. It is perfectly evident that still another force is coming into play, that that force is love for the nature of one's native land.

If we glance at the history of Russian literature, poetry, painting, music, we immediately come up with dozens of names to which our notion of, and love for, Russian nature are connected: Pushkin, Lermontov, Gogol, Tiutchev, Turgenev, Fet, A. K. Tolstoi, Nekrasov, Lev Tolstoy, Aksakov, Savrasov, Shishkin, Levitan . . .

But in art—from poetry to landscape in a novel, from the art-song to the symphony, to say nothing of painting—this feeling expresses itself clearly and definitely. Meanwhile, love for the nature of one's native land and, generally, love as a spiritual and moral principle, can color and illuminate human activity not connected at all with the direct expression or display of love.

Aksakov's book on fishing, mentioned above, and the present subject of discussion—Sabaneev's *Fishes of Russia*— both confirm this. Not once do the authors of these books cry out, sigh, or confess their love for nature. On the contrary, in a very businesslike tone they describe concrete, practical things—the structure of a fish's body, habitat, food, spawning, biological characteristics, floats and hooks, bait and longlines—and meanwhile the feeling of love for the nature of their native land involuntarily springs up within the reader and washes over him as a clear, warm wave, because this feeling is imperceptibly dissolved in a businesslike narrative, and it colors and illuminates him because it lived in the soul of the one who wrote the book and now communicates itself to readers.[40]

Sincere love for fishing links Aksakov not only with zoologist Sabaneev, but also with other prominent Russian writers of the nineteenth century who happened to be passionate anglers, most notably the poet Apollon Maikov, novelist Ivan Goncharov, and dramatists Aleksandr Ostrovskii and Anton Chekhov.[41] Serving as a soldier in Semipalatinsk, Siberia, after his release from prison camp, Dostoevsky is known to have spent happy hours during the summer of 1855 lying on the grassy banks of the Irtysh reading Aksakov's *Notes on Fishing* and *Orenburg-Province Hunter* as a young friend fished the great river.[42]

One of twentieth-century Russia's finest nature writers, Konstantin Paustovskii (1892–1968), another passionate fisherman-author, described his abiding love for Aksakov and his work. In the late 1940s and early 1950s, Paustovskii wrote a series of four essays he called "fishing notes" and gathered them under the title, "In Memory of Aksakov." He opens "A Few Words about Fishing" (1948) by referring to a famous nineteenth-century "brother of the angle": "Chekhov never got angry if he was reproached for literary errors, but took serious offense when anyone questioned his ability as a fisherman."[43] In "The Great Tribe of Fishermen" (1952), Paustovskii begins his essay with a tribute to Aksakov:

> The old Russian writer, grandfather Aksakov, was, as everyone knows, an experienced and passionate fisherman. He wrote a magnificent book about fishing. It's called *Notes on Fishing*. This book is attractive not only because it splendidly conveys the poetry of fishing, but also because it's written in language as clear as springwater.
>
> I called Aksakov "grandfather." Up to now, it was customary for Russians to use that name for Krylov, the writer of fables. For his good-heartedness, serenity and insight, Aksakov has as much right to that affectionate name as Krylov.
>
> Aksakov was the first in Russian literature to write about fishing—that astonishing activity that makes a person come to know the natural world, to love it, and to live as one with it.[44]

———

Determining the genre of *Notes on Fishing* is no easy task. In his preface, Aksakov disavowed "treatise" and "natural history" as labels for the work, calling it instead "neither more nor less than the simple notes of a passionate sportsman." "Notes" (*zapiski*) have constituted something of a catch-all genre in Russia; the definitive register of Russian literature lists more than 250 "notes"-titles published since 1801.[45] The genre was embraced by all the canonical Russian writers of the nineteenth century—Pushkin, Gogol, Turgenev, Dostoevsky, Tolstoy—and was employed for both fiction and nonfiction.

The structure of *Notes on Fishing* is simple and logical. Aksakov begins with a preface in which he defends angling and outlines his motives for writing such a book. This is followed by eleven short chapters on the various components of a good fishing outfit as well as on selecting a promising place to fish. Next come two long chapters on the skills necessary for successful angling, and on fish behavior. At the heart of the book are Aksakov's twenty-five chapters on important Russian fish species, each of which is carefully, lovingly described. Name origins, size, shape, color, spawning cycles, general habits, fishing strategies, and cooking advice are included in nearly all these chapters; occasionally, restrained fishing-stories are included. Crayfish, a favorite delicacy of Russians and of their piscine quarry as well, are accorded their own chapter before the concluding sections on set-lines and lures. Throughout *Notes on Fishing*, lyrical digressions—made all the more vivid by their pragmatic context—season the text with welcome modulations in tone and thematics. The result is an extraordinarily versatile book. *Notes on Fishing* is, among other things, an angling primer, a biological field guide, a culinary manual, a collection of literary nature-sketches, a memoir, and a philosophical case study.

As Russia's best-loved classic of fishing literature, Aksakov's book is often compared to Izaak Walton's masterpiece, *The Compleat Angler; or, The Contemplative Man's Recreation*, first published in 1653.[46] Readers familiar with *The Compleat Angler* will immediately sense the analogy to be made between *Notes on Fishing* and the Walton classic. Both works began as short booklets, then achieved immense popularity and went through numerous enlarged editions; both works were written by baitfishermen; both works open with defenses of angling before moving on to systematic discussions of important species of gamefish; both works enlist the aid of collaborators in late editions; both works subtly endorse ideological causes (Walton's "Great Tew" Christian communitarianism and Aksakov's Slavophilism); the language of both works has been especially praised; and both works generally strive for a tone of serenity, civility, and friendliness.

The differences, though, are numerous. There was already a long tradition of distinguished piscatory writing in England when Walton wrote his nonpareil of the genre; Aksakov, as we have seen, was really the founder of his nation's fishing literature. Walton frequently showed little regard for protection of the natural environment (consider the passages on slaughtering otters), while Aksakov's work boasts a more conscious and consistent sense of ecological propriety—almost an early Russian form of conservationism. Perhaps most significant, Aksakov's *Notes on Fishing* lacks the polyphonic structure of *The Compleat Angler*. The Russian writer has no Piscator, Venator, or Auceps, no comely milkmaids, no cheery inns, no dramatized dialogues, no stage directions, no interpolations of poetry, no flights of theological ecstasy.

Instead, *Notes on Fishing* is a monologue, erudite and inspired, by a single, confident intelligence who warmly invites the reader to view natural phenomena—and their skillful human manipulation—through the prism of Aksakov's systematic mind and congenial spirit. Literary and social comments, old friends, fishing companions, and fondly remembered places and times are all introduced into the text, but these refreshing asides appear quietly, as organic extensions of the author's unforced stream of expert commentary. All the qualities enumerated by Aksakov's Russian admirers—his authority, clarity, artlessness, eloquence, self-discipline, restraint, and love—are conveyed to the reader directly, intimately, often with a poignant sense of solitude. Aksakov, the gifted dramatic reader and lifelong devotee of the theater, shuns theatrical device in *Notes on Fishing*. The result is a fishing book without rival in Russia, and with few peers in Europe.

### NOTES

1. S. T. Aksakov's letter of 22 November 1845 to N. V. Gogol', *Istoriia moego znakomstva s Gogolem,* in *Sobranie sochinenii v chetyrëkh tomakh* (Moscow: Gosudarstvennoe izdatel'stvo khudozhestvennoi literatury, 1956), 3:326.

2. I. S. Turgenev, "O solov'iakh," *Polnoe sobranie sochinenii i pisem v dvadtsati vos'mi tomakh: Sochineniia* (Moscow: Izdatel'stvo Nauka, 1967), 14:172.

3. K. F. Rul'e, "Khod ryby protiv techeniia vody," in *Zapiski ob uzhen'e ryby,* 3d ed. (Moscow: V universitetskoi tipografii, 1856), 326–45.

4. S. T. Aksakov, *Polnoe sobranie sochinenii* (Saint Petersburg: 1886), 5:174–91; Varpakhovskii's notes appear on 192–95.

5. S. I. Mashinskii, *S. T. Aksakov: Zhizn' i tvorchestvo,* 2d ed. (Moscow: Khudozhestvennaia literatura, 1973), 314.

6. *Sovremennik* 6 (1847): 114.

7. *Otechestvennye zapiski* 52 (1847): 127.

8. *Finskii vestnik* 18 (June 1847); quoted from A. G. Gornfel'd, "Okhotnich'i sochineniia S. T. Aksakova," in *Sobranie sochinenii*, by S. T. Aksakov (Saint Petersburg: Tipolitografiia Tovarischestva Prosveshchenie, 1910), 5:4.

9. *Biblioteka dlia chteniia* 82 (May 1847); quoted from Gornfel'd, "Okhotnich'i sochineniia S. T. Aksakova," 5:4.

10. *Moskovskii vestnik*, no. 28 (1854); quoted from *Sergei Timofeevich Aksakov: Ego zhizn' i tvorchestvo*, ed. V. I. Pokrovskii, 2d ed. (Moscow: Sklad v knizhnom magazine V. Spiridonova i A. Mikhailova, 1912), 78.

11. *Trudy Imperatorskogo Vol'nogo Ekonomicheskogo Obshchestva* 2 (1854):98–99.

12. *Sovremennik*, no. 8 (1854): 130–31; quoted from Mashinskii, *S. T. Aksakov*, 314.

13. *Otechestvennye zapiski* 110, no. 1 (1857): 50–51; *Sovremennik* 61 (1857): 43.

14. I. S. Turgenev, *Polnoe sobranie sochinenii*, 5:416, 418.

15. Ibid., 419.

16. Ibid., 644.

17. See note 25 in *Notes on Fishing*.

18. See S. A. Vengerov, "Sergei Timofeevich Aksakov," in *Kritiko-biograficheskii slovar' russkikh pisatelei i uchënykh (ot nachala russkoi obrazovannosti do nashikh dnei)* (Saint Petersburg: Semënovskaia Tipolitografiia I. Efrona, 1889), 1, nos. 1–21:185.

19. A. S. Khomiakov, "Sergei Timofeevich Aksakov," first published in *Russkaia beseda*, no. 3 (1859): i–viii; quoted from A. S. Khomiakov, *O starom i o novom: Stat'i i ocherki*, Biblioteka "Liubiteliam rossiiskoi slovesnosti": Iz literaturnogo naslediia (Moscow: Sovremennik, 1988), 409–10.

20. Ibid., 411–12.

21. From the 1847 review in *Sovremennik;* quoted from Pokrovskii, *Sergei Timofeevich Aksakov*, 77.

22. Vengerov, "Sergei Timofeevich Aksakov," 188.

23. "Gogol' v neizdannoi perepiske sovremennikov," *Literaturnoe nasledstvo* [Moscow] 58 (1952): 706.

24. N. V. Gogol''s letter of 20 September 1851 to S. T. Aksakov, in *Polnoe sobranie sochinenii*, by N. V. Gogol' (Leningrad: Izdatel'stvo Akademii Nauk SSSR, 1952), 14:250.

25. Khomiakov, "Sergei Timofeevich Aksakov," 412–13.

26. For a useful survey of the fishing passages in Aksakov's autobiographical trilogy, see Arthur Ransome, "Aksakov on Fishing," in *Rod and Line*, The Travellers' Library (London: Jonathan Cape, 1935), 243–69.

27. "The Migration," in *A Family Chronicle*.

28. See note 5 in *Notes on Fishing*.

29. Quoted from Gornfel'd, "Okhotnich'i sochineniia S. T. Aksakova," 5:5n.

30. See A. S. Pushkin, *Kapitanskaia dochka*, Literaturnye pamiatniki (Leningrad: Izdatel'stvo Nauka, Leningradskoe otdelenie, 1985), 284.

31. Vengerov, "Sergei Timofeevich Aksakov," 154.

32. Ibid., 181, 186.

33. Ibid., 181–82.

34. Quoted in S. T. Aksakov, *Sobranie sochinenii*, 4:632–33.

35. The best bibliography of these scattered and extremely rare pre-Aksakov angling works—just over a dozen in all—is L. P. Sabaneev, "Ukazatel' russkoi literatury po rybolovstvu i rybovodstvu," in his *Rybolov-nyi kalendar'*, Chelovek i priroda (Moscow: Terra, 1992), 416–17.

36. On Lëvshin, see Viktor Shklovskii, *Chulkov i Lëvshin* (Leningrad: Izdatel'stvo pisatelei v Leningrade, 1933), 137–51, 249–62.

37. Louis Liger, *La nouvelle maison rustique, ou Économie rurale, pratique et générale de tous les biens de campagne*, 11th ed., vol. 2 (Paris: Chez les Libraires Associés, 1790). Volume 4, chapters 5 and 6 of Lëvshin's *Universal and Complete Art of Housekeeping* were simply translations of Liger (1790), vol. 2, part 4, book 1, 449–504 ("Des Etangs . . . ," and "De la Pêche").

38. The contents of Lëvshin's Chapter 6: On Fishing; On the Eel; On Lampreys; On Loach; On the Viper; On River Carp; A Method of Catching Pike with Trimmers; A Method of Catching Pike on Rod and Line; On Carp; A Method of Catching Carp on Rod and Line; A Method of Catching Carp Among Roots Under Banks; Another Method; On Gudgeon, Ruff and Other Separate Fish; On Chub, Perch, and Roach; On Salmon and How to Catch Them; On Spottie, Anchovies, and Sardines, and a Secret for Catching Trout; On Several Fisherman's Secrets for Luring Fish and Catching Them by Hand or Other Methods; A Method for Catching Fish by Hand; A Trustworthy Trap; A Method of Angling; A Method of Gathering Fish Into One Place; A Method of Attracting Fish into Nets; A Method of Catching Fish With Fire; A Way of Keeping Large Fish from Jumping Over the Net; A Method of Catching Fish with a Hand-Net; An Artificial Pen for Gathering Fish, and How to Catch Them in It; A Method of Catching Fish With Gates; A Method of Catching Fish in Top-Traps; On Catching Fish With the Net Known as the "Hawk," and on the Fishing Technique Called "Chain"; On Crayfish and How to Catch Them; On Frogs and How to Catch Them; On Live Baits Used on Rod and Line and Trimmers.

39. Lëvshin, who frequently translated for Novikov's publications, is the most likely author (or adaptor) of these items, especially when we recall that Catherine II's Free Economic Society, of which Lëvshin was a fellow, sponsored *Ekonomicheskii magazin* as well as Lëvshin's *Vseobshchee i polnoe domovodstvo;* see Lëvshin's comments on this in *Vseobshchee i polnoe domovodstvo* (Moscow: Universitetskoi tipografii, 1795), 1:vi. The articles can be found in *Ekonomicheskii magazin* 4 (1780): 330–32, 337–39; 12 (1782): 314–16, 337–51; 20 (1784): 241–302; 28 (1786): 289–94.

40. Vladimir Soloukhin, "Chistaia kliuchevaia voda," in his *Volshebnaia palochka* (Moscow: Moskovskii rabochii, 1983), 174, 176.

41. See N. Koval', "Pisateli-rybolovy: A. N. Maikov i ego druz'ia," *Rybovodstvo i rybolovstvo*, no. 3 (May–June 1961): 51–53. Chekhov admired Aksakov's nature writing; see Mashinskii, *S. T. Aksakov*, 314.

42. A. E. Vrangel', "Vospominaniia o F. M. Dostoevskom v Sibiri," in *F. M. Dostoevskii v vospominaniiakh sovremennikov*, ed. K. T'iunkin (Moscow: Khudozhestvennaia literatura, 1990), 1:361.

43. K. G. Paustovskii, *Sobranie sochinenii v shesti tomakh* (Moscow: Gosudarstvennoe izdatel'stvo khudozhestvennoi literatury, 1968), 6:596.

44. Ibid., 617. Soloukhin's title "Clear Springwater" (see note 40, above) is taken from Paustovskii's phrase in the first paragraph.

45. *Ukazatel' zaglavii proizvedenii khudozhestvennoi literatury, 1801–1975* (Moscow: Gosudarstvennaia biblioteka SSSR imeni V. I. Lenina, 1986), 2:173–77.

46. See, for example, Arthur Ransome's comments in Ransome, "Aksakov on Fishing," 270, 276.

# NOTES ON TECHNICAL MATTERS

*The text:* I have chosen to translate the complete text of the last version of *Notes on Fishing* Aksakov was able to supervise in his lifetime: the third edition, 1856. This edition was supplied with footnotes and an afterword by the Russian biologist Karl Rul'e, but I omit these (see Translator's Introduction). The only previous English edition is Arthur Ransome's seventeen-page collection of paraphrases and translated excerpts in *Rod and Line* (London: Jonathan Cape, 1929).

The two appendices contain translations, arranged in chronological order, of other fishing works by Aksakov that appeared separately from *Notes on Fishing.* Appendix 1 presents Aksakov's fishing prose, while Appendix 2 contains freely rhythmic prose translations of his fishing poetry. As the numerous cross-references in the endnotes will make clear, these supplementary works are closely related to a host of passages in both *Notes on Fishing* and the autobiographical trilogy (*A Family Chronicle, Childhood Years of a Bagrov Grandson,* and *Memoirs*).

*Illustrations:* For the third edition of *Notes on Fishing,* K. F. Rul'e supplied engraved illustrations for eighteen of the fish species Aksakov discussed. These engravings, which apparently came from a variety of sources, were uneven in quality and of unknown provenance. For this translation I therefore follow the practice, established in 1886 by N. A. Varpakhovskii, of borrowing illustrations from a nearly contemporaneous ichthyological work: Johann Jakob Heckel and Rudolf Kner, *Die Süsswasserfische der ostreichischen Monarchie* (Leipzig: W. Englmann, 1858) (see Translator's Introduction). Only the taimen chapter obtains its illustration from a different source: L. P. Sabaneev, *Zhizn' i lovlia presnovodnykh ryb* (Kiev: Gosudarstvennoe izdatel'stvo sel'skokhoziastvennoi literatury Ukrainskoi SSR, 1959), 112.

*Approach:* Fishing tackle and methods can be extremely complex, and the conviction that subtle variations in these materials and techniques determine fishing success has long been a staple of writing on the subject. Detail, therefore, assumes tremendous importance in fishing literature. And because fishing practices and terms tend to be localized, there is little linguistic standardization of fishing vocabulary within cultures, let alone across national boundaries.

In *Notes on Fishing*, Aksakov reveled in the inherent complexity and diversity of fishing, but he did so without sacrificing the clarity, simplicity, and grace of his Russian. This is due in large part to the fact that the author dictated the work to amanuenses rather than writing it down himself (see Translator's Introduction). The result was a written text that preserved the simpler grammar and syntax of spoken Russian, but also possessed the precise terminology so dear to Aksakov the meticulous angler. In his preface to *Notes on Fishing*, Aksakov clearly expressed the hope that his *Notes* would be both pleasant and useful. Its colloquial lilt and charm, which make the work pleasant, and its specialized fishing terms, which make it useful, are particularly difficult to reproduce in English. For this reason, all previous translators of Aksakov's works into English, with the exception of Arthur Ransome and Alec Brown, have simply omitted or distorted any "technicalities" in fishing passages and concentrated on approximating Aksakov's fluid style. I believe that Aksakov, whose love for scrupulous descriptive accuracy suffuses every major work he wrote, is ill served by such an approach. I have therefore opted to retain as much technical specificity and consistency—as much literality—as possible.

*Readership:* In his preface, and throughout *Notes on Fishing*, Aksakov states that he intended his book primarily for anglers; my English version, accordingly, must first and foremost make sense to modern anglers. I am keenly aware, however, that the potential readership of this translation is very diverse, and could include literary critics, linguists, historians, folklorists, botanists, ichthyologists, naturalists, cookery enthusiasts, ethnographers, and so forth. I am equally aware, however, that an attempt to please everyone would ultimately please no one. I hope that non-angling readers will find assistance in the extensive endnotes, for *Notes on Fishing* contains a wealth of material for non-anglers as well as anglers, non-Slavists as well as Slavists.

*Terminology:* To honor Aksakov's insistence on terminological precision, I have sought the most exact English-language equivalents for his Russian terms. Because Great Britain is the English-speaking region whose fish species and fishing techniques most closely match those described by Aksakov, the closest equivalents tend to be British terms (*groundbait, swim, trimmer, float,* and so forth). I have not hesitated, however, to employ Americanisms (*snell, bobber, snag,* and so forth) when there seemed to be no exact British equivalent for specific Russian terms. Readers should be aware that obscure English terms in the text (*breamet, trimmer, boulter,* and so forth) are translations of Russian terms that modern Russian speakers find just as perplexing.

The gender of pronouns for Aksakov's fish in English poses a problem with no good solution. In Russian, the word for fish (*rýba*) is feminine, while roughly two-thirds of the names of the individual species are masculine. Employing both "he" and "she" as Aksakov did, which I attempted in early drafts, sounded ridiculous, while using English "it" for all the fish, which I also tried, seemed overclinical and drained Aksakov's "characters" of their renowned animacy. In English, most anglers refer to fish as "he," and it is standard practice in English fishing literature to use "he" for all fish unless reference is specifically made to females. I have adopted the latter practice as the most euphonious of the unsatisfactory alternatives.

*Neologisms:* Quite often, there exist no English-language equivalents at all—British or American—for the uniquely Russian equipment and species Aksakov describes. In these cases I have cautiously devised neologisms based on the etymology of the Russian term: *withe-trap, muzzle-trap, toppie, redling, gutworm,* and so forth. I have made every effort to fashion terms that sound as obscure or familiar to educated English-speakers as their Russian originals sound to educated Russians.

*Etymologies:* One of the cardinal themes of all Aksakov's work is the search for origins—familial, mythological, cultural, and so forth. In *Notes on Fishing,* a prominent manifestation of this theme is Aksakov's obsession with etymology: of the twenty-five chapters on fish species, he discusses fish-name origins in twenty-one, usually as the first topic to be addressed. I have therefore elected to include his linguistic theories in full, explaining them as simply as possible in the endnotes.

*Measures:* Aksakov consistently uses nineteenth-century Russian linear measures (*arshin, chetvert', vershok,* and so forth), and these I have simply converted to their equivalent lengths in the traditional English system; otherwise, this translation would have confounded anglophone anglers who wished to reproduce Aksakov's tackle or to have an immediate, instinctive grasp of the size of the fish he describes.

To express weight, Aksakov uses the old Russian "pound" (*funt*), which I translate simply as "pound." A word of caution, however: the Russian "pound" was one-tenth lighter than its English counterpart. Thus, when Aksakov discusses a fish of "ten pounds," it would tip an English scale at only nine pounds. But because the overwhelming majority of the weights in *Notes* are mere estimates, and because Aksakov consistently claims to be conservative in guessing the weight of specimens, I felt it unnecessary to recalculate a 90 percent value for Russian pounds; readers should simply keep in mind that "pound" figures in the text are inflated by 10 percent. I diverge from this practice only in those rare cases of fish weighing more than thirty English pounds. Aksakov treats these leviathans as record specimens of significance to sportsmen and biologists; here, I have exactly converted Aksakov's Russian weight (originally in *pudy*) into English pounds, hence, for example, the 49½-pound specimen mentioned in the chapter on pike.

*Format:* The general format of the book (including chapter divisions, placement of illustrations, Aksakov's footnotes, and so forth) reproduces that of the third edition to the extent that this was feasible. I have, however, altered Aksakov's original punctuation and paragraph breaks, when this added clarity to the English version. (In later editions, Aksakov himself chose to break his paragraphs and sentences into shorter and shorter units, to replace semicolons with periods, and so forth; my alterations along these lines continue that process.)

*Endnotes:* I have attempted to identify in the endnotes all persons and places not easily locatable by the reader; endnotes are also supplied for passages and topics that could aid the various specialists—Slavists and others—who might use this translation. The works of Leonid Sabaneev, nineteenth-century Russia's foremost expert on fish (see Translator's Introduction), and Lev Berg, Russia's most accomplished fish specialist in this century, are used in the endnotes as ichthyological authorities. I have also provided cross-references to all relevant passages from Aksakov's autobiographical trilogy.

*Transliteration:* In the text, the modern orthographical forms of Russian words, and of names of persons I deem to be culturally Russian (except for Russians whose names have traditionally accepted forms in English, such as Tolstoy, Dostoevsky, Nicholas I), are transliterated according to the Library of Congress system, but without diacritics (except for the umlaut over ë): hence Kivatskoe (not Kivatskoye), Buguruslan (not Boogoorooslan), and Shakhovskoi (not Shahovskoy), Dëma (not Dyoma), and so forth. In the endnotes, the Library of Congress system, without diacritics, is followed. In words being discussed as such, I mark the Russian stress. In the endnotes, I give the transliterated Russian titles of Russian works; English translations of those titles can be found in the bibliography. I diverge from this practice only in references to Aksakov's own works, for which titles and chapter-names are given in English in the endnotes.

*Dates:* Dates for events occurring in the Russian Empire before 1918 are given according to the Julian calendar (that is, "Old Style"); all other dates are given according to the Gregorian calendar (that is, "New Style").

Finally, I hope that Aksakov's book will be profitably used as a manual by modern anglers interested in testing the Russian master's techniques. Nonetheless, I entreat all readers to obey their local fishing laws and to practice catch-and-release angling. Under no circumstances should readers attempt the trimmering, boultering, trapping, netting, snagging, stunning, poisoning, shooting, or spearing of fish described herein.

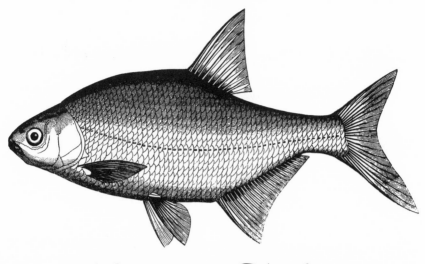

# Notes on Fishing

There is a time for business and an hour for amusement.

Written by Tsar Aleksei Mikhailovich in

*Rule of the Falconer's Way*[1]


Indulging sport is no calamity.

Sport outcompels coercion.

Russian proverbs[2]

TO MY BROTHERS AND FRIENDS,

*N. T. and A. T. Aksakov*[3]


There is, though, a conciliator,

Eternally young and alive,

A miracle-worker and healer—

I go to him sometimes.

I venture into nature's world,

The world of serenity and freedom,

The kingdom of fish and sandpipers,

To my own native waters,

To the expanse of steppe meadows,

Into the cool shade of forests

And—back to the years of my youth.

   Excerpt from "Epistle to

   M. A. Dmitriev," January 1850[4]

# PREFACE

I wrote these notes on fishing to reinvigorate my memories, for my own pleasure. I publish them for those inclined to be fishermen, for sportsmen to whom *fishing rod* and *fishing* are magic words that stir the soul. I believe my notes can be pleasant and even rather useful to them. The former, because any sympathy with our proclivities, any special view or special aspect of these pleasures, the occasional brightening of some murky feeling hitherto incompletely recognized, can and must be pleasant. The latter, because any experience or observation made by a person passionately devoted to something can be useful to those people who share his love for that same subject.

Fishing, like other forms of sport, can be both a simple pastime and a strong passion, but it would be out of place and useless to discuss this here. The Russian proverb puts it well and profoundly: "Sport outcompels coercion." Nonetheless, hardly any other sport is attacked so roundly and contemptuously as quiet, innocent fishing. One person calls it the sport of do-nothings and idlers; another, the amusement of old men and children; another still, the occupation of dullards.[5] Even the most lenient of judges shrugs his shoulders and says, pityingly, "I can understand hunting with borzois. In that case there's a great deal of movement, agility—some kind of liveliness, something active, even martial. And this is to say nothing of the splendid passion for card-playing. But catching fish? Well, I confess that this is a passion I cannot understand . . ." The critic's smile betrays his belief that fishing is, quite simply, ridiculous. So speak not only those unfortunate people who are born and raised in the city with no chance of escaping it, under the sway of artificial notions and intellectual currents, people who have never lived in the country, never heard about the simple inclinations of country folk, and possess almost no conception of sport. No, thus speak sportsmen themselves, but only about other kinds of sport. The latter I decidedly fail to comprehend. All forms of the hunt—with guns, dogs, hawks, falcons, snares, seines, nets, and fishing rods—

they all have the same foundation. All the various kinds of sportsmen should understand one another, for sport, which unites them with nature, should unite them with one another.

Some feeling for nature is inborn in all of us, from the rude barbarian to the most educated person. Unnatural upbringing, enforced doctrines, false tendencies, and sham existence all strive to stifle nature's mighty voice and often smother or distort one's feeling for nature. Of course hardly a single person can be found who is absolutely indifferent to so-called natural beauty, that is, to a lovely natural scene, a picturesque vista, a sunrise or sunset, or a bright moonlit night. This, however, is still not love of nature. This is love of landscape, stage-sets, prismatic refractions of light, and such things may be loved by the stalest, driest people, who have never experienced a single poetic feeling, or who have now irretrievably lost such sentiments. Their love of nature therefore ends with these trifles. Take such people to the secret canopy and cool shade of a dense forest, to the plain of an endless steppe covered with succulent, tall grass; or place them in a quiet, hot summer night on the bank of a river glimmering in the silence of nocturnal gloom, or on the shore of a sleepy lake overgrown with rushes; or surround them with the fragrance of flowers and grasses, with the cool breath of waters and woods, with the unceasing calls of night birds and insects, with all the life of creation. To them, none of this qualifies as "natural beauty," and they will understand nothing! Their love for nature is shallow and obvious. They prefer pretty pictures, and even then not for long; even as they look at them, such people already begin to think about their trifling affairs. They hurry home, into their filthy whirlpool, into the dusty, choking atmosphere of the city, and onto their balconies and terraces in order to inhale the fragrance of the fetid ponds in their wretched gardens or the evening vapors issuing from a roadway scorched by the afternoon sun . . . God help them!

Only in the country—not the outskirts of Moscow, mind you, but the distant countryside—is it possible to sense the full life of nature, undefiled by people. The country, peace, quiet, serenity! Artlessness of life, simplicity of relations! There you can take refuge from idleness, emptiness and insufficiency of interests; there you can flee from irrepressible external reality, from trivial, self-seeking errands, from fruitless, useless—even if conscientious—thoughts, worries, and cares. Here—on a green, mossy bank, above the depths of a river or lake, in the shade of bushes, beneath the canopy of a gigantic black poplar or curly alder quietly rustling its leaves in the bright mirror of the water where your fishing floats tremble or lie motionless—imaginary passions will subside, imaginary storms abate, prideful daydreams disperse, and impossible hopes fly away. Nature will assert her eternal rights, and you will hear her voice, hitherto drowned out by vanity, travail, laughter, shouting, and all the vulgarity of human speech! Along with the fragrant, free, invigorating air, you will breathe in tranquillity of thought, gentleness of feeling, mercy for others and even for yourself. Imperceptibly, little by little, your dissatisfaction with yourself will disappear, as will the disdainful lack of faith in your own abilities, strength of will, and the purity of your intentions. This epidemic of our age—this spiritual epilepsy that is so foreign to the healthy nature of a Russian, but that visits us for our transgressions—will be cured . . .[6]

But I have digressed from my subject. I wanted to say a few words in defense of fishing and a few words in explanation of my notes. Let's begin at the beginning: the accusation of vacuity and idleness is entirely unjust. A true sportsman is necessarily bound to be very hale and very active: consider the early rising, often before dawn; enduring the damp and cold weather or the sultriness of midday; tireless attention during the fishing itself; searching for suitable swims, to which end it's sometimes necessary to test them a great deal, venture out a great deal, and go out in a boat a great deal. Taken together, this is not to the taste of a lazy man. If one meets with idlers who have no real fondness for fishing but simply don't know what to do with themselves or how to occupy themselves, and who prefer sitting on a riverbank with a rod to running among the bogs with a gun, then is it really possible to call them sportsmen? Is fishing to blame, if such people resort to it? Another imprecation, that fishing is the amusement of old men and children, is likewise unfounded: no one has made himself a true fisherman in old age who was not one in youth. Of course, children almost always begin with fishing because other kinds of sport are less accessible at their age, but is it really true that children mimic the amusements of adults only when it comes to fishing? The feeble oldster or invalid who may not have the use of his legs is able to fish and in doing so finds a certain comfort for his meager existence, and in this we recognize one of the important and precious advantages of fishing over other kinds of sport.

It remains to defend angling from the charge that it constitutes an occupation of the weakminded, or, put simply, of fools. Good heavens, where are fools not to be found? What activities do they not attempt? In which intelligent and useful undertakings do they not participate? It doesn't follow that all other people who engage in the same activities must also be stupid. To point up the ridiculousness of such an accusation one can name several renowned historical figures who could hardly be suspected of stupidity but who were nonetheless passionate about "doing a little fishing." It's well known that our famous military leader Rumiantsev[7] was ardently devoted to this sport. Also well known is his response, uttered with feigned humility, to an important diplomatic question: "This affair has nothing to do with us; our business is to catch a little fish and take a few towns." The renowned Moreau,[8] who hastened from the banks of the Mississippi to the aid of Europe when it rose up against its conqueror, could not pass up a chance to go cod-fishing for a few hours—hours precious to the armed world that awaited him—so passionately did he love this sport. Louis Philippe—also, it seems, an intelligent man—devoted all the time he could spare from affairs of state to fishing at his charming Neuilly.[9]

Now let me explain my notes. As far as I know, not a single line has thus far been printed in Russian about fishing in general or angling in particular that was written by a literate sportsman who knew his subject intimately. In French and English we find many whole books on the topic and even more small booklets strictly about angling. In London there even exists a society of anglers that systematically researches the sport, perfecting it in every regard. Several works on the subject by Frenchmen are written colorfully and engagingly. But we have no translations of them, and if they were translated, they would afford more pleasure in the reading than utility in practical application. The reason for this is the difference in

climates, species of fish and their characteristics. The conscientious observations of a native angler, however insufficient
they may be, will thus enjoy an important advantage.

All this persuaded me to make the first such attempt yet in
the Russian language. There are many anglers in Russia, especially out in the countryside, and I'm sure that I'll find sympathy among them. I ask only that they remember, as they read
my little book, that it's neither a *treatise on angling* nor a
*natural history of fish.* My little book is neither more nor less
than the simple notes of a passionate sportsman: sometimes
superficial, sometimes one-sided, and always incomplete by
comparison to the exhaustiveness of the two aforementioned
genres.*[10]

1847

*I'm printing my little book in its third edition. Over the course of six years,
while constantly continuing to fish—with more attention and less animation—
I was able to make many new observations for the second edition and treat
more expansively and fully what was discussed too briefly before, as certain
sportsmen rightly pointed out to me. Over the course of the last three years,
however, I've been able to add almost nothing new. 1856.

# THE ORIGIN OF THE FISHING OUTFIT

Of all the kinds of fishing gear, rod and line were probably the first to be invented. Some savage, while wandering the banks of a river or sea to gather himself some humble victuals, or while carelessly resting in the shade of a steep bank and the trees growing upon it, noticed schools of fish swimming near shore. He saw the hungry fish greedily snatching the various insects and leaves falling onto the water's surface, and perhaps he himself threw them into the water, at first simply amusing himself with the rapid movements of the fish. It's entirely natural that the thought should occur to him that if something resembling a hook (of bone or strong wood) were to be concealed in the insects, and were attached to a thread made of animal gut or the fibers of plants, and that if the fish should strike and swallow such a bait, then the hook would hold fast and it would be possible to drag the fish out onto the bank. This is probably how the fishing outfit came into being. Even today it's almost the same in villages among the little peasant boys: a headless nail bent into the shape of a hook, or a hook made of wire or a pin, tied to a thread, with a little pebble instead of a sinker and a stick of dry wood or cane instead of a float ... this is almost the tackle of the savage. Even among us, among the most refined sportsmen, the fishing outfit in its modern form has strictly preserved all of its original basic qualities.

*Outfit* is a general term. It consists of the following parts: the rod, the line, the float (or bobber), the sinker, the leader, and the hook. We shall examine all these elements carefully, separately, and in order.

# THE ROD

It's hardly necessary to mention that by this term is meant a long switch or stick to which line is attached. Rods may be artificial or natural: I decidedly prefer the latter. The well-made artificial rod is fashioned from sea reed (cane) of varying thickness, or even simply whittled out of wood so that one section, being slimmer, may be inserted into the other, thicker one. The whole rod consists of three or four such sections, and they all screw into one another or are simply inserted into one another. The uppermost section is made of baleen or slender cane with a small wire ringlet on its upper end to which the line is attached. Such jointed rods, made well, with a butt and terminal ferrule, have the appearance of a handsome walking stick. At first sight one fails to recognize that this object is, in fact, a fishing rod.

In the first place, however, such a rod is very expensive. Second, it's unsuitable and unreliable for large fish since only its tip bends (that is, the top section, which is made of whale-bone or reed), and for landing large fish it's necessary that the bend gradually extend through the rod at least to its middle. Third, one must always hold it in one's hands or lay it on something dry: if you start to set it down in water, which is sometimes unavoidable, then it will get wet, swell, and, in time, even snap. Moreover, the damp segments, since they cannot dry out, are not easily inserted into one another. Fourth, all this must be done methodically and neatly—qualities opposed to the nature of a Russian: each time there's the disassembling, rubbing dry, inserting, screwing, unscrewing, tying and unty-ing the line and float, sinker and hook, and then the line again needs to be wound onto something, put into a case or little box and stored somewhere. . . . Isn't all this tedious and dreary? Just such jointed rods are fabricated in Russia from ordinary wood, but there can be no doubt that the latter are good for nothing. In many places composite rods are used: to a normal willow or walnut rod is affixed a tip of whalebone or slender juniper switch. Even in this case, however, we encounter the same drawbacks: the bend will once again be uneven and the tip will flex only to the point where it's attached.

Simplest and best of all are one-piece, natural rods of walnut or willow: the latter is sturdier and can be found more easily everywhere. They say that elm rods are also good, but I haven't had occasion to use them. The most reliable time for cutting rods is in the spring, before any leaf has yet opened, but when the tree's sap has already moved up from the roots and swelled the buds on the boughs. It's possible, however, to cut them at any time of year. One must choose shafts that are slender, long and straight. Carefully cut off all knots, leaving the main shaft undamaged along its entire length up to the last knot. One should take care that the rod not be thin at the butt-end. The lower half, running toward the hands, must be scraped, even planed, if it's too thick, while the upper half must be left in its bark *without fail.* Several rods prepared in this way should be firmly tied to a straight pole or board and in such constrained position cured, that is, dried indoors (or outdoors in a sheltered place), where they'll be touched by neither rain nor sun. Such a rod, if not broken out of carelessness, can serve for two or three years.

The choice and preparation of a good rod are extremely important. The straightness and flexibility of its upper end are crucial for successful hook-sets. Accordingly, the quantity of fish caught sometimes depends on the rod's quality, but its true merit is revealed only when a large fish takes on a light line.[11] Then one can admire how on a good rod, which has been half-bent into an arc, a huge fish will circle until the skillful hand of the fisherman wearies him and leads him to the bank where the other, free hand can grasp the prey, or, most reliably of all, capture it in a net.

Everyone knows what a net is, but here are the qualities it must have:

1. The net must be light.
2. For the rim to which the mesh is attached it's best to use iron and, to keep rust from devouring it, one can sew around it a sleeve of canvas and then sew the mesh to that.

3. The net bag should be fine but not close-woven.
4. The bag should not be small, but about twenty inches deep, so that the fish cannot jump out and so that he can be wrapped up in it.

# THE LINE

"Line" is the name given to a thread attached at one end to the rod and at the other to the hook. It's usually twisted from the hairs of a horse's tail, but there are lines of silk and of cotton, as well as those prepared from a kind of Indian plant,* which in their transparency perfectly resemble white horsehair. All these kinds of line have their advantages and disadvantages. I prefer the first, for its durability as well as the convenience with which fresh horsehair is obtained. It's not difficult to find someone expert in twisting or spinning from it a line of any thickness desired, but it's best to braid horsehair: braided line is sturdier, never twists and never gets tangled.[12] It's best to know how to do this oneself. Lines of silk and of cotton are not manufactured in Russia for sale. They're obtained from England and Austria; with a hook, float, and sinker, they're sold in stores for not less than two rubles fifty kopecks in assignats—too high a price.[13]

Such lines can be prepared at home. Any woman knows how to spin (by hand, or on the small wheels used to manufacture fine twines) a few silk or cotton—or, better yet, hempen—strands of any desired thickness or length. The advantage of such lines is that, being knotless and having no elasticity, they coil according to the water's motion and vary the appearance of a small baited worm or some other morsel, making it look natural, as though it were stirring. But when the bait and the end of a green silk line lie on the bottom, the line perfectly resembles the fibers of a long aquatic moss called "water silk." It must be confessed that fish take keenly on such lines, but, on the other hand, they rot through fairly quickly and tangle unbearably, which takes up a great deal of time and is dreadfully vexing. Both of these shortcomings can be mitigated somewhat by steeping the lines in melted

*This is what rumor previously led me to believe, but now I think that this is silkworm gut fashioned according to some special method.

wax,* but because of this they will partially lose the "fluttery" property that makes them alluring to fish.

With regard to line made from the Indian plant, fine as horsehair, its entire advantage consists in transparency and lightness. If the bait is also light (for example flies, grasshoppers and the like), then it stays up over all depths of water and floats for a long time at the surface without sinking. It lacks, however, the *flutteriness* of silk and cotton lines and is better suited to floatless angling for small fish, especially in clear waters, around midday, when fish linger at the surface. Such a line (whether made from the Indian plant or silkworm gut) is at first very strong, and, with the help of a good rod and due caution, one can land a fish of four or even five pounds on it. But this line soon gets mossy; that is, it becomes rough, and in places grows thin. As it dries up in the sun, it cracks lengthwise at bends and becomes unreliable, even dangerous, for catching good-sized fish. They say it's possible to avert all this by wiping the line dry each time after fishing and by rubbing it with oil, but I, true to my carefree Russian nature, have never tried this and have lost both fish and tackle many times; I'll discuss this in more detail in the entry on leaders.** And so we turn to lines of horsehair. Those acquired from abroad are very good, but, on the other hand, they're also very expensive and not available in sufficiently varied thicknesses. Those purchased in Russian shops are usually spun unevenly and often from old hairs that are no longer sound, but you can tell this by their yellowish color. And so it's best to prepare them at home.

*Here again it must be said that such a line lacks durability: the wax will soon come off and the line will start to get fouled as before. The wax, however, can be reapplied.
**In 1853 I was brought a present from Le Havre of many wondrous lines, very fine and translucent, having at the same time (when they're dry) a certain elasticity and the resonance of a musical instrument's string. I used them for a whole year and must say that at first they were astonishingly strong and could withstand the largest fish, but after about four months of everyday fishing, they rot through and require replacement. When damp, they become as soft as silk, but when dry they regain their stiffness; they're woven from several extremely fine filaments, apparently raw ones. In Le Havre they call them "American." Fish take very keenly on them. Perhaps these are the fibers of some American plant.

It's necessary to pluck the hairs from the tail of a white* horse. Choose the longest, most even, whitest and clearest ones and spin or twist from them lines of whatever thickness is desired: from two, four, six, and up to twenty hairs. One can twist and spin lines in one piece or with small links. Lines with links are made very simply. For example, six horsehairs of identical length are taken, matched in thickness,** tied at one end with an ordinary knot, divided into two equal groups, and spun or twisted (whichever method one knows best) up to the very end of the hairs. Then an ordinary knot is again tied: this is called a "link." Links are then connected to one another by a double "fisherman's" knot, pulled as tight as possible, and the tag ends trimmed quite close. There you have a line of the desired length.

Explaining in words the manufacture of a line without links is rather difficult, but once one sees how this is done, it's easy to imitate. Hairs of various length are used, and these are spun in or twisted in one after the other. As soon as one hair comes to an end, then another is introduced in its place, while the tag ends of both are trimmed so close that afterward it's impossible to tell where the individual hairs end and where they start. Lines made in this fashion may serve three or more years, even if they're fished every day in spring, summer, and fall, if, at the end of every fishing trip, and for the duration of the winter, they're kept in a dry place and not forcibly torn. There's no need to expatiate on how important strength of line—which principally depends on its evenness—is to the angler. Especially good lines are made from hairs the way a girl's plaits are braided. They're much stronger than spun or twisted lines and they never tangle.

*Lines are also prepared from black hairs, but the transparency of white hairs, when immersed in water, obviously makes the line invisible to the fish, and therefore better.
**That is, half the hairs are positioned with the root-end at the top, and the other half with the root-end at the bottom.

# THE FLOAT

"Float" is the name given to a small, usually round or oval, stick,* the length and thickness of a finger, of light wood (or of the woody bark of the black poplar, or of cork), fastened to the line at the desired distance from the hook. The size of the float must depend on the thickness of the line, the weight of the sinker, and the size of the hook and rod. If the float is too small for its sinker, it sinks; if too large, it doesn't stay upright in deep water, and this is sometimes necessary. The float has two purposes. First, it ensures that the baited hook will rest at that distance from the bottom required by the fisherman, or will lie on the bottom, as necessary. Second, and more important still, it shows by its movement any bite on the baited hook and, finally, indicates the moment when it's necessary to set the hook (that is, to pull up the line with the rod) and land one's quarry.

Consequently, any light substance that floats on water can serve as a float. Floats are prepared in various ways:

1. They're carved or turned from the bark of the *black poplar*, which has a beautiful dark red color, very light, and doesn't get waterlogged. In my opinion, these are the very best floats.

2. They can be made from any dry wood: onto one sharpened end of a small stick, a finger's thickness in the middle, is firmly mounted the lower half of a goose quill, while into the other end, similarly sharpened, is inserted a small loop made of wire through which one passes the line, the other end of which is put through a ringlet cut from a feather; the ringlet is slipped over the quill-end of the float (the ringlet must be somewhat wider than the quill) to hold the line in place.

*Nonetheless, the float's shape is an arbitrary matter. I've seen floats, most artfully carved from black poplar, which represent a fish, a bird, and even a man. Generally, however, floats tend to be thicker in the middle.

3. Instead of wood one can use cork: a slender wooden stick is put through it and then it's fashioned in precisely the same way as floats of the second type.

There are other floats, acquired from abroad, made from one thick goose-feather and put together in exactly the same way as the floats I've just described, but they're suited only for surface fishing, without a sinker, because they're too light. Moreover, the thick end of the feather, to which the loop is attached, is ordinarily glued up with sealing-wax or a special resin. If water somehow gets in, then it will fill the cavity of the feather and the float will sink. What's more, they're not easy to see on the water. Though floats of black poplar are less convenient to change, because it's always necessary to loosen the double knot with which the float is bound to the line, they're less complex and more rarely go wrong. With floats of the second and third types, on the other hand, the wire loops often pull out and the quill ringlets often crack. You have to carry spare ringlets, but putting them on is bothersome since you must untie the line, if the hook and sinker are too big to pass through the quill ringlet.

One can also use floats of green and dry reed of a certain species—soft, thick, and porous on the inside—but this plant isn't sturdy and doesn't grow everywhere. The size of the float must be commensurate with the construction of the entire fishing outfit, as I've already said. The float must therefore have such a weight, relative to this general arrangement of the outfit, that the fish feels no impediment when touching and taking the baited hook into his mouth.

# THE SINKER

"Sinker" is the name given to a small piece of metal, almost always lead (for lead is heavy and soft), attached to the line a short distance from the hook in order to make it sink. Sinkers may be of various weights depending on the size of the whole fishing outfit and on whether the water is flowing or standing. For the smallest outfit, one little pellet is sufficient. For a middling outfit, one, two, or three large pellets; for the most enormous one, a small bullet is used.

Attaching lead sinkers is done in the following way. A little piece of lead of the appropriate size is taken and pounded into a long, narrow plate and wrapped onto the line or leader. Its sides are then crimped together with a light hammer-blow so that the sinker won't slide about. Pellets are attached even more simply: the pellet or bullet is taken, cut almost in half with a knife, and into this aperture the line is laid and the edges of the sinker are then pinched together. It's always necessary to attach the sinker to a hair line a little higher than the silk leader, for lead eats through silk more rapidly than it does horsehair. In the absence of shot and bullets, one can make a sinker from any small piece of the aforementioned lead, taking care only that its shape be oval: an angular sinker will more likely snag the weeds or uneven bottom. After lead, tin is best, and in the absence of both the one and the other, bronze or iron can be used. These latter metals are sometimes attached to the line with a special thread.

# THE HOOK

Without doubt this is the most important part of the fishing outfit, for all success in angling depends on the quality of the hook. The best hooks are English ones. Their size varies and is divided into twelve numbers.*[14] In choosing them it's necessary to observe the following:

1. The hook must be well tempered: an undertempered one will straighten out, while an overtempered hook will break. A blue color, the sign of good tempering, is easy to fake, and therefore you should test every hook by bending it by hand. When no tempered hooks are available, it's best to take undertempered hooks. They'll straighten a little, while the overtempered ones will break; the latter are good for nothing.

2. The bend of the hook must be round, not too deep and not small, but wide, and bent a little to the side toward the sharp end. The point must be sharp, long, and kirbed. The advantage of the first two characteristics requires no clarification, but the advantage of the last—that is, why the end of the hook must bend slightly to the side—one can discover only from experience. If you fish two outfits identical in size and construction, one of which has a kirbed hook, while the other has a hook whose bend is parallel to its shank, you'll see that on the second outfit there will be three times as many missed strikes as on the first. Without doubt the reason is that, when you strike, the straight hook more easily pulls itself out of the fish's mouth without having caught on either side of it.

3. The barb must be well, but not steeply, separated, and be held fast while cleft, for this is the device that keeps the hook from slipping back out of a hooked fish's mouth. Hooks often break during cleaving if the cut is too deep.

*It used to be twelve. Now a multitude of numbers is reckoned, but I don't know them properly.

4. The hook must not be thick. A thick hook is inconvenient because on it a small bait (a little worm, grasshopper, small fish and so on) loses its natural appearance and immediately dies, and especially because a slender hook more quickly pierces the lip. It's even more difficult for a thick hook to penetrate the upper part of a fish's mouth, which tends to be very tough.

5. The hook's shank should not be long; this also hinders the liveliness of the bait, which is usually threaded onto the bottom, while the upper part of the shank remains uncovered. This may frighten a fish, but apart from that, even if he takes the bait into his mouth, which is almost always done on the move (except when one is bottom-fishing), he'll immediately feel the hard, uncovered shank of the hook and promptly spit out (throw back out) the bait. Any observant sportsman will see this with his own eyes when he fishes in clear waters.

6. The shank ends in a little nub whose shoulders must be wide and not sharp, so that the attachment of the leader or the hair line is not cut but holds fast. This last condition is very important. The snell may also be severed on the inside imperceptibly to the human eye, even though the solicitous fisherman may examine his outfit every day. All goes well when a small fish takes, but as soon as a big one bites—it's farewell to both hook and quarry. . . . The line rises to the top as if the fish had freed himself, the chagrined fisherman hastily obtains a fresh worm, goes to bait it up and instead of a hook sees the cut-off end of the leader or the line to which it was attached. . . . Conclusions will follow: "The fish was so big that the leader didn't hold," or "a pike bit it off," and so on, but this is nonsense! Under careful examination it will be revealed that the length of the leader or line has not diminished, but that it was broken off at the hook itself, at the snell.

I particularly direct the attention of sportfishermen to the *connection* of the hook to the leader or directly to the line: from contact with iron and dampness, the connection, that is the little knot itself, is often eaten through by rust. To guard against this, one can wind a slender silk thread under the connection in one layer, but no more—otherwise the connection will be too thick. It's best to scrutinize hooks carefully every day. As soon as yellowness appears near the connection, change the leader immediately. Even hair line is subject to the action of rust, though hair resists it longer.

# THE LEADER

"Leader" is the name given to a special kind of small attachment, with the hook already fastened to it, which is tied to the end of the line. Leaders may be made of

1. fine copper or iron wire;
2. strings from bass instruments, or any such thick string;
3. the spine of an entire length of goose quill, with the pulp removed;
4. silk.

The first three kinds of leader are used for pike angling because the pike, due to the sharpness of his numerous teeth, bites through, sometimes in a single second, all types of line: hair, thread and silk, though almost no one uses silk leaders. Their use was actually devised by an old fisherman on our estate. My thirty-year experience with silk leaders, and their employment by several other sportsmen who adopted this device, have utterly convinced me of their usefulness. All fish take (or, as the sportsmen say, "bite") much more eagerly on an outfit with a silk leader. Almost everything I've said about the advantages of a silk line (its flutteriness) also holds true for a silk leader, and, to that end, it should be no shorter than ten inches. The hair line to which it's attached won't get tangled or decay like an all-silk line. Each year, then, it's necessary to change leaders four times or so, but this isn't difficult. Another advantage is that the hook can be attached to a silk line much more securely than to a hair line, for the obvious reason that hair is stiffer. The leader's thickness depends on the thickness of the line. For the thickest line, I usually attach a leader spun of six English silk threads; for a medium line, four threads; for a fine line, two threads. This latter, of course, is a *small* outfit— or *roach* outfit—with four-hair line; for a surface-fishing rig, a leader of two silk threads would be too heavy. For leaders, it's best to use green silk, for it resembles aquatic weeds in color, though, if necessary, any color will do. Good silk is so strong that a five-pound fish may be carefully landed on *one* thread of it. Such leaders, if one fishes constantly, must be changed once or twice a week.

There are other leaders, obtained from abroad, made from the Indian plant (or silkworm gut), with hooks already attached, and these have all the advantages and disadvantages found in whole lines of the same material. Fish take very well on them, but I warn sportsmen not to tie their lines to mail-order hair leaders with the *little loop* they always have, but instead to attach leader to line by means of the usual fisherman's knot. Looped Indian hairs tear easily, and therefore I'm not particularly keen on them. I have, unfortunately, experienced this many times.

Line of a single horsehair is used without a leader. It's possible, however, to dispense with leaders altogether and attach the hook directly to the line, which is what nearly all sportsmen do.

# ASSEMBLY OF THE FISHING OUTFIT

Once you have all of the outfit's components ready, it only remains for you to assemble the entire rig. Fishing outfits vary in size depending on their purpose. *Small* ones are for little fish: stone loach, gudgeon, ruff, bleak (called "bluelet" and "white-eye" in Orenburg Province), dace, small perch, and roach. *Medium* outfits, which are the most widely used, are for large perch, ide, chub, bream, tench, and crucian carp. *Large* fishing outfits are intended for the largest fish: for the occasional large specimen of the aforementioned kinds, but especially for predatory species: pike, asp, carp, zander, and taimen (or "redling"). Such divisions are of course arbitrary, and if one fishes waters that hold all species, then a huge fish may easily bite on a medium or even small outfit. Such a fish loves to play pranks: without touching the largest, tastiest baits, he'll snatch the daintiest wheat kernel, pinhead-sized morsel of bread, or fly. . . . Then the fisherman has an adventure both dreadful and delightful in store for him! . . . The angler is wretched when a fish breaks off or snaps the line, but what joy is his in landing a large ide or chub on light tackle. One thing is certain: that on a large outfit, due to the size of the bait, small fish don't take.

Now then, take the hook, attach to it the leader, attach the leader to the line and then fasten a sinker to it. If you have a float with loop and quill, then put it on from the other end of the line. Measure out a length of line a half or a third longer than the rod, and attach this to the slender end of the rod, at the very tip, with a double knot. As the entire line is always much longer than the rod, the excess has to be kept tightly wound around the rod, descending from tip to butt. Where the line terminates, tie it smoothly to the rod with waxed thread.

Now you have at the ready a typical fishing outfit, the kind most often used. But there are two types of outfit—the "bottom" rig, and the "surface" or "casting" rig. The first type, or rather its line, can be six yards or more in length. Its sinker consists of a bullet fastened twenty to thirty inches up from the hook, which is usually taken from the largest sizes: number one, two, or three. The type of outfit with the thickest (about thirty-hair) line is used on large and swift rivers without a float. The line is attached to a small, very flexible rod, and since it cannot be cast in the usual manner, the line is taken—coiled—into the hand, right up to the sinker, and in this fashion the baited hook may be thrown a great distance. The aforementioned type of rod is always held in hand and serves to indicate whether a fish has taken, to set the hook, and to play and weary the fish, which, for the most part, will be of the largest size. He may be very simply landed on the line and removed from the water by hand or net. This kind of angling is done largely at night, from a boat. In 1827, I myself saw an angler employ this method on the Moscow River to take an enormous chub of around nine pounds. He assured me that fourteen-pound chub are sometimes caught.

The surface (or casting) outfit is assembled with line of two horsehairs (or even one) and without a sinker, float or leader. The smallest hook (no. 10, 11, 12) is attached to a long line, which is tied to a slender, light, and flexible rod. The bait consists of flies and the smallest red worms, called "mosquito wrigglers," which I've never seen anywhere but in the vicinity of Moscow. The hook barely sinks, and fish strike the bait on the water's surface. This sort of angling must be done in swift water. Preferably, dace, small ide, small chub, and bleak will bite. The rod must of course be held in hand. I'm a proponent of neither the bottom- nor the casting-outfit. The latter is especially difficult to cast. It's normally fished from a bridge or while wading up to the knee or deeper. In these situations it's best to wind-cast—fussy angling that demands great skill. The sense of touch in one's hand must be developed enough to indicate when the hook should be set, and even then for each fish caught there will be several missed strikes. Bottom and surface rigs represent the gamut of fishing outfits.

I might mention here that in general I don't care for angling without a float, not only because it's fussy, but because one must constantly hold the rod and, chiefly, because angling without a float loses a great deal of its charm. Careful observation of the float's movements, of their differences and significance, as well as the expectation that the float will suddenly go under or be dragged off—all these things provide enjoyment for the sportsman. Moreover, there's a kind of bite where one can only discern visually when the hook must be set. If you judge by the force of the pull (and, without a float, there's no other way to judge), then you'll consistently go wrong. You won't set the hook at the proper time, and you will lose the real moment for striking—that little "tug" which the hand is incapable of feeling. Our outfits of all sorts are now ready, and we must be able to attach the bait, or, as many sportsmen say, "to bait up."

# THE BAIT

"Bait" is the name given to anything intended to attract a fish and mounted on the sharp end of the hook, which, if the bait is large, is entirely concealed. While enumerating the multifarious types and kinds of baits, I'll also discuss baiting techniques, for they too are numerous. There's one general rule: the hook point must be hidden in the bait so that it's neither visible nor easily felt. It should not pierce the fish's mouth on first contact, but at the same time the hook should emerge freely so that, when the hook is set either by the angler or the fish's own movement (the fish, in taking the bait into his mouth, sometimes veers to the side), the point instantaneously thrusts forward and sticks into the interior parts of the fish's mouth.

1. The most common bait—which is found everywhere in dung in the spring, summer and autumn, and is used by everyone—is the red "dungworm," called "gutworm" in southern districts.[15] It's only in midsummer that fish take less avidly on them. All species of fish bite on the dungworm except asp and pike, but even they occasionally permit themselves this treat, especially pike. It stands to reason that, because of its small size, the dungworm is usually taken by small and medium fish, but sometimes even a large one will strike it. The red dungworm must be baited by inserting the point into its head,* and the entire hook must be covered by the worm. It's best if the worm's head is kept on the snell or on the shoulders of the hook, with the worm's middle concealing the hook and point, while the tail is allowed to curve freely. Thus a worm whose sides haven't been pierced will live for quite a long time and retain its natural appearance, and both these qualities are very important in attracting quarry. Fish take the little tail very eagerly, but for small fish, especially roach, such bait isn't

---

*Sometimes one can bait this worm from the tail, if small fish are consistently biting off the little tail alone. This baiting method is especially good for ruff-fishing. In this case the hook point ends up concealed in the worm's head.

desirable. The fish will take the long end and drag off the float, and half the worm will harmlessly remain in his mouth when the fisherman pulls up. The smaller the outfit, therefore, the smaller the worm to be baited. For a large fish, several dungworms—even ten or more—are baited on the same hook by impaling them crosswise and hiding the point in one of the worms. This is called angling "on a cluster of gutworms."

2. The "earthworm" is very similar to the dungworm in shape. It's around five or even seven inches in length, and about the width of a little finger. The earthworm is pale brown in color, while the very largest specimens are brown. Earthworms aren't baited in exactly the same way as dungworms. There are two techniques: to pierce the worm about a finger-and-a-half below its head, lodging the entire hook in the remainder of its body, while concealing the shoulders of the hook in the slit; or to bait it about two fingers up from the tail, while concealing the sharp end of the hook in the worm's head (which will hang slightly), and leaving the blunt end in its middle. Many prefer the latter method, claiming that fish take the worm more eagerly from the head, but I don't entirely agree. It's been my observation that small fish take the worm more avidly by the tail, while large fish, especially perch, as it happens, most often take it crosswise. I haven't seen this species of worm in Orenburg Province, but here, near Moscow, they're very numerous. One must use fishing rigs of the largest size. Ide, chub, tench, and, especially, perch, take very well on this worm. It has the added advantage that it won't be touched by small fish.

There's another gutworm, or worm, which is also an earthworm, though it differs from both of the species of worms just described. It's whitish, very long, but not thick. Its body is mealy and tears easily. This worm is suitable for baiting medium outfits. Both species of earthworms live not in manure, but in soil. The second kind can be found everywhere, while the first can sometimes be very difficult to find. When it's dry, they burrow deep in the soil and crawl out onto the surface only after it rains, especially at night. The porous beds in vegetable gardens are their favorite habitat. There, after a rain, one can stock up on them, but for safekeeping they must be stored in a large clay pot filled to four inches from the top with common soil. The pot must be put in a cellar and worms taken from it for angling a few at a time. Thus they may be kept a few days, even a week, during severe hot spells.

3. In the Moscow River, in its tributary streams, and in lakes fed by it, one can find a small worm that is called the "mosquito wriggler," probably because it wriggles in all directions, as it consists entirely of tiny joints. This worm is bothersome to bait, for as soon as you pierce it, red liquid oozes out and only a transparent pellicle remains. Nonetheless, local fishermen manage to bait wrigglers on small outfits by impaling two or three crosswise and skillfully hiding the hook point in the fourth. All small fish bite very eagerly on them in summer, just when they're taking poorly on earthworms. But bothering with them is very tedious.

4. There's another fairly big worm, as thick as a finger, two inches long, with a hard, red head, which is called the "white worm." In the Simbirsk region it's called the "greaser," while near Moscow, God knows why, the "eel." This is the grub of a dung beetle. It's baited in exactly the same way as the common worm (but always from the head), with the only difference being that one must gently squeeze the black filth out of its lower half and then rinse the worm. Otherwise, it will soon turn blue, or even black, in the water. Large ide, perch, and especially chub take eagerly on this worm. Small greasers, which we call "milkjugs," are baited without being squeezed out.

All species of worm must be kept in small wooden or metal boxes which can be shut tight and filled with moist earth. Excessive moisture and dryness alike are harmful to them. After fishing, it's best to put such boxes in a cellar or other damp, cool place.

5. Crayfish always make an excellent bait and enticement for fish in those waters where these crustaceans are found. In waters where they're absent, fish won't take them, but can probably be made accustomed to them. Raw, peeled tails are commonly employed, but it's possible to use the innards of the crayfish as well as its little pincers. The only pity is that this marvelous bait is mercilessly torn about by the roach; this fish, where he's numerous, will exhaust the patience of even the

most patient fisherman. It's also possible to fish with boiled crayfish. Fish don't take quite as well on them, but the roach won't tear up and pull apart this bait as severely. But the tastiest morsel, which will be greedily attacked by any large fish, is *molting* crayfish. It's well known that crayfish molt, that is, change their shell, in the summer, in June and July.* At this time they're indisposed, so they sit in holes from which they must be extracted by hand. The molting crayfish is ready for baiting when it's possible to carefully peel the old, hard shell away from it and from all its parts, even its little legs. Beneath it will remain a thin, new membrane, and it will be so tender and soft that the largest crayfish can be swallowed by the ide, chub, and tench, whose mouths are very small in relation to their size. All kinds of large fish, including predatory species, are incredibly greedy in their pursuit of molting crayfish. It's baited whole, except for the pincers, which constitute an especially dainty enticement. The hook is first put through the middle of the tail, starting from its end, along the alimentary canal, and brought out on the underside, next to the first two legs, so that the tail remains penetrated by the leader. About two fingers down, the hook is again inserted completely into the interior of the crayfish, and the hook point emerges slightly, near the crayfish's eyes. The leader gently straightens, and the crayfish attains its natural length and shape. This baiting must be done very skillfully. If you tear through the new skin somewhere and the liquid insides of the crayfish come out onto the surface, the avaricious and impertinent roach will begin to nibble the torn place and utterly ruin your bait.

The claws of large crayfish are torn out right at the body. Along their entire length they can be relieved of their old skin with no damage done to the tiny tips, and just as carefully mounted from the upper, narrow end, onto the hook, which is concealed in the pincer itself at its branch. It becomes smoothed out on the leader and has the appearance of a long, stretched, women's glove. It's taken very eagerly by fish of medium size and even by large ones.

If the molting crayfish is already torn through, then one

---

*I've been told, but don't claim, that in some places crayfish molt twice a year.

can bait its separate parts. The tail can be baited separately. The body is cut in two lengthwise, and its two halves can be baited separately, according to the general rule. These halves of the crayfish body are covered on the inside with some kind of moss, and large perch readily take on them. Angling with such bait is called "fishing crayfish moss." All crayfish baits must be pulled up and examined frequently if the float doesn't remain completely still. They're easily spoiled by the biting of small fish, that is, the hook point may thrust out through the surface of the bait.

It's best to have live crayfish, but since this isn't always possible (incidentally, crayfish can live out of water for two, even three days), one must remove the tails and keep them on ice during hot weather.

6. *Baked bread and cereal grains.* Soft rye bread, kneaded well by hand until it has the consistency of sticky dough, rolled into several round balls, is also a very widely used bait, especially among peasants who live along rivers abounding with fish. The size of the balls varies—from a small pea to a small walnut—depending on the size of the hook and the fish you wish to catch. Roach take on bread most avidly of all, but so do all other species except predatory fish, ruff, and stone loach. Aside from the convenience of its preparation, bread bait has two advantages: (a) bites are more sure, since fish can't drag a round piece of bread from place to place with impunity, as they often do with the tail of baited worms; and (b) by baiting a large piece of bread the size of a small walnut, you can thereby defend against the tugging of small fish and safely wait for a large one, which can't be done with tails of nonmolting crayfish or with worms. One can fish with white bread and bread made from sifted flour, but rye has more odor and fish take it more eagerly.

Among cereal grains, oats, barley, peas, and, best of all, wheat, are used after first being stewed in hot water, which makes them large, soft and easy to impale with the hook point. They're baited one kernel at a time, or two or three, depending on their softness, size, and the fish. Here it's especially important to ensure that the point of the hook emerge freely. For the most part, fish that have already been groundbaited are caught on grain. Except for the predatory species, all fish, even very large ones, take grain.

7. *Live bait, baitfish.* Small fish are taken by perch, pike, asp, zander, and chub. Burbot also take willingly on them, but only at night. In late autumn, roach and rudd take on little pieces of cut-up fish. A small fish is usually baited by inserting the sharp end of the hook into its back, from head to tail. Many sportsmen hook live bait by the lip and claim that this method is much better, that a baitfish mounted in this fashion will be more lively, stay alive longer and attract predatory fish better. All this is partially true, but no less true than the fact that a small fish baited by the lip often tears away by itself and even more often is torn off if it is not struck by the largest fish, and if it's not entirely swallowed at once. All species of fish, except predatory ones, are used for bait. If necessary, even they can be used, but of course only when they're young. Gudgeon, stone loach, and minnow, however, make superb baitfish at any age. Baitfish must be kept alive, which is fairly difficult. The simplest method is to keep them in a bucket of water, which must be changed as often as possible. Best of all is a small, woven keep-net, which can stand next to you or in the water, although carrying this net from place to place is inconvenient.

8. *Grasshoppers, beetles, flies.* All kinds of jumping insects are used for angling, from the locust to the grasshopper. Large fish take most eagerly of all, as I've happened to observe, on a large green grasshopper, while medium and small fish prefer a very small gray one. One must fish them with a light sinker and not early, but around midday, when fish cruise at the surface. One can even remove the sinker altogether and slide the float down as far as possible—sometimes around five inches from the hook—thereby converting the standard outfit into a surface rig. All species of insects are baited the same way, by inserting the hook into the back from the head to the tail. This kind of angling is more successful in clean and rather swiftly flowing waters, especially *steppe* rivers, because in the steppes there are more grasshoppers to be found than in other places, and the fish have grown used to them because they frequently fall into the water.

The so-called May beetles are used for angling, though in

Russia's central belt they appear in June and remain until mid-July, which means they're called "May beetles" erroneously. Ide and chub take on them. When baiting them, one has to take care that their hard outer wings are lifted and the long, soft, transparent secondary wings are sticking up from beneath them. Some sportsmen even tear off the hard outer wings.

Common flies represent a tasty enticement for small fish, who will take greedily on them from spring to autumn, on a surface, or casting, outfit. Rarely, fish of decent size, especially chub, will also take.

It's necessary that flies and all insects used for bait be fresh and alive, to which end one should catch them just before fishing and put them into a clean, dry, glass jar, because they'll die immediately in a damp one, or in one that has some sort of odor.

It's possible to fish with dragonflies, butterflies, flying cockroaches—in a word, with all insects and even with snails (slugs). All kinds of large and predatory fish are caught on small pieces of raw meat.

I've never tried it myself, but I've heard that hooks can be baited "with greenery," that is, with aquatic blossoms when they become thick enough.

For want of other bait, I once had recourse (on a good fishing river, the Dëma, in Orenburg Province)[16] to try baiting my hook with sandpiper entrails, and all kinds of fish took it! I've tried the same thing a couple of times in other places and always been successful. I caught small fish because I was fishing slender intestines. Perhaps on thick ones large fish would have taken.

And so, we have ready not only the outfit, but also all kinds of bait. We must now choose a place to fish.

# ON SELECTING A SWIM

If you chance upon or live in an area that boasts a river with a mill and millpond, hasten there. You will encounter there the most diverse kinds of angling and freedom in choosing a swim, which I will discuss below. I should confess that I'm partial to dammed rivers. The appearance of the pond and mill, the clatter of its rigging, and the rush of falling water bring serene and sweet emotion to an old fisherman's soul. The water and its plants appear as something cherished of years gone by. The spinning wheels rumble, the millhouse trembles, and the roiling waves foam beneath it! A dam overgrown with bushes; paths beaten through by passers-by, grain-carriers, proprietors; log bridges over the water—all this speaks of something long familiar and dear to my heart. Where there's a mill, there will also be fish, for the millpond is their lair and promenade!

In such a swim there's an abundance of every kind of food; there the fish can spawn freely and the small fry can hatch. Near a mill, the sportsman will find and bag fish at all times of year and any time of day. In early spring, in late autumn, in foul weather, fish hold more in the mainstream, in the upper reaches of the pond. In warm weather, during summer hot spells, they cruise along flood-pools, weeds, and rushes. In cold weather, they draw close, along the mainstream, to the warm manure dam. But they especially like to hold in holes, below the release of a flood-gate or under waterwheels. In vain does the stream crashing down from above carry back schools of tiny fish, for a bit to the side they ceaselessly return to the same swift current. Meanwhile the predatory fish snatch the little fish, who've been weakened by their battle with the current. The fisherman clambers onto a wet beam, on which the millshaft turns ponderously, and—under an overhang of waterpipes, overgrown with green moss, under drops and streamlets of seeping water, shuddering in his place at every turn of the wheel—he casts his line, baited with a worm or, better still, a small fish, into the midst of the swift current, into the waves and foam—and he pulls out greedy perch and small pike. . . . But having described the mill in particular as a good place, I shall turn to choosing a swim in general.

The choice of a swim can vary not only with the time of year, but also with the time of day. In the spring, while the water is still a bit cloudy, fish wander about aimlessly, as sportsmen put it, and bite everywhere in all the deep swims, for the banks of the rivers have not yet taken shape; they have not yet become overgrown with thick sedge, sweet flag, or bulrush. Aquatic weeds have not arisen from the bottom, and lily-pads have not yet risen to the surface. Bankside trees and bushes have neither put on their leaves nor covered the transparent waters with a shadow of overhanging verdure, beckoning the fish with food all day and cool shade at noontide.

When undertaking early spring fishing,[17] which can start at the end of April (when there's still a great deal of water in the rivers and they run faster than usual), one must add weight to the line in order to get the hook to sink as deeply as possible, since the angling will have to be done "taut." In other words, the line will be stretched by the streaming water and the hook won't touch bottom, but this is inevitable in the spring. Fish usually hold on the bottom and along the banks, especially steep ones, where the current is calmer. One should choose swims that are neither small nor too deep. Due to the strong current, a baited dungworm or earthworm (fishing with bread in swift water is impractical) will wash ashore, and therefore one is obliged to place or plant the rod in such a way that only the bait touches the bank and the line and float don't fall upon it. Otherwise, they'll start to snag the shore when the hook is set, and this is no good: the fish, seizing the moving bait in ambush, will immediately encounter resistance from the snagged line or float and instantly reject the hook. Moreover, the hook can never be set soundly, for the sportsman's hand will encounter the same impediment, and the raising of the rod won't be communicated to the hook instantaneously. When the water hasn't quite receded and cleared up, it's difficult to get crayfish and there are no insects, so the natural bait is worms. But as soon as the river has reached its lowest level and still places are formed, then every sort of nonpredatory fish will begin to take bread very eagerly in such swims.

In undammed rivers that flow freely, as dictated by their own mass of water, *whirlpools* are commonly chosen for fishing. These are deep places where the water suddenly loses its swiftness as it falls into a depression, and then, spinning backward near the bank, meets the flow of the upper current, struggles with it, and finally loses momentum. A still place results from this struggle, and in such quiet whirlpools fish constantly hold.

In the summer one must choose a moderately deep swim, with a sandy or gravelly bottom (that is, consisting of small pebbles) that slants or slopes from the bank into deep water. In such swims it's good to fish early in the morning and late in the evening. It's even better if the water about a yard and a half from shore has sprouted weeds and been covered by their leaves, as if by a green carpet. In this case there are many benefits for the sportsman: the fish have both food and shelter from the bright sun, but, most important, the fisherman sitting on the bank is hidden, and he may conveniently lay his long rods on the grassy fabric. Deep swims overgrown with green lily-pads, as round as plates, present the same advantages. Swims where trees have bent their green boughs over the water—where supple bushes wash their long leaves in limpid currents, quietly murmuring at their touch—are reliable for fishing not very early and not very late in the season; at those times the fish, having risen from the bottom, swim at moderate depth and like to hold near the green foliage. Sportsmen know this well and on rivers and lakes whose shores are utterly bare they resort to cunning and create artificial greenery. They cut off the top of some young tree (or two or three, if they're small) or take an entire sallow or willow bush, choose a suitable swim, lay them half-submerged in the water, and stick their sharpened ends into the bank. Small fish won't hesitate to rush to the green leaves, and large fish will come after them. In about two days the fish will be accustomed to holding near these bushes, which can thereafter be changed at night when the leaves wither. The same thing is also done on large rivers, where they fish from a boat to which a sheaf of treetops or a bush has been attached. If the swim isn't too deep, then the boat *idles;* that is, it's attached to a long stake driven into the bottom. If, on the other hand, the water is deep, then the boat is held by a rope tied to a stone that's been lowered to the bottom.

In the autumn,[18] when one seeks to angle for large fish in the morning and evening, it's necessary to select the deepest swims. Around noon, however, fish no longer hide from the sun's intense heat under weeds, bushes, or in the shade of overhanging banks or even bridges, as they do in summer. On the contrary, rejoicing in the warmth of the sun's rays, they swim out in schools to the water's surface and strike at the fading leaves and all the various insects as they fall. In this case one must fish the lightest possible outfit, preferably with some sort of insects.

There's also autumn "whipfishing," as the fishermen call it, which I haven't had occasion to try, though they say it can be very successful. It's especially productive and pleasant because at that time of year it's hard to get good fish by other angling methods. It's done in the following manner. Two people set out in a small fishing boat. Drifting along the current, one person quietly works the oar, keeping the boat at a distance of fifteen to twenty feet from shore, while the other continually casts and retrieves a long-line surface rig baited with worms, grasshoppers (if they haven't disappeared yet) or small fish. The bait is thrown toward the bank, toward weeds, and under bushes and leaning trees, where the water is still and littered with dry fallen leaves. All kinds of fish, sometimes fairly large ones, usually rise to the bait and strike it while moving. Certain kinds of insects may fall into the water along with the leaves, which is probably why falling leaves attract fish.

I myself have observed many times how fish strike at fallen leaves and take them down. A few of the leaves float to the surface, while others disappear; perhaps fish swallow some of the leaves, which are still green. In calm weather and on still water, in the upper reaches of ponds, where the mainstream is even with the forested bank-tops, leaves sometimes cover the water so densely that it's difficult to cast the rig, and, if the sinker is light, then the baited hook lies on top of the leaves. One must, of course, find a way to get the bait to sink and the float to stand upright. One has to fish in every way possible, that is, both on the surface and deep, because the fish sometimes take very shallow, just beneath the leaves, and sometimes on the bottom. This kind of angling has one drawback: it's difficult to make out one's float among the leaves. On the other hand, fish bite eagerly and boldly under this leafy cover, and the transparency of autumn water improves the fishing, for the fish can see from a distance any bait that has fallen into the water, even though the angler can't see it. Perch, ide, medium-sized chub and large dace tend to bite, though all kinds of fish may. The pleasure afforded by this kind of fishing consists in the fact that it's tranquil and that in late autumn there are no other swims in which decent fish, other than predatory species, can be caught. While fishing under leaves, I've caught good ide, chub, and very big roach. The latter would bite on bread, while the former would take large earthworms.

Good fishing at any time of year may be had in *riffles* (shallow places in the river), the mouths of tributary streams and brooks, and holes carved out by water falling beneath mill-wheels and flood-gates. Riffles provide a thoroughfare for fish swimming from one whirlpool to another, as they slip downstream when the water recedes and struggle upstream when the water rises. Riffles are always swift, which means bottom-fishing must be done with heavy weights. The water's current will drag and shake the baited hook, and passing fish will start to strike it.

Where streams and brooks join the river, little fish always hold, and near them you will find all the species of predatory fish: pike, asp, zander, perch, and even chub. This last fish, though he would seem to belong to a nonpredatory race, swallows little fish very eagerly. In deep holes carved out by water dropping beneath flood-gates or weirgates, large fish are always numerous. Below the roar of water falling from mill-wheels, too, there are always fish present, though they're not as large.

It would not be proper to conclude from all this that fish will bite only in the swims I've enumerated. Where there's water, they can be found, and, consequently, taken by rod and line. The fish make good use of this freedom and often their biting will be sufficiently capricious to bewilder an experienced fisherman.

Thus far we've been discussing rivers. There's nothing special to say about selecting a swim in small streams and brooks, where trout (spottie), grayling and taimen are caught by rod. Such swims, that is, small whirlpools or little holes, are constantly changing, and this will be discussed in the section on trout-fishing.[19]

Choosing a swim in flowing ponds overgrown with weeds and rushes has its own peculiarities. Fishing in their mainstream ("mainstream" refers to the channel of the actual river) is simply river-fishing. There's no way to choose a swim depending on the position of the banks, for the water has flooded them and stands higher than the surface of the submerged ground by a yard and sometimes more. One must know the character of the bottom, having observed it when the floodwater is released, or, if you're familiar with the pond, having sounded the bottom with a fisherman's plummet. ("Plummet" is the name given to a small weight or large lead bullet tied to a long string.) Without doubt the best place is a hard bottom, free of snags and not overgrown with weeds, which slopes away from the bank into deep water. Here, however, fishing might be done better from a boat or from a wooden platform or raft built expressly for it.

For fishing in *flood-pools*, that is, in the overflow of a pond overgrown with weeds and rushes (especially common in the black-earth provinces),[20] one must choose swims that are a little deeper, and free of weeds and bulrushes. In summer, all the fish hurry there and flood-pools become the sole and most abundant place for fishing. This will be discussed more fully in its proper place.

In lakes, if their shores are overgrown with weeds and bushes, selecting a swim is in many respects similar to choosing a river-swim. In an artificial pond, the banks and bottom are identical everywhere, and you may therefore fish where you like, though you must always adapt yourself to the habits of the fish themselves—fish where they're more numerous. Here, experience is the best guide.

Groundbait renders special benefits to swims.

# GROUNDBAIT

"Groundbait" is the name given to bread, cereal grains, *kvas* dregs,[21] small worms, and generally any fish food that is thrown into the water. There are many sportsmen who have fished their entire lives without groundbaiting and even see no particular advantage in it, though the latter claim is unjust. Groundbait is an important matter: it not only yields the most abundant catch, but also allows one to take fish in a swim where, without groundbait, you would never catch them, and at a time of year when that species of fish has stopped biting. We're speaking, of course, about permanent groundbait, which may be well prepared in the following fashion. Kernels of rye, oats, wheat, or whatever is available, are taken and mixed with bran and rye-bread crusts (especially burnt ones, whose odor fish detect from afar). All this is put into an iron pot, water is added, and the pot is placed in a hot oven for about two days, until it has become completely soft.

Groundbaits may be *temporary* or *permanent.* By "temporary" groundbait, we mean the scattering of the aforementioned during fishing, or the evening before, or just before fishing. One can also throw in worms and crayfish chopped into bits. By "permanent," we mean the lowering to the very bottom of a bag containing the groundbait I described above. The size of the bag is arbitrary, but ten inches by twenty inches is quite sufficient. The bag should be sewn of cheesecloth so that liquid leaks through, and kernels, too, spill out in places. The bag of groundbait must be set near the bank so that one's baits move in front of it; in this way a fish approaching the groundbait will first encounter the baited hooks. The bag must be tied with string to a small peg which is stuck into the bank or under the bank so that no one will notice it and only its owner can find it. The string is necessary, first, so that you can carry the groundbait bag to another swim if the need arises, and, second, so that if you snag it with your fishing rig, you can pull up the bag and extract the hook, for without a string you will tear the bag. In spite of all caution, you can get snagged when the fish himself drags your hook over to the bag. I once got caught on the bag, and, when I pulled it up by means of the string, I found a roach pinned to it by my hook.

Permanent groundbaits should be in place about a week before your fishing will begin. It's also a good idea to throw out about two handfuls of groundbait specially every day in the morning and evening. If you start this kind of groundbaiting in the spring (as soon as the water recedes, until weeds grow near the banks and on the bottom of the river, pond or lake, and the aquatic insects have yet to develop—at the time, therefore, when the fish are hungriest), then it's possible to train the fish. Even though they'll suck the groundbait out of the bag, they'll keep visiting it, especially if you support their habit with a daily scattering of groundbait at the same hour. It then stands to reason that one should preferably go fishing at that same time of day.

Permanent groundbait has the added advantage that it attracts fewer small fish than does temporary groundbait.

There's no doubt that one not only can, but must fish with what's been groundbaited, that is, with bread or stewed cereal grains as bait. But sportsmen rarely maintain such propriety and hasten to offer their dear guests the bait they consider tastiest and their favorite: worms, crayfish, and so forth. In defense of these sportsmen, one can argue that certain species of fish, especially the predatory ones, simply won't bite on grain, and that the fisherman would otherwise voluntarily prevent himself from catching them and deprive himself of that diversity of quarry so pleasurable to any sportsman.

Some bread-groundbaits are made with hempseed oil, and with cheese. Sometimes small pieces of castoreum (which are even put on hooks), wrapped in a small rag, are sewn to the bag. I have tried all this, but did not detect any special benefit. With bread, or *kvas* dregs with hempseed oil, in my experience, you are more likely to drive the fish away. I've twice experienced this firsthand with crucian carp. I'm certain, by the way, that there must exist an irresistible food for fish that has the power to gather them into one place, but this important discovery has not yet been made.

Though after what I've said one cannot dispute the fact that permanent groundbait is very beneficial to angling, I nonetheless repeat that there are sportsmen who prefer fishing without groundbait. "What kind of satisfaction is there," they ask, "in catching fish which, thanks to long conditioning, have been made almost tame, trained to eat food without the slightest fear, at a certain time of day, like barnyard fowl? The art of angling vanishes, and skilled and unskilled fishermen are made equals. No labor, no care, and no sleepless nights are required. No: to study, to guess the location, character and taste of a cautious, skittish, wild fish, to attract and deceive him with an artificial bait, to be on the watch for his contact with the hook—that's the pleasure of fishing! One such fish is worth ten groundbaited ones!" Despite the fact that I've done a great deal of fishing with groundbait, and even now continue to do so and defend its advantages, I must confess that there's a great deal of truth in the objections to groundbaiting—if one approaches fishing only from its poetic side.

# ON FISHING SKILL

There would seem to be nothing simpler than taking a rod, baiting a worm or piece of bread, throwing it into the water, and pulling out a fish when the float goes down. All this is true, but it's no less true that great fishing skill does exist.[22] For the complete acquisition of this skill, one must have a good deal of experience and even a few special qualities. For example: deftness of hand and the art of preserving the natural appearance of baited worms, crayfish and insects; sharpness of eye for observing the movements of the float, sometimes barely perceptible and utterly incomprehensible to a person unversed in the secrets of fishing; unshakable concentration, for the fish's bite, depending on the season and bait, is constantly changing; acumen; imagination . . .

Do you chuckle, dear readers, thinking that I wish to enumerate all the requisite sportsmanlike qualities published in *The Perfect Huntsman,* and that I shall eventually reach the virtue of "sharp, straight teeth"?[23] Though they're not a bad thing for any person to have, I intend to discuss something else with you. The true fisherman—an artist among sportsmen— must study the ways of the fish, and this is a most difficult and inscrutable subject, even though fish dwell in transparent mansions. Their ways must be guessed. Because there are few clues, one must have perspicacity and thoughtfulness, but how much toil there is too, how much distress! . . . Dusk and dawn are the best time for observing the feeding habits of fish, but in the summertime, as they say, dusk meets dawn, and the observer gets only a few hours' sleep.

If someone took it into his head to ask me as a joke what I mean by the phrase "ways of the fish," then I would reply that by these words I generally intend the natural characteristics of fish, that is, in which waters certain species of fish predominantly like to live, what their favorite food is, what season and what time of day fish hold in certain places, and so forth.

I must confess that we know very little of this curious side of natural history in the life of these aquatic denizens. All that

I've chanced to read is very unsatisfactory, and at times blatantly untrue. Commercial fishermen's accounts of their craft, which rarely and inconsequentially concern angling with rod and line, could, of course, be very useful, but these men often view with disgust their laborious everyday occupation—work that provides a meager scrap of daily bread. They have no love for their business, and therefore lack an educated man's attention and powers of observation, but, I repeat, their stories can most certainly be useful. In discussing each species of fish separately, I'll tell all of what little I know about their ways, how they bite, and angling methods. I warn my readers that although everything I say is perfectly true, it could easily prove unsuccessful and even faulty in practice. Not only do the same species of fish in different waters have different tastes and characteristics, but in one and the same river their ways change with the passage of time. This probably depends on changes in the characteristics of the water, the evenness of the bottom, and the usual piscine food. For example, because of increased human habitation, cattle-raising, and mill-building, the water becomes murkier and warmer; riverbanks lose the grass that previously covered them, and in the overflows of ponds there grow new plants characteristic of shallow, dammed water; the original fish species are partially replaced by others; and because of abundant food, the fish are made less eager; along with this, their biting habits change.

And so, it remains for me to discuss just a few general rules pertaining to fishing skill.

*One.* The most important part of fishing skill is knowing how to construct the fishing outfit properly. This was already discussed, but I'll recapitulate briefly. The rod must be straight, smooth, light, easy to strike, and have a flexible end. The line must be even and spun without being twisted. Twisted line will get tangled, the float will start to rotate, and the baited hook will rise up. If a fish takes in this situation, you'll tend to miss the strike. This is intolerable in angling and even frightens the fish. Such a line must be untwisted, which is fairly bothersome, or thrown away. The knots connecting the leader to the hook and to the line must be small and not ragged. The leader must run from the inner side of the hook. The hook must be well bent, and always sharp; as soon as it becomes dull, change hooks immediately. The bait should be fresh, alive, and well mounted on the hook. The entire outfit should be well proportioned in its parts, and handsome, even elegant. Such a rig is a great guarantee of success.

*Two.* It's no less important to take advantage of propitious weather and time of day. The most precious hour for angling is early morning. There can be no doubt that at this time the fish are hungrier, and take more actively and boldly because the water isn't yet very clear, and the fish therefore begin to bite more surely. In the evening, too, especially late evening, fish take more actively than during the rest of the day. At that time even large fish will begin to swim boldly near the banks even in very clear and shallow places. Though fish eat at all times of day, in the evening they search for food more eagerly. The hotter the weather, the earlier one must fish. In the middle of summer, on clear, very hot days, the sportsman must be at his swim by the time a band of white barely flashes in the east (I have in mind angling for large fish, especially in a ground-baited area). While the fisherman throws out the groundbait, unwinds his line and painstakingly baits the rod, the sun will have come up, fish moving on all sides will begin to send bubbles from the bottom to the water's surface, and the biting will immediately start. It doesn't last long—only until about six o'clock. As soon as the sun is thoroughly warm and its rays have dispelled the morning chill, proceed to another swim to angle for medium or small fish, or proceed home with your catch and go to bed. In rainy and cool weather one need not begin to fish so early, especially in spring and autumn, when one can even fish nearly all day long.

*Three.* It's also very important to know in what places, at what time of year and in what kind of weather fish hold. One can get some idea of this by reading everything I've written, but it's impossible to attain this knowledge well and truly by means of description alone. Practical knowledge and personal observation are required. Sometimes the swim and the time seem very good, with all the favorable indications, but there are no fish or they won't take. Sometimes the reverse is true: fish bite at both the wrong time and in bad swims. But one cannot dispute that fish do have their favorite lies, apparently without any particular reason. The best days for fishing are warm and gray, with intermittent rain, especially on calm days. For perch- and roach-fishing alone, even strong wind can be helpful at times. On very hot, cloudless days one can fish only in the early morning and late evening (I shall discuss midday fishing separately), but on overcast, intermittently rainy days one can fish all day. Sometimes a thundercloud and strong wind blow in, and frequent, heavy downpours drive your floats under the weeds; the smooth surface of the water, if it's not deep, is chopped up into noisy spray and bubbles, and muddied; long mats of aquatic weeds are carried to places where they'd never been before, and the condition of the swim is so altered that you yourself don't recognize it. . . . But the cloud passes, and a moist, steamy warmth fills the air. Momentarily a deep silence ensues, and order is restored all around: the round green lily-pads slowly float back to their former places, the long leaves of the shoregrass spread themselves wide over the water once again, and the fish, frightened for a time by this sudden perturbation of the elements, attack with renewed eagerness the hooks you have adjusted in the meantime. We shall now specifically discuss the process of fishing.

*Four.* The sportsman must observe all possible silence and try to ensure that the fish not see him, especially if the water is clear, if the swim is shallow, and if the lines are cast close to shore. In turbid or quite deep water, or amid the roar of mill-wheels or falling water, or if the rigs have been cast a fair distance, one may exercise less caution.

*Five.* The outfit must be cast without slapping the water with the rod, always a bit farther than necessary and then brought to the place where you've chosen to situate the float (without letting the hook lie on the bottom). A cast outfit must in no way be *dragged* back to the bank. If this is necessary, then take it all the way out of the water and cast it closer. By dragging the rig, you'll immediately snag it on some kind of irregularity on the bottom.

*Six.* One should not pull up the rig often unless necessary, especially when angling for large fish. This can frighten the fish. If, however, small fish are constantly nibbling, then one must pull up often without fail and check or change the disturbed bait. This should be done carefully and quietly.

*Seven.* One should never use too many rigs. If you're bottom-fishing, you must never cast more than three outfits, having set them up with different baits (if you have them), and if the swim is spacious. At the slightest movement of the float you must immediately grasp the rod, without shifting it, so that you can set the hook the minute the fish takes down the float or drags it considerably to the side. If your bait is hanging suspended, then you should not use more than two rigs, for sometimes the float goes down immediately following its first movement, and, if there are too many rigs, they will get in the way. If, though, you're angling for small fish, which take often and nibble constantly, then you must fish one outfit and hold the rod. Otherwise, you'll rush from one rig to the other and on both of them miss the most favorable moment for striking.

*Eight.* Knowing the time and instant for setting the hook is, without doubt, a most important fishing skill. But it's impossible to make a general rule about when to strike, for all fish have a special kind of bite and an appropriate hook-set that changes along with the character of the bite and time of year. Though this will be discussed in the separate descriptions of each fish, it's such a crucial angling skill that it merits special treatment. I have always heard from old, experienced fishermen that it's imperative to let fish *bite thoroughly,* that is, to let them swallow the baited hook and drag the float down to the bottom. For a long time I blindly believed this, but later, thanks to my own careful observation, I became convinced that this rule should under no circumstances be accepted unconditionally. With regard to predatory fish it's always true that the float does indeed go down. But with other species, especially small ones, this rule is dangerous: rather than swallowing, such fish take the bait into their mouths and swim to the side, very often without dragging the float. If some impediment is encountered (and without fail it results from the drag of the line being drawn tight), especially if the fish feels the hard shank of the hook, or, as happens most often, if he's stung by its point, then he immediately throws off the bait and hook. And so, when there's a *tug* on the float, that is, when it moves to the side, especially if you see some inclination of its lower end—that is the actual moment for striking a fish. Setting the hook must always be done quickly, but not too forcefully, always upward and in a direction somewhat opposite to that in which the fish is dragging the float. It's especially necessary to observe this last rule when bottom-fishing.

*Nine.* One should endeavor as much as possible not to put rods in the water and not to submerge the rod-butts. If the place permits, one can gently stick the rod-butts into the bank, or put them on tall shoregrass, or place rod-rests beneath them; these can be planted in the water near shore at swims where you often fish. This is especially crucial for swift and sure hook-setting. It's necessary to place rods in the water only if the water along the bank is so overgrown with weeds that the rod can barely extend to the edge of the weeds, and at times does not even reach it. In this sort of awkward situation, you must, if possible, play the hooked fish away from yourself or straight to the very surface of the water, and then toss him out onto the bank. This is done to keep the fish from getting fouled in the weeds to which he immediately rushes, especially if he's large.

*Ten.* The line, from the rod to the float, especially if it's long, must not be left in the water too much. It can snag something on shallow bottom near the bank, and you'll miss the strike.

*Eleven.* One should not land fish in one pull, with all one's might. You will tear a small fish's lips and toss it so far onto the bank that it will take some time to find in the weeds, and you may even lose it. With a large fish you can rend the line or break the rod. One must strike swiftly, and if the fish is not large, then gently pull him out. If, though, you feel a large fish, then after the hook-set (which should be strong enough so that the point is made to penetrate deeper), you must give him freedom to move in circles without weakening the line, and not suddenly pull him up to the water's surface, but patiently wait until the fish tires and becomes submissive. Then, depending on the suitability of the bank, either lead him in a little closer and take him by hand under the gills, if the bank is steep, or haul him out, if the bank slopes gently, for which you must run backward or to the side. Incidentally, it's unforgivable to fish without having a net with you in swims where you might take a large fish. When landing a large fish without a net, having seen and felt him, one must lead him up to the bank, especially a steep one, such that the fish's head and upper torso are out of the water and raised up. It goes without saying that this can be done with a thick, strong line; otherwise, one has to play the fish for a long time, first in the water, then on the surface, and pull him up to the bank very carefully, without lifting his head, and then take him by hand, but this must be done, without fail, *in the water.*

*Twelve.* If a very large fish takes and you either don't know how to (or can't) make him swim circles in deep water, and he rushes to the water's surface and runs directly away from you, then you must try to turn him to the side, having plunged the rod halfway into the water. If this doesn't help and, contrarily, the fish, coming up and away from you, begins to drag the line and rod in one straight line, then immediately throw your rod into the water. This is your only hope. If you are unyielding, you'll lose both the fish and the outfit, for without the bend originating in the end of the rod, the line will unfailingly break off in a second. The fish will grow weary swimming with the rod you've thrown, and will make his way to shore or entangle himself in the weeds in a shallow place. There you can take him more easily with your hands.

*Thirteen.* When landing a large fish one must never take the line in one's hand, even though this seems very convenient. Doing so can result in the same loss I've just discussed.[24] In only one instance must one resort to this measure. If your rod breaks very high, then there's nothing to do but catch the broken-off rod-tip and gently lead the fish to shallow water or to a mildly sloping bank and, having taken the line in hand about a yard or less from the fish, drag him to shore. But if the swim is deep and the bank steep, then, as you lead the fish to shore and hold the line gently with your left hand, take the fish under the gills with your right and toss him out onto the bank, as I've already described. One must always remember that the line, especially fine line, will only support the weight of a large fish because it's moving in water, which is much denser than air and can therefore support the fish better, and because the flexible rod-tip functions, so to speak, as a continuation of the line.

*Fourteen.* If you have a fish on and he becomes fouled in the weeds, then under no circumstances should you drag him out. On the contrary, slacken the line to give the fish freedom to extricate himself from the weeds, which he will almost always do—one need only have patience. The float or line will instantly indicate to you whether the fish has moved. Then, one must expeditiously lead him out to a clear place and proceed as I've described above. If, however, the fish has not untangled himself after a long time and your hand feels that he has become firmly stuck and snagged at the bottom on weed-roots or branches, then you must crawl into the water and clear the line by hand. This way, both fish and rig will sometimes be saved. One may also find a long pole, cut a notch into its narrow end (like a forked rod-rest), and, reaching with it along the line down to the hook and the weed-roots upon which it's become snagged, gently pull up the weeds from the bottom or disengage the line from the branch. In this case it's difficult not to lose the fish.

*Fifteen.* You must never leave a swim without having tried to fish outfits of different sizes, at different depths, and with every kind of bait you have. Fish are incomprehensibly idiosyncratic and capricious; at least it seems so to us in our ignorance. How many times it's befallen me that fish have taken constantly on a poorly assembled rig not lying in the right place, with the same old scrap of worm or crayfish; and then that the floats of other rigs, which surpass the first in every way, with live and tasty bait, have lain motionless. You must not disregard this instruction, and I, without *slyly playing the sage*,[25] advise you simply to quit the other rods and continue to fish the outfit on which fish are taking, that is, on the *lucky one*, without baiting it with whole worms and crayfish, but with small scraps of them, and casting it to one and the same place. Who knows—perhaps the contour of the bottom is favorable for the presentation of the bait, making it visible from all sides?

*Sixteen.* Though it's true, as all fishermen recognize, that fish swim shallow in August and September and deep in the other months, one must add to this that the state of the weather certainly alters the movements of the fish. If the weather is hot and sunny, then at the end of July fish rise to a shallow depth and hold under an overhang of weeds, predominantly broad-leafed ones, and this continues in August and even September, until the arrival of the cold season. On the other hand, fish stay deep not so much due to cold weather as to rains and strong winds. Generally, large fish hold deeper than small ones. And so, the most important rule is that one must be able to reckon with the time of year and state of the weather. If it's warm out, clear and calm, then fish will move about everywhere, even along the shallowest swims (especially in the evening), and hence that is where one must fish. When inclement weather arrives, especially if a wind comes up, fish rush into the weeds and hide under banks and bushes, which is where one must seek them. When the severe cold begins, fish begin to cluster, that is, they group themselves according to species, gather into schools and lie on the bottom in deep water, where one must pursue them by fishing very deep. Such schools, well known to fishermen, allow the possibility of fishing even in winter, regardless of the hard frost, through holes cut in the ice above them.

I believe I've covered everything that more or less relates to or constitutes fishing skill. In speaking as generally as possible, I've been unable to avoid certain particulars that will inevitably be repeated in their own place.

Now I intend to make a few general remarks about the way fish "bite," and the reasons for fishing failure that depend on the character of the fisherman himself.

Fish do not always bite the same way. It's impossible to guarantee that wonderful biting won't suddenly change. Fishermen are of various opinions on the matter. Some say that fish stop taking just before foul weather, that they *sense* foul weather, and I consider this opinion sound. Many times I've happened to note that in fair weather fish have suddenly stopped taking, and almost always, within a day or less, persistent inclement weather has set in, that is, strong, lengthy rains driven by a cold wind. I've also remarked that fish have subsequently grown used to the foul season and begun to take again, though not so well as before; a day before the arrival of fine weather, however, their former biting is restored. Other fishermen are convinced that fish take splendidly "on the waxing moon" and very badly "on the wane." I can't agree with this because my observations don't confirm it. Here are some indisputable observations I've made based on extensive experience:

1. Fish bite more eagerly when there are no weeds, and preferably in the spring just after the floodwater recedes.
2. The hotter it gets in summer, the worse fish bite, and during severe summer hot spells only early morning and late evening can yield anything decent for the fisherman.
3. In the middle of summer fish bite very sluggishly on earthworms, but better on bread than at other times of year; they bite best on crayfish, especially molting ones.
4. Cool weather, not clear and sunny weather, is the most favorable for summer angling because the fish move about less and hold deeper in swims known to the sportsman.

It's impossible to dispute that in fishing, as in everything else, much depends on luck, and that there are lucky fishermen, just as there are lucky gamblers. Otherwise it would be a tall order to explain the groundless success of one man and the unearned failure of another. Nonetheless, just as the lucky gambler who lacks skill often comes off the loser, so the lucky fisherman who lacks skill manages to catch little. In all things one requires firmness, patience and the ability to make use of luck. The impatient fisherman—vexed that his fisherman-neighbor has fish biting all the time in a terrible swim, on a crudely fashioned outfit, with ridiculous and unseasonable bait, while his own rigs, skillfully assembled, baited in sportsmanlike fashion, lie motionless—often quits a good, groundbaited swim, moves to another, and another, misses the best time, and returns home with empty hands, while his neighbor, moving to the abandoned swim, regardless of his poor rigs and lack of fishing skill (because of which, it stands to reason, he should lose half his fish), returns home with a full bag. This, though, is more a matter of character than of fishing skill. In general one must never be angry with failure. I've known many fishermen who, when anything went wrong at the start—for example, their rig fouled or snagged, or, worst of all, they lost the first good fish—would grow enraged, begin to bait their hooks terribly, set the hook too early and too abruptly, and would stop fishing. Thus, being entirely at fault themselves, these impatient sportsmen blame their bad luck.

As to fishing with ready-made, artificial insects with hooks

I can say nothing, because no matter how many times I've attempted it, my trials have been unsuccessful.

Fishing for trout (spottie), grayling, and taimen (redling) has an altogether different character, if it's done on swift, small streams. But in the upper reaches of ponds on such streams, in which these species of fish are sometimes found, it in no way differs from ordinary fishing, for the water there is deep and not quite transparent. Trout-fishing in small, undammed—hence, absolutely clear—streams must be done with the greatest circumspection. The slightest noise or human shadow falling on the water's surface will instantly cause the frightened fish to hide under the bank or the roots of trees, and sometimes they won't come out from under them for several hours. Having spied out a good swim* from afar, one must creep up from the bushes and pass through them a long, straight rod on whose tip is wound a short line with a small sinker, a hook baited with a red earthworm, and no float. Quietly unwind the line and lower it into the water. If the fish doesn't see you, then he'll bite that very second, sometimes barely allowing the worm to enter the water. If, though, you let down the hook and the fish doesn't take immediately, then he's either not there or you've scared him. One must immediately go to another swim. For stream-fishing, as I've already said, small whirlpools are chosen. In one swim you'll never catch more than five fish—six at the most. Sometimes it's possible to cast the outfit after concealing oneself behind steep banks, thick trees or bushes, *without passing the rod through them.* In that case the line should be a little longer. One must recognize that this fishing is fairly troublesome and fatiguing. Spottie, and especially taimen, according to several sportsmen, take avidly on baitfish.

Sometimes, though very seldom, fairly large spottie are caught. I've taken one of more than two-and-a-half pounds, though I have it on good authority that other fishermen have taken fish of five pounds and more. The taimen reaches enormous size. I saw a taimen of twenty-seven pounds; during the

---

*Good swims are to be found in small whirlpools, holes where the water turns and runs more quietly and where trout sometimes jump at the surface, catching small worms that fall from trees, as well as midges and other insects.

spring flood, he'd moved into a small brook and been caught with a burlap dragnet. Tinkering with a fish in a small stream and shallow water is very difficult. Playing him is awkward, roots jut up from the banks, and there are trees and bushes along shore; lines are for the most part fine, hooks small, rods inflexible, and fish of the liveliest sort. . . . Now that's trouble for you! Under such circumstances it's difficult to avoid an unfortunate loss. A large fish, though, rarely takes in small whirlpools, but more often in the upper reaches of ponds in deep water. There the sportsman with medium outfits of the usual configuration has nothing to fear from the desperate leaps of this fish—who fights furiously when hooked—and the precious quarry won't escape the fisherman's net.

Angling around midday, which I promised to discuss separately, is done on hot summer days in those places where dense shade covers the water, namely, under bridges, boardwalks overhanging the banks, thick stumps and snags that often protrude into the water, and under thick overhangs of weeds spreading over fairly deep water. Perch especially love to hold in the shade and take at midday quite well. Sometimes ide and chub will bite even on a rig fished shallow. But only in flowing ponds overgrown with rushes and weeds does midday fishing come into its own. On a hot day in summer, from around nine in the morning, all the decent fish will leave the mainstream and the clear sections of the overflow to enter flood-pools set about with weeds and thick, green stalks of bulrush, over which the cattail is already raising its fluffy, dark-brown plumes. Among the weeds and rushes there are always some spots a bit deeper than others that never get overgrown and are called "channels." In these swims it follows that one must fish from a boat. In the weeds near such swims, at the proper distance and time, stakes are driven in, and the boat is tied to these to keep it from rocking. Here long rods are definitely required, for the boat must stay some distance from the swim and the rods are placed on the weeds. If one is among bulrushes, however, stakes are not necessary: having brought the boat to a clear area, one must place it sideways to the clearing so that the boat and fisherman are completely hidden in the rushes, a couple of handfuls of which are taken and bent underneath oneself. The fisherman sits securely on top of them and the boat will stand motionless. The rods must lie across the boat. For the most part the water will be shallow— all the more reason for silence and caution while moving about, especially when landing fish, which take very well in such swims and tend to be very large. This kind of angling in flood-pools is especially important because during torrid summer weather, apart from early morning and late evening, and also in groundbaited swims, it's difficult to catch anything decent either in the pond's mainstream or in its upper reaches, or in a river, whereas in flood-pools the catch will sometimes be abundant and varied. It's delightful to watch the keep-net,* attached to the opposite side of the boat, in which great perch, ide, chub, tench, bream and even pike are swimming about!

Aside from the aforementioned reasons, midday fishing by boat has, at least for me, its own particular kind of charm. For many, this seems incomprehensible. Many people find unbearable the piercing rays of summer's midday sun, which, as it's reflected on the water, acts with redoubled force. I, however, always loved, and still do love, the heat of our short-lived summer. . . . The torrid noontide blazes, and perfect silence reigns over the unstirring meadow, as green now as it was in spring. It's just as if the pond, woven over with weeds, is sleeping between its sloping banks. The rushes stand motionless. The mainstream and its channels, cleansed by the weeds, gleam like mirrors, and all the remaining expanse of water is thick with myriad aquatic plants. Now bright green, now dark, leaves spread along the water, though their roots have gone down deep into the muddy bottom. There are the white and yellow water lilies (blossoms of the lily-pad), informally called "juglets," and the little red flowers of the dark grass, sticking out over the long, sculpted leaves. All this adds variety to the green carpet that covers the surface of the pond. What opulent warmth! What languor and luxury for one's body! How pleasant are the water's nearness and the chance to cool one's head and face with it! The fish are hot too. As if sleepy, they hold beneath the shady weeds. Coveting tasty foodstuffs, they strike

---

*"Keep-net" is the name given to a sack of strong, fine netting. A hoop is inserted in its middle, the lower end is tied shut, and the upper end is gathered on a strong line with which it's tied to whatever necessary.

at prey and hurry back under their green overhangs, having only for a moment swum lazily out into clear waters shot through by the sun's rays.

Any fisherman knows that one often chances to snag the hooks of one's outfits on uneven bottom, bank, rocks, weed- and tree-roots jutting invisibly into the water, or on branches of intact trees that often lie in it. Many hooks and lines are lost because of this. It's impossible to avoid such afflictions, especially if you're fishing in unfamiliar waters. Moreover, the fish, predominantly perch, like to hold in precisely such fastnesses, and, when caught on a rig, they pull it over the snag. Thus for unsnagging rigs one must always have a smooth iron clearing-ring, about three inches in diameter and a pound or less in weight, tied to a long, slender, and strong line. Having put the rod-butt of the snagged outfit through the ring, one must then allow the ring to slide down at first along the rod, then along the line, which is meanwhile held a bit slack. The ring, on reaching the hook, will disengage it with its weight.* In the absence of such a ring one can fairly successfully free fishing rigs with a pole in precisely the same way in which I described freeing a fish that has become tangled in the weeds. But it can happen that there's no ring, no pole and no one to climb into the water to free the hook, whose loss is now inevitable. It remains to break it off, preserving as much line as possible. There's no other means of doing this than winding it around the rod until it breaks off.

One must never rush the unsnagging of a fouled fishing outfit. It's very often the case that a crayfish drags the hook into a hole, or a fish drags it under the bank. One must lay down the rod without tugging on the line. It frequently happens that after a little time the outfit will disengage itself; that is, the fish will free it, or the crayfish will release it, or it will be washed away from the bank by the water.

Sometimes fishing outfits come unsnagged in some mysterious fashion, but, without doubt, this has been done by a fish.

---

*In one French booklet I read that such a clearing-ring can be made with two hooks soldered securely, opposite one another, to the outside of the ring, so that, having hooked it to the snag on which your fishing outfit is stuck, you can tear the snag out and thereby save your hook.

With my own eyes I've seen a rig that was snagged by the sinker on a steep bank get disengaged by a roach who tugged the hook downward. This is no great marvel. I once saw a hook—stuck fast into a block of wood because I'd tugged hard on the rod several times, even risking a break-off—get freed by a fish who, having struck the baited hook from behind and pulled it down, very easily removed it from the wood. As if that weren't enough, I once snagged a hook in deep water so badly that, having struggled more than an hour, I abandoned the outfit in order not to scare the fish and to be able to disengage the rig later. After an hour and a half, I saw the float go down, the line tighten and the rod even get dragged into the water. I seized it and pulled out a big perch. The line was baited with crayfish.

Now we'll examine generally all those species of fish to whose capture we devote ourselves.

# ON FISH IN GENERAL

The fish's element is water, and his purpose is to swim in it. To this end he's supplied with a large number of fins as well as a tail trimmed with them. For submerging himself in the water and holding at various depths, he has an internal bladder that lies along the spinal column, is filled with air, and stretched into two unequal halves. One might assume that by contracting and expanding this bladder the fish sinks down or rises up. Further details of the fish's internal anatomy are a subject for natural history. I shall discuss how and where fish live, and how they reproduce.

The fecundity of fish is difficult to comprehend. Many of them have such tiny roe, and in such abundance, that if all of it were fertilized and hatched, then each fish would annually produce, say, a million facsimiles of itself and there would not be enough water on the earth's surface to accommodate them. But this is not what happens in the event. Nature did not supply every female fish with such an astonishing abundance of roe idly, because, apart from the fact that roe often goes unfertilized, it's destroyed every minute by predacious foes who surround it in the water and live in the air above the water, and for whom the roe serves as a tasty food. I cannot determine at what age female fish begin to *cast* (or *thrash*) *roe* that is capable of accepting fertilization, or when the males' milt attains the ability to fertilize. There can, however, be no doubt that small, young fish, which have not yet reached one-tenth of their natural size, possess roe and milt annually, starting one year after birth. Each species of fish casts its spawn at its own specific time, which means that this operation is taking place almost all the year round.* When the season

*Many sportsmen claim that certain species of fish spawn twice a year, but I completely disagree. Though roe inside fish of the same species can be found at different times of year, this only proves that individuals spawn at different periods. I am convinced that each female fish spawns once a year. My conviction is based on the *slow rate* at which roe develops inside the fish; there would not be enough time to complete the process of spawning two times in one year.

arrives,* females feel the desire or necessity to cast off their burdensome roe, and the males their milt, and both gather in schools. The males crowd right up to the females, even mixing with them. The latter release their eggs, while the former pour their milt over them. The spawners are followed by other species of fish, for the most part predatory ones: pike, perch, zander, asp, burbot, and so on, and even those not classified as predatory—chub and ide.** They all greedily swallow the little eggs, tiny as poppy seed, enmeshed in slime, which float in clusters with the appearance of tufts of fur or spiderwebs and hold at the surface or any depth of water. The spawning females and males, especially the former, try to press themselves, or strike themselves, against something hard. They hang about the banks and aquatic plants, preferably bulrushes and water lilies, and near underwater snags, roots and stones. Certain species—namely, bream, crucian carp and roach—constantly leap from the water and plop about its surface so that the eggs and milt might flow more freely because of these movements and jolts. Sitting quietly and placidly with a fishing outfit on the bank of a lake or river cove overgrown with weeds, and, sometimes, hiding in a boat in the thick bulrushes of a pond, I have often had occasion to observe, though superficially, the curious scene of this *piscine thrashing*.***[26]

While the air is perfectly still, the water's surface is dis-

---

*This season will be recognized by anyone who has glanced at a fish caught at the proper time, especially if the fish is taken in hand. Besides being unusually fat, even pot-bellied, the females excrete liquid roe, while the males expel a whitish slime resembling milk.

**I submit that all species of fish, without exception, eat any spawn, even their own.

***Even with the three aforementioned species, it's very difficult to observe the process of casting, or thrashing, roe not only because it takes place for the most part among weeds or rushes, but chiefly because fish fear the proximity of people. Certain fishermen claim that it's not the males who chase the females, but the other way around, with the females after the males. They say that there are far more females than males, and that the former hang about the latter, chase them into a shoal, into dense weeds, and, when the male, having turned his little belly upward, starts to excrete milt, the females release their eggs directly into this fertilizing liquid. I won't take it upon myself to decide which opinion is more just. In warm, sunny weather, the eggs hatch in ten, twelve, or fourteen days.

turbed, as though by the wind, because of the fidgeting and jumping fish. Spray flies on all sides, and the splashing water is audible from far away. I was very surprised by this spectacle the first time I saw it. With gun in hand, I had come up to a small lake, surrounded by a shoal of tall, dense bulrush, and suddenly heard some strange noise in the water. Supposing that this was coming from brooding ducks, I carefully entered the rushes, made my way through the water on hands and knees to the lake's edge—and saw a veritable piscine dance being performed by a roach of medium size. I didn't immediately guess what this phenomenon meant, but I had heard of it. Several times thereafter I've had occasion to observe this process with roach and especially crucian carp, but despite all my desire to examine it in detail I haven't been able to do so. I myself have never witnessed the devouring of eggs by other fish, though I've often found eggs in the stomachs of caught fish.

When this operation is accomplished by other species of fish, especially *bottom fish*, that is, those that usually move or swim along the bottom—namely, rudd, gudgeon, stone loach, tench, and, most of all, burbot, which spawn around Christmastide—they probably hang about the banks and underwater snags or on gravelly, stony bottom. The latter supposition is proved by the fact that precisely in these places, at precisely this time of year, burbot are caught in muzzle-traps or mouth-traps.[27] Roe excreted by the aforementioned species of fish, it would seem, must be exposed to less destruction because the waters are covered with ice and in winter the fish don't swim about everywhere, but stay in one place. It seems that these species should multiply much more than the others, but one certainly can't make this claim, especially about burbot. Without doubt, there must be other reasons why their countless, fine-grained eggs vanish.

Thus, at the very appearance of the tiny piscine eggs, their destruction commences. It continues until the complete formation of the little fish, who, being surrounded by the same enemies, can at least hide from them and save himself by his nimble swimming and small size. Besides predatory and non-predatory fish, birds also eat a considerable quantity of roe. The chief extirpators are ducks, gulls, and crows. Ducks and gulls seize roe as it floats in the water, and even dive after it, while crows get at it from land as they walk the banks and shallow water, for the most part near weeds, where the eggs are washed in by the wind. Here, having adhered to sedges or bulrushes where they're splashed up by the waves, the eggs often dry out and go to waste. One must assume that in the first year or years the fish grows very quickly, because after he hatches from eggs as tiny as poppy seed, he attains in one month the size of an oat grain in the husk. My own observations convinced me of this. Regarding the further growth of fish, and likewise their longevity, I know absolutely nothing. It's said and written that pike live up to three hundred years, while carp live more than a century, to prove which, we are assured in print, incontrovertible experiments have been performed.[28] Small pike and carp with gold or silver rings put through their cheekbones were released into ponds that never dwindled but were refreshed by flowing water or internal springs, and the year was indicated on the rings. Such fish were caught afterward (by the experimentors' descendants, it stands to reason), and their longevity was confirmed by the inscriptions of the years.

Fish have maladies that are often revealed by black spots over the entire body. If these spots are located only on the surface of the skin, then the fish will safely endure them, but if the black color penetrates deeply and touches the internal organs, the fish dies. I've noticed that almost every autumn black dots appear on roach in streams, for the most part dammed ones, near Moscow. Local fishermen have assured me that this is because the roach feeds on weeds beaten down by autumn frosts, and that he's done no harm by it. This seems to be true. In small ponds without flowing water, in which crucian carp are found in great abundance, it often happens that these fish—especially the white ones—develop spots that are first sanguine and then black, but I've rarely noted crucian carp languishing from this alone. At first I thought the spots appeared due to internal causes, but on close examination I've seen that they result from the biting of minute green worms that in some years—especially during a hot, dry summer—appear in stagnant waters in unbelievable multitudes. They creep under the scales of the crucian carp and suck their blood. In one small wound I would find more than ten little worms. Moreover, in such ponds there live water-lizards, beetles, and large, greenish, aquatic worms (probably grown up from the small green ones) that wrap themselves up in a little tube, as if glued together of sedge.*[29] They all bite and do damage to the poor crucian carp, thereby obstructing their reproduction and full growth, and even biting to death those fish placed in wicker pens or slit-pens. In addition, all these filthy pests will take on a fishing outfit baited with dungworm, and it's often befallen me to disengage the repulsive vermin from my hooks. Nowhere have I encountered such an abundance and variety of this subaquatic fauna as near Moscow.

Sometimes one catches a sickly fish without any external or internal signs of illness, but the intestines and bladder appear wrinkled and somewhat dry.

A fish's health doubtless depends on good water and food. All sportsmen know that in one particular body of water the fish tend to be plump, tasty, and lively, while in another they are emaciated, bland, and sluggish. But which qualities of water and what kind of food are healthy or harmful for fish, we certainly don't know. Water even affects the color of a fish: without altering his natural spotting and other marks, the fish's brightness or hue is changed solely by his being transferred from one body of water to another. This has been established by many experiments. Lake crucian carp, for example, usually tend to be bright, deep-yellow or gold, while those transplanted into clayey, turbid, artificial ponds turn a pale pinkish color. Perch in some rivers are very dark and brightly spotted, but, after living in a pond for a long time, they become light, or whitish. Exactly the same thing occurs with more or less all the other species of fish as well.

Very rarely, fish suffocate in winter beneath the ice, even in

---

*These aquatic worms have the capacity to crawl halfway out of their tubes and to hide in them completely. Water beetles are flat and chestnut-colored, with shells that are whitish along the edge. They nimbly crawl about the ground and fly quickly in the air, rising straight up from the water and descending straight down into it. I've been told that peasants near Moscow use them instead of leeches.

huge lakes and in ponds with flowing water.* At first, after the passage of a certain amount of time, such fish show themselves in the apertures of ice-holes, thrusting their mouths from the water and gulping air, but they don't yet allow themselves to be caught, and swim away when a person approaches. They'll appear thereafter in much larger numbers, as if besotted, so that they can be caught by net and even taken by hand. Sometimes dead fish also rise to the surface. As soon as the number of ice-holes is considerably increased, the fish recover and conceal themselves. This latter condition has produced universal certainty that fish will die from insufficiency of ice-holes, that is, due to a lack of vents through which stale aquatic vapors can escape and where fresh air can be obtained. This is partially true, but to agree unreservedly with such a conclusion is impossible, for the following reasons:

1. All lakes and ponds, both large and small, that are not located near human habitation, never have ice-holes because there's no one there to make them, and no reason to make them. They also lack leads, that is, unfrozen places, which, as is well known, occur only on large and swiftly flowing rivers. Consequently, in such ponds and lakes there should be no fish at all, let alone in great numbers, but experience shows that the reverse is true.

2. In ponds and lakes located in or near settlements and having permanent ice-holes for the watering of livestock or for other purposes, fish in some years die off under the ice in the presence of an identical number of holes.

3. Such dying-off occurs not every year, but every ten or more years, even under exactly the same conditions.

From the aforesaid one must conclude that there are some other conditions under whose influence fish will perish beneath the ice, but that, independent of these reasons, fish recover if the water's communication with the atmosphere is increased. For the preservation of the fish's health, there's

---

*Of the many such curious phenomena I've seen myself, the most remarkable occurred in Kazan' around 1804. There, Lake Kaban, an enormous body of water, stagnated in the winter, and the fish seemed besotted. A multitude of people came running and riding from all around, caught them with all means, and loaded down entire carts with fish.

great benefit to be derived from maintaining large ice-holes that are cleared daily not only on ponds having no current, and on lakes, but also on flowing ponds and placid, whirlpool-laden rivers that are completely covered with ice.

Fish are sometimes killed off by the introduction of harmful outside substances, to wit: manure run-off from cattleyards and spoiled water from factories and foundries, if either one somehow percolates into a lake or pond (usually one without flowing water). But widespread and sudden fish-kills can occur for utterly unknown reasons. The last time I happened to see such a fish-kill was in 1841, when I spent the summer in the village of Il'inskoe, near Moscow. About two miles away there was a fairly large, deep pond and mill on Somynka Brook at the village of Oborvikho.[30] Large numbers of every kind of fish inhabited this pond because the multitude of underwater stumps, snags, and thick weeds made it impossible to seine or dragnet there. I used to go there almost every day to fish. Once, at the end of July, while driving up to the pond, I saw that all the banks had turned white, just as if snow had fallen along the edge of the water. Drawing nearer on foot, I saw that it was dead fish: perch, roach, small ide, chub and young pike. The miller told me the fish had started to die the day before. There appeared to be no signs of illness in the dead fish. Large ide and huge pike swam about near the surface, circling. Peasants were catching them and safely using them as food. Remarkably, the tench, crucian carp, and ruff remained unscathed. Out of curiosity, I began to fish immediately. The fish took from time to time, but very quietly and sluggishly, and those I caught seemed almost dead. The fish-kill continued for five days and suddenly ceased. Several days later the fish started biting as before, and there was no perceptible decline in their numbers. In surrounding waters the fish remained perfectly healthy. This was obviously no general epidemic, so its cause had to be local, located only in the Somynka pond, in whose water, however, I could discern no change of any kind. The peasants told me a story to the effect that some drunken soldier, after quarreling with the miller in a tavern, threatened him and threw something into the pond as he walked past.

Leaving it up to the judgment of every reader to be satisfied or not with such an explanation, I, for my part, will say that we still know very little about both those medicinal and poisonous substances, especially herbs, which are familiar to the common people. One thing is sure: that the fish in the Somynka did not die of thorn-apple, tobacco, or snailseed poisoning, for the effect of their toxins is short-lived and lasts less than a day. These poisons are produced in the following way. Tobacco, thorn-apple, or, most often, snailseed (for it's much, much more potent), is ground into a fine powder, mixed with baked bread or raw dough, and scattered in small pieces about those places where fish tend to hold, and they avidly swallow the pieces. In an hour or less, depending on the quality and quantity of the poison, the fish become inebriated, besotted. They run up on shoals, float to the water's surface, swim in circles, wriggle, ram the banks (sometimes even flopping out onto them), and especially tend to get into rushes and weeds if these are present. The poisoners, for the most part country lads and little boys who have impatiently awaited this amusement, run along the banks and weedy shallows with loud and joyous shouts, picking up the dead fish and catching by hand the ones that fall asleep, while using nets for the big fish. Although compared to past practices this destructive bagging of fish has declined considerably, nonetheless, unfortunately, everyone is certain that fish poisoned in this way, even the dead ones, serve as harmless food for people. While it seems difficult to agree with this, even if we assume that such certainty is justified, this poison is still very harmful to the fish. The ones who have swallowed a good deal of snailseed die quickly, float to the top, and are gathered and eaten. But a considerably larger portion of the poisoned fish swim, unconscious, under banks, snags, rocks, bushes, and tree roots, into the dense rushes and weeds that sometimes grow in deep water—and there they die, unnoticed by the poisoners themselves. These fish are therefore *lost utterly in vain*, while their rotting fouls the water and air. I even think that all fish fed on snailseed who then recover because they've eaten only a little of the poison must be sick for quite some time, lose the capacity to reach full size, and, perhaps, to reproduce their progeny. I've noted that where fish have often been poisoned they have considerably declined, and that the number caught by means of poisoning pales beside the quantity of fish caught annually before, in the same water, with ordinary fishing rigs. It's also evident that, after snailseed-poisoning, fish stop taking on rod and line.

The predatory species of fish feed on small fry, while the nonpredatory ones swallow whatever falls their way. Nonetheless, the feeding of the latter is sometimes a mysterious affair. In ponds, lakes, and rivers with some or a great deal of aquatic weeds and plants, fish feed on them as well as on the insects and vermin to be found near them. This makes sense, and all fishermen know that the most nourishing food available to a fish is young reed, whose first shoots are sweet to the taste. If you quietly approach a reedy and grassy pond or lake and listen carefully, you will be astounded at the strange and incessant noise—the munching sound—made by fish eating the weeds. But what provides nourishment to nonpredatory fish in large rivers that flow constantly between sandy banks on which not a single blade of grass grows, whose bottom is also sandy and clean, and where very few aquatic insects are present? And finally, what lends sustenance to fish in those wooden tanks, with wooden bottoms, called *slit-pens* (because they are *slit*, or perforated), in which fishermen usually keep caught fish, occasionally for up to several months without ever feeding them? I'm incapable of answering these questions satisfactorily. One must reluctantly agree with the opinion of the commercial fishermen, who say that fish feed on slime, silt, soil, sand, and even on water itself. That fish live in pens without food can only be explained by this, if we assume beforehand that all water contains within it a multitude of infusoria not visible to the human eye but that must by itself be nourishing for the fish.

In spring, when the runoff begins, as soon as the water becomes murky, the rivers start to swell and rise, and the fish also rise to the surface and move against the current, near the banks at first. They're caught there in great numbers by nets. But when the rivers overflow their banks and spill into low-lying places, fish too disperse about the flood-pools, never ceasing to struggle doggedly against the current. This instinctive struggle is so strong that it's difficult to believe if you haven't seen it.[31] Despite the terrible speed with which

heavy floodwaters rush, breaking loose at flood-gates or releases from overflowing ponds, the fish reach the very last,
steep waterfall, and, with no chance of swimming against the
pounding vertical cascade, leap upward. Ceaselessly battered
by the water's force, falling backward and often beating themselves to death against wooden scaffolding or against stones,
new schools of fish continually repeat their attempts, and
many are successful; that is, they end up in the pond. During
spring floods, fish visit the very headwaters of rivers, streams,
and brooks. When one stands in summer near the places they
go, it's hard to believe that large fish were caught here with
wing-traps or withe-traps placed at first with the current, then
against the current.[32] But as soon as the water "falters," that is,
recedes, the fish turn back and head downstream with the
same striving they had displayed before while making their
way upstream. To this end, they instantly rush from shallow
places into deep ones, from the overflows into the mainstream.
It often happens, though, that when they make their way too
high or far into the water-meadows, they can't find a water
route for returning to the river and therefore remain in small
holes and potholes. If they are seen by people, they are caught.
If not, and the potholes dry up in isolation, the fish perish and
become food for crows and various other birds, sometimes
even for pigs. Fish that are unexpectedly stranded in holes, or,
as they say in Moscow, "hollows," by a shallowing of the water
passages, will pass from one to the other *overland*, jumping
along a damp trail where water has recently run. If, however, a
tiny brooklet remains, they will bound down along it without
fail. By this same means, fish escape even from artificial pens
or small ponds through which brooklets run, provided the
banks are low. Such vernal journeys of fish upstream and back
are partly repeated at every fortuitous but considerable rise of
the water: the sudden breach of huge ponds, and freshets
resulting from heavy and prolonged rains.

Not all species of fish can live with the same water temperature. Some require clean, swift, and cold water, while others
need warm, quiet, and even stagnant water with a rather silty
or muddy bottom. I'll discuss this in a bit more detail in the
descriptions of the fish, but here I'll mention only the succes-

sion according to which one species lives after the other in any river. Most rivers begin in springs as cold as ice. Flowing in the open air, warming themselves in the sun's rays, augmenting themselves with various tributaries, they grow warmer. In the very headwaters of such springs or sources, live trout (that is, spottie), grayling, and taimen (or redling); after them, minnow, stone loach, and burbot. Then appear chub, roach, perch, pike, and gudgeon; next, bleak, dace, ruff, ide, zander, and, if the river is large, asp; finally, bream, tench, carp, and crucian carp. Certain of the aforementioned species—namely, stone loach and crucian carp—can live and be found in the coldest and warmest water, as well as in the cleanest and dirtiest water. It stands to reason that such a succession is sometimes violated in its exact details, but where are there not exceptions to be found thanks to regional causes and conditions? Thus, all species of fish can live in the selfsame river if its flow is *protracted*, but some live upstream, where the water is colder and cleaner, while others live downstream, where the water is warmer and murkier. It's not hard to become convinced of this if one has researched the flow of any respectable river. During the spring floods, water is the same everywhere—murky and cold—and fish that normally inhabit comparatively warm water ascend to the coldest springs. If, however, during their return downstream, something accidentally detains them in such places where the water is still too cold, or, vice versa, they move so far downstream that the water turns out to be too warm, then the fish will either ascend higher or descend lower, but they'll unfailingly seek out their accustomed temperature. If the fish can't do this that same year because of pond-gates or grating, then they'll certainly do it the following year. Many sportsmen have witnessed the insuperability of this struggle toward the customary temperature when they attempt to rear for themselves those species of fish that lived in the very same river, but several miles downstream. All efforts turn out to be useless. They plant fish small and large, day and night, at all times of year; at first they hold them for about two months in pens fenced off in the same pond. But there's nothing for it: in spring, the fish ascend the river and are caught about ten miles upstream, and then every last one of them heads downstream. There thus remains only one means that's occasionally successful: to force the fish to spawn in the same water you've designated for their offspring.

In small, flowing, spring-fed ponds, which always have fresh and even cold water, which scarcely rise because of spring floods and *never overflow,* whose outlets are always protected by grates and whose upper reaches are shallow, any kind of fish will live, even though the water's temperature bears no likeness to that which is natural for the fish. But here they'll only *survive,* not *thrive,* and won't even attain their full natural size. The best and most successful method for rearing certain fish species, in flowing and still ponds in which they don't ordinarily hold or start to live of their own accord, consists of the following. Catch the fish you wish to rear just before they spawn. For every six gravid females select about two milters, and put them into a long, spacious enclosure or pen built in a pond designated for the purpose. When fry hatch from the eggs that were voided in their turn, and have grown a bit, remove the enclosure and release the fish into the pond. The old fish will depart, while the young ones will remain and sometimes breed, if the water temperature isn't too different from that in which the old fish were caught. In precisely the same way crayfish are raised.*

I was just discussing how difficult it can be to cultivate certain species of fish in water where they were previously absent. On the other hand, however, fish by themselves can breed incomprehensibly in places where neither they nor their roe, it would seem, could possibly end up, as, for example, in steppe lakes lying a great distance from rivers and therefore never flooded by spring runoff, or in mountain lakes. In the Sterlitamak district of Orenburg Province, on the River Be-

---

*I had occasion to convince myself that crayfish can live in thick mud or in river silt more than a yard below the surface of the bottom. Once, while I was present, the shell of a spring-well was being cleaned at the end of summer. The well was more than two yards deep, would rise with the spring floodwater, and was very densely filled to the top with mud and earthen silt (I don't know why it hadn't been cleaned out earlier). At a depth of almost four feet, where the soil became a little moister, we began to catch large, live crayfish. About twenty of them were tossed out, and they were perfectly plump and tasty. Crayfish are thus able to manage with almost no air.

laia,[33] there are very high mountains located some distance apart from one another and visible from meadows about twenty-five miles away. When the sky is covered by clouds, the mountains shine white against the dark horizon in picturesque fashion.*[34] I don't know what one can find now on their summits, but about fifty years ago on two of them there were small lakes with clean, cold water. In one tarn, on Iurak-Tau I think, there were crucian carp, and perhaps other fish. How they could get there is difficult to explain. I also used to know one of the so-called *gaps* (round, more or less deep, funnel-shaped holes) of Orenburg Province in the upper reaches of the River Ik.[35] From time immemorial, this gap, like many others, kept its snow long after spring, while in summer it was so perfectly dry that forest raspberry grew down along its sides. All of a sudden, I heard that it had filled with water, and after about two years, that crucian carp had bred in that water. I verified both phenomena with my own eyes. I repeat my question: How could crucian carp get there, when the nearest lakes with crucian carp were located three-and-a-half miles from the gap? One must acknowledge the well-known assumption that a bird (probably a gull or crow), having swallowed fertilized fish eggs somewhere, then flies to various places and waters where no fish were found before, excretes the eggs in its droppings, and that the digestive juices of the avian stomach or craw do not deprive the roe of its capacity to hatch into fry. This is the only way to explain the appearance of fish on the mountain of Iurak-Tau and in the Ik gap, though I must also confess that such an explanation fails to satisfy me completely.

Fish have sensitive hearing and keen eyesight, especially trout, but, it seems, fish generally fear the sound of a person or animal more than the sight of them. At least they quickly get used to both, but fish are unbelievably sensitive to sound, and by exploiting sound one can deafen them to the point of unconsciousness. The universally known "stunning" of fish by cudgeling thin autumn ice serves as proof of this.[36] Fishermen know that the faintest sound affects fish. Who among them

*I recently read with pleasure a few lines about these mountains in the article by Mr. Avdeev entitled "A Journey on *Kumiss*," which was printed in the December issue of *Notes of the Fatherland*, 1852.

hasn't happened to be standing quietly or sitting near deployed fishing outfits, waiting for big fish, and seen small ones rising to the top, covering and rippling the whole surface of the water near his floats? Suddenly the fisherman coughs or sneezes—and like spray the silver schools of little fish scatter to all sides, just as if a momentary rain had sprinkled the water. The same thing happens after any sudden sound, or the appearance of a pike, large perch, asp, or other predatory fish.

Almost all young fish, especially a few from the smaller species, are so handsome, or, to put it better, pretty, sportive and bright, that people in the south of Russia use the phrase "little fish" (*rýbka*) as a term of affection, of tenderness—in praise of maidenly beauty and charm. The phrase is often encountered in Little Russian folksongs, in which, if the feeling of love isn't so deep or serious as in the Great Russian songs of old, then, on the other hand, it's more tender, more aesthetic, so to speak. In Gogol's story "May Night, or The Drowned Maiden," the young cossack Levko, summoning his dear Galia from her peasant house with various tender words, says, among other things: "My heart, my *little fish*, my necklace! Peep out at me. Put just your little white hand through the window . . ."[37] To a Great Russian peasant this sounds mawkish, but he too loves to look at any fish in the water, merrily glimpsed at the surface, as the fish flashes his scales now silver, now gold, now rainbow-striped—sometimes swimming quietly, imperceptibly, and sometimes holding motionless in the river depths! . . . No one, young or old, will pass by a river or pond without watching "the free little fish swim about." And sometimes the peasant, who was hastening on foot about some necessary business, forgets for awhile his life of toil, stands for some time, without stirring, and, leaning over the blue whirlpool, intently gazes into the murky depths. He admires the frolicsome movements of the fish, especially as they play and splash, when, having swum to the surface, they suddenly turn abruptly and plunge into the water, splashing with their tails and leaving on the surface a spinning ring whose edge, ever widening, doesn't immediately merge with the tranquil smoothness of the water. Or he admires how the fish slices the water's surface with just the edge of his dorsal fin, and like an arrow flies straight to one side, while behind him runs a long wake which, dividing itself in two, presents the strange figure of a radiating triangle . . .

Must one say after this that the sportfisherman gazes at every fish with even greater, more particular love? And that he looks upon a large one—a rare sight, for some unknown reason—with rapture, with a joyously beating heart! Perhaps only sportsmen won't find such statements ludicrous. I won't take offense at this, for I'm addressing sportsmen, and they'll understand me! Each of them, having reached old age, finds joy in the recollection of that vigorous feeling which animated him in youth, when, with rod in hand, forgetting both sleep and weariness, he would passionately devote himself to his own beloved sport. He must recall that golden time with plea-sure. . . . I too remember it, as a long-ago, sweet, and some-what vague dream. I remember the torrid midday, the bank set about with tall, fragrant grasses and flowers, the alder's shadow trembling on the water, the river's deep whirlpool, and the young fisherman—clinging to a tree stump that leaned over the water, his hair hanging down—who motionlessly strained his enchanted eyes into the clear, dark blue deep. . . . And how many fish roiled within it! What ide, chub, and perch. . . . And how the youth's heart froze, how his breathing would slacken. . . . This is long ago now, very long ago! Young sportsmen even now experience the same thing, and God grant they long preserve this vigorous, innocent feeling of the passionate fisherman.

———

I'll now set about a description of the fish species known to me that can be taken on rod and line. I'll begin with small fish that never reach considerable size, then discuss the large but nonpredatory species that very rarely feed on fish, and, finally, the strictly predatory species for which small fry constitute the vital and nearly exclusive foodstuff.

# 1. MINNOW

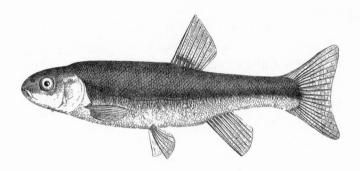

The very name (*loshók*) of this lovely little fish is a diminutive of the name "taimen" (*lokh*), and it's not bestowed upon the minnow idly.*[38] The red, black, and white speckles with which he's mottled are very similar to the spots of taimen, or redling, which reach huge size. But the little fish I'm discussing is among the smallest: a minnow of four inches is a rarity in size. They inhabit small, spring-fed streams and always appear in large schools. Sometimes in the small whirlpool of a clear brook you suddenly notice that the uniformly light-colored bottom is covered with something black; these are minnows, which school in several ranks, one on top of the other, usually with the larger ones above and the smallest below. It's not difficult to catch as many of them as you like with a *burlap-net* of coarse material, a close-woven net, or a *nosebag*** attached to its two narrow sides to two sticks. If, however, even these simple fishing rigs do not happen to come to hand, but you do have a small fishing outfit, then minnows will consistently take on dungworms (without the little tail, that is) and ordinary flies. The smaller the outfit, the better. No one, of course, will catch minnows unless there's some special need to do so, and I myself remember that I used to catch them only when I was a child. They can, however, come in very handy, for

*I recently learned that in the Mozhaisk district minnows are called "barebelly," while in the Vereia district they are known as "pigpunch." These fish probably inhabit other provinces as well.

**Nosebag* is the name given to an open sack of coarsely woven material in which oats are given to horses.

they're a superb bait for perch and any predatory fish of medium size. I've seen minnows only in Orenburg Province. There they were found in great abundance, and not only in small rivers, but also in those on which there were mills with about four pairs of millstones. I well remember the countless schools of minnows lying on the bottom under the mills' waterwheels. But the growing human population muddied the purity and transparency of the lovely streams and brooks there, and minnows have become much scarcer. Minnows prepared in a skillet make a tasty dish. They are cooked without being gutted; their innards are instead squeezed out by hand and the fish thoroughly washed.[39]

## 2. TOPPIE

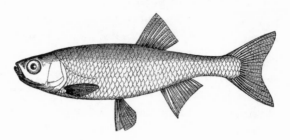

This is also a minute fish, no bigger than the minnow, though the latter is rounded, while the toppie[40] is flat. Toppie so resemble bleak that many consider them one and the same fish, only in different sizes, but this is incorrect. I know many rivers in various provinces where bleak are found in abundance under the name *bluelet* or *white-eye,* but there are certainly no toppie in them. The name "toppie" is given to him because of his habits: he loves to swim at the water's surface and often lies on his side, gleaming a rather bluish white in the sunshine, precisely as if he were a dead fish that had floated up to the surface. Where they are numerous, toppie can be very annoying. Whirling about the fishing rig with the swiftness of lightning, and with a running start, they ceaselessly touch and knock your hooks, sinkers, lines, and even floats, especially if you aren't bottom-fishing. They can be caught only on the very smallest outfit, baited with slender worms or a tiny piece of bread, or, best of all, a fly. The float must be attached as shallow as possible; toppie rarely submerge the float, but swiftly drag it to the side. . . . Toppie are also good simply as bait for predatory fish, and it's only with this aim that a commercial fisherman will catch them. They are found in great multitudes in all the rivers and clean ponds near Moscow, while in Orenburg Province there are none.

## 3. STONE LOACH

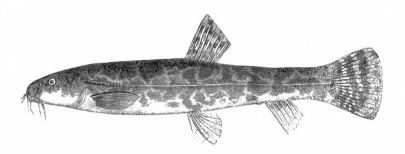

His name (*goléts*)[41] comes from the character of his skin, which is naked (*golá*); that is, there are no scales upon it. The skin is very fine, slippery, and of some kind of indeterminate color: grayish-yellow or pale pink with irregular, indistinct, more or less dark spots. In the selfsame water some stone loach can be lighter, while others are much darker. In general stone loach are darker in streams and brooks, while in ponds, especially in pens, they are yellower. The stone loach grows no longer than five inches, and larger fish are a great rarity. He's perfectly round and paunchy. The largest ones can be the thickness of a man's thumb. The stone loach has whiskers on his little mouth. Spawning takes place in April. The distinguishing characteristic of the stone loach is that he inhabits all waters, from an artificial pond that is muddy, dirty, and warm in summer, to a mountain spring as cold and clear as ice. Together with the trout (if not before him), he's the first to appear in the headwaters of springs, sometimes lying under the very rocks from beneath which the virgin stream of water issues forth.

Stone loach are generally so small that it's rare for someone to spend time fishing specifically for them, and they bite very little in rivers. In the small whirlpools of brooks and ponds, however, where they sometimes reproduce in unbelievable numbers and take consistently, it's great fun to angle for them. They bite exclusively on a single dungworm. One has to use the smaller sort of medium-sized hooks because it's difficult and tedious to be continually baiting the smallest size, while having to select the very smallest worms as well. One can safely allow a short length of their tails to dangle, since stone loach even take worms with no tail at all; this is because these fish do not bite on the run and do not swallow the bait at once. Instead, they take the worm's tail into their mouths and quietly swim to the side, which means that one must strike immediately, as soon as the float is carried sideways or straight. Because of the softness of their skin, stone loach serve as a tempting bait for all predatory fish, but also constitute a most delicious food for people. Fish soup prepared solely from stone loach that have been carefully cleaned (that is, without squashing their little gall-bladders) is so rich and tasty that it's scarcely inferior to burbot soup.[42] Fried and pickled stone loach are superb. They take on rod and line until the hard frosts. I've heard that stone loach are such greedy devourers of other fishes' roe that in small ponds they exterminate the other species, but I doubt this.

## 4 . GUDGEON

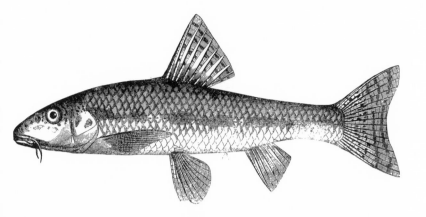

His name (*peskár'*)[43] comes from the fact that he always lies on sandy (*peschánoe*) bottom. Nonetheless, he's often called *piskár'*, not *peskár'*, but this is only because the former is easier to pronounce. Many people, however, are certain that this little fish must be called *piskár'* because, when being squeezed in a person's hands, he lets out a sound that resembles "*pisk.*"[44] The largest gudgeon is no more than six inches long and no thicker than a thumb, and even this size he attains very seldom. He's bar-shaped and fairly flat. His back and sides are covered with dark blue speckles, while his belly is quite whitish and silvery in color. Gudgeon are very handsome, or nice-looking, and most tidy little fish. They always gather in schools, which can be incredibly large. Gudgeon inhabit both small and large rivers, preferably sandy ones. Fishermen say that gudgeon spawn several times a year, but this is untrue; they probably undertake this operation during the winter months. When planted in ponds, they reproduce abundantly, especially if the water is clean (sometimes, though rarely, they live in dirty water). In small ponds they tend to be small, while in big ponds with flowing water, and in rivers, they are unusually large.

Gudgeon are deliberately sought by anglers, and for many sportsmen this is very pleasant fishing, for if gudgeon bite, they bite constantly and very surely. To catch them, anglers even attach two or three hooks, on separate leaders, to the same line, and sometimes the fish suddenly take all three. For angling, ordinary dungworms are used, and medium outfits are the most convenient.

In the course of my angling career, I've noticed an inexplicable oddity connected with gudgeon-fishing. In rivers and flowing ponds, especially near a wicket or flood-gate, they bite on rod and line with unusual eagerness. In large, still ponds, they don't take as well, while in small ponds or artificial pens they don't take at all, even though they may be present there in abundance. Another oddity: in the latter they sometimes take on bread, but in rivers they never do. I've chanced to fish a great deal in artificial ponds containing only crucian carp and gudgeon, and many times I've had the opportunity to watch my hooks baited with worms lie on the bottom or dangle among schools of gudgeon without attracting their attention (and I've often caught gudgeon by snagging them on their sides from without), but then, just as soon as a hook baited with a little piece of bread touched bottom, they immediately surrounded it. The gudgeon would touch, knock, pull about, tweak, and suck the bait until it fell off the hook. If the hook and piece of bread were very small, then I sometimes chanced to catch a gudgeon. Gudgeon have vexed me dreadfully with such pranks, for they did not bite in serious fashion and obstructed the crucian carp.

Gudgeon-fishing begins not in early spring, but when the water becomes absolutely clear, and it continues right up to winter. They bite at any time of day. In spring and summer they're usually sought in rivers, over riffles, and in shallow, sandy, gravelly swims where the water flows fairly quickly and one can see their schools lying on the bottom. Three methods of gudgeon-fishing are employed:

1. It's possible to fish with a float and moderately heavy sinker, going down deep enough that the sinker is suspended but the hook drags along the bottom. This is good in moderately fast current.

2. It's possible to fish without a float, and with a very heavy sinker located fifteen or even twenty inches from the hook. The sinker will lie on the bottom, while the line with the worm will undulate according to the water's

flow. This is the best method, especially in very strong current.

3. It's possible to fish without a sinker at all, with a float, or, better still, without a float. Let the water carry the hook baited with a worm where it will. Because of the current's speed, the hook won't immediately touch bottom, but as it gets close, gudgeon will expeditiously rise and strike the hook. Nowhere have I caught gudgeon in such quantity, and such big ones, as in the Moscow River. When the frosts arrive, gudgeon drop from shallow places into deep ones, where they remain for the winter. There they'll take until thick ice covers the surface of the water, and one must bottom-fish for them *without fail.*

The gudgeon bites boldly and surely. His take and hook-dragging are visible through the float and palpable to the hand. It's necessary to strike him swiftly, and therefore one must fish a single outfit and always hold the rod in hand. He makes an excellent bait for predatory fish and a most wholesome food for people. Gudgeon soup—so light and free of fat—is usually prescribed by doctors for their patients. Gudgeon cooked in sour cream are exceptionally tasty.[45]

I've already mentioned that gudgeon are caught on two and even three hooks, each shorter than the next, tied to the same line. It's true that if one must fish a swim where there's an enormous school of gudgeon, they take eagerly, and one may chance to land two or three gudgeon at once. But I don't care for this kind of fishing outfit. It gets terribly fouled and is suitable only for gudgeon, which, if the biting is good, can be caught in abundance even on one hook. The French are very keen on double and triple outfits, and they use them for going after big fish. Hooks of various sizes are attached, and the droppers are put down at widely varying depths, so that one hook lies on the bottom, while another hangs a yard above the bottom. It stands to reason that various baits are also used. This fishing method makes sense in its own peculiar way, and I've tried it, but without success. The double or triple fishing rig is ungainly, ugly, often snags, and fish don't strike it enthusiastically.

# 5. BLEAK

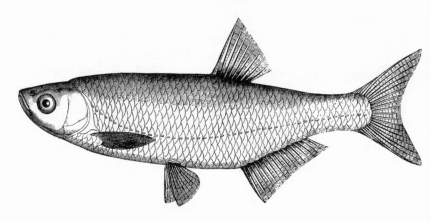

I've already said that the toppie perfectly resembles the bleak,[46] but is four times smaller. He's just as flat, slender, bluish-silver and white-eyed. For these last two qualities they call him *bluelet* and *white-eye* in Orenburg Province. I've never seen a bleak longer than seven inches or wider than two inches. Why he's called "bleak" (*ukléika*) near Moscow, I simply haven't been able to ascertain.[47] He's found in great quantities in all clean waters, especially rivers. When you stand above the blue depths of a whirlpool in a river or lake and the sun illuminates the water's surface from behind, then without fail you'll see at a fairly considerable depth the flashing of bluish-silver bands piercing the water in various directions like curving rays; these are bleak.

Sportsmen rarely engage in bleak-angling, but no matter what you fish for, if the hook is baited with dungworm, bleak won't cease to strike and spoil it or to be caught on the rig at the first immersion of the hook. This, of course, occurs where bleak are very numerous. If the worm reaches bottom safely, however, then they won't touch it much. The bleak makes a nuisance of himself by ruining a bait of worms that was in no way intended for him, but he attacks only small worms. If someone wishes to fish for bleak, then that angler must use small outfits, attach the float very shallow, with a tiny sinker, or even without a sinker at all. The bleak takes most eagerly and surely on a fly, and bites well on a worm with a little tail, but not so surely, because he often strikes only the dangling half of the worm. His bite is swift, and he attacks from a running start, suddenly dragging the float off to the side, sometimes plunging it into the water. If a bleak hooks himself, which happens infrequently, then he'll pull the line tight and even tug at the rod if you fail to set the hook immediately. There are no special swims for bleak. They hold along the entire river, though I've noticed large numbers of them in deep and quiet places. Bleak are good as bait for all predatory fish, even large ones, which they can entice from a distance since they toss about with extraordinary speed in all directions and flash a sparkling white. Bleak are never oily and therefore not used for fish soup, but they're very good when cooked in sour cream and when dried, or, better yet, smoked.[48] Their flavor is generally better than that of small roach. Bleak bite until late autumn, but, after the hard frosts, only in deep whirlpools and on the bottom.

# 6. DACE

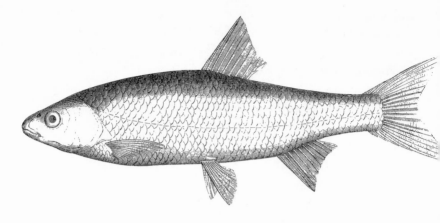

This fish[49] is unknown in the southern provinces. Perhaps he was given his name (*eléts*) because he first appeared in the renowned Elets River, on which the city of Elets stands.[50] With his shining silver scales he resembles the bleak, but the dace is whiter, and not flat, but bar-shaped, and thus similar in form to the chub. He can be a little over seven inches long and about a finger and a half thick. His eyes, fins, and tail are a kind of indistinct grayish-bluish color, but his back is a bit darker. In general this little fish is very lively and handsome. Dace are found fairly abundantly in all the rivers of Moscow Province as well as in flowing ponds and lakes flooded by river water in the spring. They can't live in small, stale, artificial ponds. Just like bleak, dace are very nimble in their movements, but appear broader, brighter, and whiter in deep water. For the most part they bite at the bottom and hold most willingly in swift, gravelly, stony shallows.

The dace's bite is fairly sure. If he strikes on the bottom, then he first carries the float without diving, and this is the time to set the hook. If, though, the bait doesn't touch bottom, then he takes actively and drags away the float altogether. One must fish for him with dungworms, but large ones take more avidly on small earthworms. It's said that dace also bite on bread, but I've never happened to catch a dace on bread bait. In autumn, dace love to play in the sun, and at that time one has to fish for them by tying on the float very shallow, sometimes lowering it right down to the leader. After the hard frosts, however, in October, they take only on the bottom, in deep whirlpools. Dace of medium size make good bait for pike and large burbot. The flavor of dace is something between roach and bleak, and therefore has little merit. They begin to bite very early, even in April, when the water in rivers is still excessively swift and turbid.

## 7. RUFF

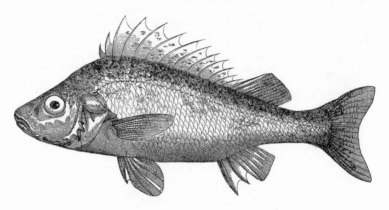

The name "ruff," obviously, is given to this fish[51] because of his exterior: his whole back, almost from head to tail, is armed with sharp, strong spines, which are united by a thin, spotted membrane. His cheeks, which cover the gills, also have one long row of spines. When you pull him from the water, he has the ability to spread his gills so wide, to flare his spiny crest and bend his tail so much, that the name "ruff" was probably given to him the moment he was first seen by man. A ruff in this state, quickly plucked from the water, doesn't even seem to be a fish, but some kind of round and shaggy object. Even when hefted, he seems heavier than other little fish of equal size.

Russians love the ruff, and use his name, in adjectival form, for any unattractive, quick-tempered man who gets angry, bristles, or flies into a rage.[52] Russians have composed an entire fairy tale about the ruff that probably everyone knows, in chapbooks of whimsical originality, and sometimes with amusing assonances instead of rhymes.[53] In my view, the ruff is the best fish of those that don't reach large size. In shape he resembles the perch, though the ruff never feeds on other fish. In the rivers of Russia's central zone, he's scarcely seven inches long, but in Saint Petersburg, in the mouth of the Neva, ruff of unusual size are caught. I myself have seen them over seven inches there. I've also heard of enormous Siberian ruff.

The ruff has unusually large, bulging eyes of dark blue. From his very head, as I've already mentioned, runs a rigid crest almost two inches tall. It ends about two fingers short of the tail, and this area too is occupied by another small crest, but a soft one, similar to a normal piscine fin. The ruff pricks like a perch if you grasp him incautiously. He's mottled everywhere except on his belly, but the speckles are some sort of darkish, indistinct color. His whole body shines with a greenish-yellow luster, especially his cheeks. His skin is covered with thick slime in such abundance that the ruff surpasses even the tench and burbot in this regard. His tail and upper fins are speckled, and the lower fins are whitish-gray. Ruff inhabit only clean waters and are found in great quantities in sandy or clayey rivers, as well as in lakes inundated by spring floodwater. Where ruff are plentiful and large, the fishing for them is unusually productive and pleasant. They bite only on red dungworms, and on earthworms, though not as eagerly. It stands to reason that one must select the very smallest worms for this kind of fishing. Medium fishing outfits are used. Ruff bite much more avidly on the bottom than at medium depth, and therefore one must refrain from bottom-fishing for them only if the bottom is weedy or has snags.

Ruff start biting very early in spring and stop at the very end of late autumn. If you come upon a school of ruff, it's possible to catch the majority of them. You can bait the worms with tails or without tails, but the former method is always better. Ruff take and bite surely, without deception, and almost always sink the float, but sometimes they carry it sideways and shake it. On rare occasions, when simply lifting the rod, you will land a ruff who was holding the hook in his mouth. This, however, can sometimes happen with any fish. I've never found ruff in greater numbers than in flood-lakes near the Moscow River. There you could catch as many as you wished: two hundred, three hundred, and more. Large ones would therefore rarely be caught, which deprived the fishing of its allure. Ruff are not used for bait, probably because predatory fish don't care for their pointy armaments, but for people the ruff is a superb catch. Soup made from ruff is the healthiest, most nutritious, and tastiest of foods, but—especially if they are large—ruff are best prepared cold in jelly, which tends to be unusually thick. In my opinion, nothing can compare with the most delicate flavor of this dish.[54]

I've always prized large ruff and sought them out tirelessly, but their bite in rivers is very capricious—sometimes in the shallows, sometimes in deep water; today they bite well, tomorrow they don't bite at all. Ruff at the end of April are packed with roe to the point of disfigurement. They void it in May, after which they bite more avidly.

I shall now discuss those fish that, though born as tiny as the ones I have just described, nonetheless reach large size.

# 8. ROACH

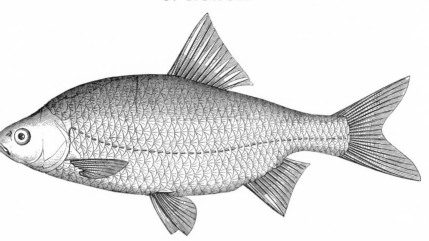

The roach[55] obviously got his name (*plotítsa*) from the fact that he's flat (*ploská*). In some provinces he's called *soróga*, or *sorozhniák*, but I'm unable to explain the origin of this name.[56] Without doubt, this is the most prolific and numerous species of fish. Roach inhabit rivers small and large, lakes, and flowing and artificial ponds, as long as the water is fairly fresh. In a word, roach are found everywhere in abundance. This has so debased him that fishermen have no respect whatsoever for the roach. Only when he begins to weigh over a pound does he acquire a certain significance. I myself have seen roach of four pounds, but elderly fishermen in Orenburg Province have told me that roach of seven pounds used to be caught in the old days. Landing a roach of that size is very enjoyable. The roach is somewhat wide and roundish (especially a large one), flat, and colored a pure silver that becomes darker along his back. He has red or reddish-brown eyes, and the larger the roach, the redder his eyes become. The upper and lower fins are a dark-reddish color, and his scales are rather large. As he increases in size, the roach becomes wider and more rounded. He has a small mouth.

The roach's biting starts in earliest spring, even when the floodwater hasn't altogether subsided and is still fairly turbid. In a word, the roach is the first fish to begin biting, and almost the last to stop biting. He avidly attacks any bait—ordinary dungworm, or, if he's a big one, even earthworm, bread, all kinds of stewed grain, crayfish tails, and any sort of insect. He can be caught in all swims and at any depth, but a large roach bites better and more surely at the bottom, in deep and quiet places, especially on bread bait. But in rushes, flood-pools, and in shallow water, he takes at fifteen inches, and even less, below the water's surface, especially in windy weather. In waters where big fish lurk and the fisherman seeks them specifically, roach are unbearably irritating. There's no defense against their tugging and dragging. The sole salvation lies in baiting the hook with huge pieces of bread, the largest earthworm, an intact greaser, or a molting crayfish mounted whole on the hook. I remember how, in my childhood, when Orenburg Province was still much less populous and its rivers teemed with all kinds of fish, especially roach, they used to catch roach on little pieces of the intestines of small birds, grass stems, and all sorts of rubbish. But one can despise the roach only where there are many other, better fish. I myself have chanced to live in places where I was even glad of a decent little roach, and, as this can befall other sportsmen as well, it would be fitting to discuss roach-fishing in greater detail.

The roach's bite varies endlessly. It's most reliable to angle for him with little pieces of bread and stewed wheat kernels, but he must be trained for this by being groundbaited with both the one and the other. I've encountered rivers in which roach took nothing but earthworms,*[57] and only then with dangling tails, but their bite was most uncertain. I don't know how to explain this oddity. Was it due to their lack of familiarity with bread and grain, or to an abundance of nutritious weeds and various aquatic insects? Large roach especially like to take early in the morning. One must try to train them to bite at the bottom, because there they drag and plunge the float into the water, which makes striking them easy; only this way is it possible to fish two outfits. If, however, you fish at intermediate depth, then you must strike the very moment

*One estimable sportsman (S. Ia. A.) has informed me that the abundant roach in the River Nëma, which flows near the town of Vereia, altogether refuse to take on rod and line, so that in some years you'll catch only one or two of them.

they drag the float or begin to sink it. Roach of medium size, but especially small ones, seldom take with certainty. Watchfulness, vigor, and swiftness and dexterity in setting the hook are thus indispensable. The rod must be held in hand. Pay no heed to the many missed strikes, for there will also be many fish. In swims where the groundbait bag was put down long before, roach grow very accustomed to eating stewed grains and take on them without trickery. In that case, you can catch as many as you like by baiting one outfit with one or two kernels of wheat that has swelled in hot water, while each time checking to see whether the hook's point is freely protruding. The largest roach, however, are more likely to take on pieces of pressed bread the size of a small Russian hazelnut. For wormbaits, one must use medium fishing outfits, and small hooks for tiny bread-balls and wheat kernels. Little roach can serve as bait for predatory fish. Soup made from roach is not tasty and often smells of aquatic weeds. It's better to cook them in sour cream and dry them. Small roach bite until late autumn and even in winter through ice-holes. They spawn in June.

# 9. RUDD

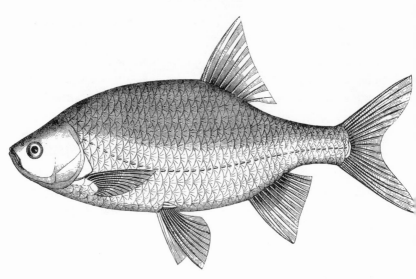

Because fishermen call him the "roach-rudd," it might seem improper to discuss this fish[58] as a separate species. I, however, find between the rudd and the common roach an essential distinction apart from their difference in color, which one also encounters among fish of the same species, though not quite so dramatically: the rudd is much wider than the typical roach, and with his roundish figure and shape is quite similar to a *breamet.* He's covered with scales of a brilliant yellow-golden color, and the edges of these scales appear to be trimmed with a dainty selvage of golden brown. The rudd's fins, especially the lower ones, are of the bright ruddy color that gave him his name,[59] and his eyes are brown. All this together makes the rudd one of the loveliest fish. The rudd can probably reach the same size and age as the common roach, and rudd spawn at the same time as roach.

Once in my presence a fisherman caught a three-and-a-half-pound rudd (on crayfish tail), and the fish was so handsome that we admired him for a long time. The rudd is not found everywhere the common roach is. Near Moscow no one has heard of him, and even in Orenburg Province, in the numerous rivers, ponds, and lakes teeming with all species of fish, including the roach, there's not a single rudd, while in other places he's found in abundance. His bite is utterly different from the roach's: the rudd does not peck, pluck, or drag the hooks after seizing the worm's tail. Either he takes surely, or he doesn't take at all. Very seldom will you catch him in a river, but at the end of summer or beginning of autumn the rudd is caught in great quantities from boats in the flood-pools of ponds, among the weeds, and, especially, in clean places among the bulrushes as well as in lakes flooded in spring by the same river. Here he takes very well on red dungworm and even better on stewed wheat (at a groundbaited swim). He doesn't bite so eagerly on bread, but by the end of autumn, the rudd descends to the depths of the pond's mainstream, especially near a wicket, weir, or flood-gate, and holds there until the hard frosts. Here he takes on bread and small pieces of fresh fish, for which roach fry caught in the same swim, or other small fish, are normally used. This characteristic alone utterly differentiates the rudd from the common roach. Small rudd are very good as bait for predatory fish because they're tenacious of life and don't rapidly grow weary while swimming on a large hook. In flavor the rudd differs little from the common roach. For fishing with grains, small outfits are used, while medium ones are employed for worms and pieces of fish. Because of his unusually handsome appearance, and the fact that he's not found everywhere, doesn't bite all the time, and doesn't even appear in large numbers every year, fishing for rudd is incomparably superior to roach-fishing.

# 10. IDE

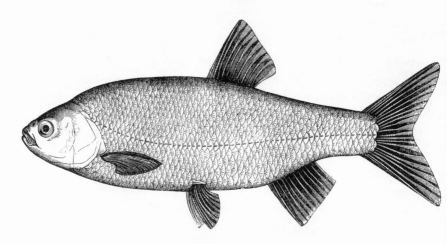

I'm unable to determine the origin of his name (*iaz'*).[60] The ide[61] is, so to speak, a capital fish and occupies a place of honor in large-fish angling, in the real sportfishing that predominantly attracts true fishermen. He who casts a small outfit after little fish in a swim where large ones are biting is not a sportsman. It's better to sit or stand a few hours without catching anything, watching motionless floats while every minute expecting a rich catch, than to set about landing wretched little roach, and in so doing, perhaps, startling the big fish. Ide for some reason are rarely caught small. For the most part they begin to take on a fishing outfit when they've reached decent size, but this observation isn't universally true.\* Near Moscow, small ide of up to two pounds are called *ideling*, but in other regions of Russia I've heard of no such subdivision. Though ide can reach nine pounds, fish of close to four pounds are caught most frequently of all. The largest ide I've succeeded in catching weighed almost seven pounds. The ide is fairly broad, but not round, and he's flatter than the roach. He sometimes reaches twenty-one inches in length and four inches in thickness through his back. The ide has a red tail and lower fins, gray-blue upper fins, and eyes of bright brown. He's covered

---

\*This observation is valid only for Orenburg Province. Near Moscow, the reverse is true: little ide are caught much more frequently.

with scales that are, for the most part, silver, and larger and darker near his back, but from time to time ide caught in the same river are yellow-golden. They only inhabit clean waters: rivers, flowing ponds and large lakes. They spawn in May.

Ide are easily accustomed to groundbait, especially permanent groundbait, and only under this condition is it possible to catch many large ide in one morning in the same swim. By "many" I mean about ten. From the beginning of spring ide eagerly take on pieces of pressed bread the size of a small walnut, then on large earthworms and a cluster of dungworms (or gutworms), as well as on crayfish tails. In the beginning and middle of summer they take on molting crayfish and large white worms (greasers), and, later, on grasshoppers, though in autumn ide almost never bite. If some naughty little fish does take, then it's not on a large outfit with large bait, but on a small rig put down shallow and baited with a bit of wheat, a fly, or some other similar trifle. I caught one of my biggest ide on a large greenish mosquito of a particular species, with a tiny fishing outfit, and therefore spent nearly an hour playing him. The ide's real bite is at the bottom. In ide-fishing, large hooks are used if the bait is large, and medium ones if it's small. After the floodwater recedes, ide start to take just after roach. According to fishermen, their best biting takes place when the guelder-rose is in bloom. If you fish without groundbait, angling *in the fish's run*, then, after choosing a narrow place in the river, you must cast one outfit into the middle, another a bit closer, and a third near the bank. If you fish at a groundbaited, sloping swim, then it's better to place all the floats near weeds, a little closer to the bank, and to lay the rods on the weeds. Without the slightest doubt, the most precious time for both kinds of ide-fishing is early morning. Then they take long before the sun comes up, so that you can make out your floats only if you sit facing the sunrise, bending to the ground. Only a true sportsman can fully appreciate all the enchantment of this early morning angling.... The east grows pale in magnificent silence and chases night's darkness to the southwest, while objects begin to emerge from the murk and take shape. But the rushes remain motionless, and the surface of the water gives off no light vapor, for the sun is still far off.... Suddenly you begin to hear, at first from far away, the gurgling of bubbles from the bottom—air released through the nostrils of a big fish—a sure sign that ide are about. . . . The bubbles rise closer, and you can already see them. . . . Now the biting will commence. . . . Ide take surely and drag the float straight into the water. Your strike must be swift and decisive, but not too forceful and not jerky. The ide is one of the strongest fish and he fights very boldly when hooked. Having first wearied the fish, one must carefully lead him to the water's surface and ensure that the circles in which he begins to swim are not too wide. Otherwise, it's easy for him to draw the line tight and break off after throwing himself sideways.

Large ide tend to be very oily, and soup made from them is fairly tasty, but it's best to prepare them cold, covered with a sauce of sour cream and horseradish. The only pity is that ide are very bony. The color of their body is a pale pink.

Ide constitute the greatest share of the large fish I've caught in the course of my whole fishing career. The Buguruslan River, on which I grew up,[62] abounded mainly with ide in those days. The chub were fished out, and the bream hadn't yet taken hold, so large ide were what the fishermen yearned for. And how gloriously they used to take on bread then, without any groundbaiting, along the entire river without exception. But you also used to hear about snapped lines, and straightened or broken hooks and rods. Of course, they pulled up the ide carelessly, just like little roach—so is it any wonder they'd only land a quarter of the fish they hooked? . . .

To the number of extraordinary incidents I've seen while angling I can add the following. Once I was fishing on the bank of my own pond (in Orenburg Province), while another fisherman sat on a wooden platform built in the weeds above the very mainstream, at the middle of the pond. Suddenly I saw the fisherman stand up and begin to fight what seemed to be a large fish. This scene went on so long that I was greatly astonished. I tried to make inquiry, but the distance was so great that we could only hear the noises we made and not make out words. It annoyed me to watch the fisherman's monotonous gestures, and I concentrated on my own fishing outfits. From time to time I glanced up at him and saw the same thing. Finally, after at least an hour, I saw the fisherman, now in a boat, hurriedly sailing straight toward me. In a net he was carrying an enormous ide (over five pounds), still hooked, and the man was inviting me to examine the manner in which the fish had been caught. It was extraordinary indeed: a silk leader (two strands thick) was wound around and holding fast to the tip of the ide's dorsal fin, while the hook, baited with a worm, hung untouched at the fish's side. I tried hefting the fish (and in air they are much heavier than in water), and the line held fast. With the same fisherman another adventure of the same kind, though even more astonishing, occurred later—but I'll relate this in my discussion of the pike.[63]

I have some news to report that may be of interest to sportsmen. Last year (1851), on the night of the fifteenth of September, I caught a three-pound ide on a hook baited with crucian carp and intended for burbot in a hole below a flood-gate. Thus, ide may also be taken on baitfish.

# 11. CHUB

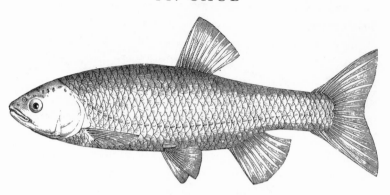

Though it's obvious that the chub's[64] name (*golóvl'*) comes from his large head (*golová*), his head is nonetheless not so big.[65] If it seems larger than the heads of other fish, this is solely because the chub's forehead is very broad and blends right into his bar-shaped form. The chub isn't so broad as the ide, and he's longer and much deeper through the back than the ide. According to many fishermen, the chub reaches twenty-seven inches in length and weighs up to fourteen pounds, though I myself have never seen one over nine pounds. He's much handsomer than the ide. His scales are larger and more silver, while each scale is shaded along the edge with a narrow, shiny, brown trim. He has a fairly large mouth and dark eyes. The lower fins are reddish, while the upper ones, especially the tail, are of a dark gray-blue color, so that when fish rise from the bottom to the surface of the water in the warmth of midday, you'll immediately distinguish the chub by their dark blue, almost black, tails. The chub likes clean, clear water and even inhabits water too cold for the ide, so that in rivers chub appear just after the trout species. I don't even know if they live in large lakes, but in flowing ponds on rivers they reproduce abundantly. They hold exclusively in sandy, gravelly, and even stony places. In flood-pools the chub is a rarity; his place is in the river, or the pond's mainstream. He's extraordinarily swift in his movements, which is facilitated by the shape of his body, in which he somewhat resembles the pike. He's not so easily groundbaited with cereal grains as the ide, and is generally more cautious, but sometimes he takes on bread. He likes worms best, especially greasers, as well as crayfish tails and whole molting crayfish. The largest chub take on baitfish, preferably at night. For this kind of fishing, hooks baited with gudgeon and stone loach (or, if those aren't available, little bleak and roach) are set out for chub in the autumn, when it gets colder. I've already mentioned chub-fishing in the summer, at night, in a boat, with long lines.[66] For the most part, a large chub takes on the bottom. His bite is unusually swift, and he almost always sets the hook by himself, after which he leaps out headlong, furiously thrashes about on the line, sometimes even jumping completely out of the water. The fisherman must try to prevent all these dangerous tricks, and, having guessed by the speed of the fish's movements that he's hooked a chub, mustn't allow the fish to rise from the bottom to the surface until he's grown weary and quiet; to accomplish this the fisherman must sometimes plunge the rod tip into the water. There's no stronger, bolder, swifter, or more tireless fish. A huge chub taken on rod and line is a magnificent spectacle! Even the most experienced, skillful fisherman cannot watch without fear the chub's lightning-fast, unyielding leaps, and will only compose himself after the quarry is netted. Chub are also caught without a sinker or float, on a surface rig of medium size baited with grasshopper, small beetle, fly, or dungworm. Such fishing is done in the swift flows of a river and for the most part yields medium chub, and, rarely, large ones. A large chub, however, is almost impossible to land on such a line. Though he's similar in taste to the ide, the chub is somehow cleaner, more delicate.

Because of this fish's skittishness, extraordinary swiftness, boldness, as well as his reluctance to take, I consider fishing for large chub to be first-class angling. To land two or three big chub in one morning is a rich, even magnificent catch. But I simply can't figure out why large chub take so rarely, when every sportsman has probably chanced to see them much more than any other large fish. Chub have always and everywhere driven me to despair—in the rivers of Orenburg, Simbirsk, Penza and Moscow provinces. Most annoying of all is to see the way they sometimes swim about in schools at midday, along the very surface of the water, and sometimes lie on the shallow, stony, or sandy bottom of a river riffle as clear as glass! You put their favorite baits right up under their very mouths—crayfish, enormous earthworms, fat greasers, gudgeon—and all for naught! The bait might as well be invisible! Sometimes one fish will suddenly approach as though sniffing (and take the expectant sportsman's breath away), nudge the bait with his snout, and swim off! Sometimes a piece of bait chances to fall directly onto a chub lying on the bottom—and what do you think happens? He moves away to the side a bit and lies on the sand again, stirring his black tail like a scull. Fishermen usually explain this by saying that chub see the sportsman and, out of skittishness, refuse to take. But heaven only knows if this explanation is right. It's understandable that any shy, timorous fish, having seen a moving figure, whatever it may be, might swim away and hide. But I can't account for the further skittishness of chub: why do they seldom take even in deep places, in opaque water, where the fisherman is surely invisible? No, there must be other reasons for this that we simply don't understand.

In discussing the chub, I don't consider it superfluous to relate an incident that serves as proof that one must never take the line in hand while landing a large fish, which I mentioned above.[67] Once in early spring I was fishing in the afternoon above a large pond (in the mainstream, that is) overgrown with rushes. I was standing on a slender "point"—that's what we used to call a promontory surrounded by water on three sides. The big fish were not biting yet. My three large fishing outfits were lying motionless. At last, there was a touch on my white worm (greaser). It was dragged down twice, and the third time I swiftly struck once and landed a little chub. Because no big fish were taking, I tossed aside the large rig and took up a medium one, with six-hair line, baited a small greaser and cast out. Before I had time to put down the rod, the float disappeared. . . . I set the hook, and—a huge fish was on! . . . The flexible rod bent into the shape of a ring, right down to the handle. At first, because of the fish's straight runs, I thought he was a pike, but the fish wasn't long in dissuading me. This was an enormous chub whose like I'd never seen before, nor have I since, and he flew to the water's surface and commenced his desperate jumps. . . . My slender line was so strong, the rod so flexible, and I played the fish so cautiously, that after half an hour the chub had grown weary. I led him to the bank in order to net him, but the net was *too small and shallow*, and the fish would not fit in it.*[68] Meanwhile, the chub suddenly made a desperate leap and catapulted into the dense sedge that hung over the bank and was buoyed by the water partially flooding the shore. I had only to grasp the chub carefully by hand or cover him with the net and land the fish by dragging him in. But I—such a wise, patient, and, one might say, skillful fisherman—was seduced by the fact that my fish lay almost on the bank, that it was necessary to drag him a distance of only about seven inches to get him to a safe place. So I seized the line with my hand and had only just pulled it, when the chub leapt up as if rabid, the line snapped, and he rolled over into the water. . . . I'd lost a catch so precious to the sportsman, especially so early in the spring, that I was literally in despair, and to this day I'm unable to recall that loss with equanimity, though afterward I consoled myself by writing the idyll "The Fisherman's Woe."[69]

*This is the proof of what I said above: the net must always be deep and not too small.

# 12. BREAM

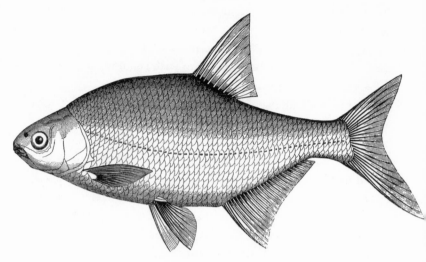

It's rather difficult to determine with precision the origin of the bream's[70] name (*leshch*). It could easily be that the words "slab" (*léshched'*) and "crotch" (*leshchëdka*) came from the same root as "bream," for a wide, flat slab bears a certain resemblance to him.[71] "Crotch," on the other hand, is the name given to a small, forked treestump or stick with which one holds down anything that has to be pressed or flattened.

The bream is differentiated from all other fish by his round, flat, wide figure. His head is small, and seems especially so because of his wide form. His mouth appears even smaller in relation to the size of his entire body. Bream can reach huge size and weight, attaining almost twenty-seven inches in length, fifteen inches in width, and almost four inches in thickness through the back. I've heard from many people that bream of eighteen pounds are caught, but I myself have never seen a fish of more than twelve pounds. Bream are yellow-golden and grayish-silver, though the former color is rare. Their bellies are white and their scales large. The tail and fins are gray-blue and very small; the eyes are white, with dark pupils. The bream's figure is disagreeable, and has a deformed appearance. He can't bear cold water and appears in rivers after all the other fish. He's found in large numbers predominantly in quiet, deep, muddy rivers that have many runs and coves. Bream especially love large ponds and lakes. They spawn in April, during the spring flood itself. I remember that in Orenburg Province's Buguruslan River, when that region was still not very populated, there were at first many chub and few ide. Then an abundance of ide reproduced, and the chub became few. The bream, on the other hand, no matter how many were released into the pond, simply wouldn't reproduce, even though about thirteen miles downstream, where our river flows into another—namely the *Nasiagai*[72]—there were plenty of bream. Today, however, in both the pond on the Buguruslan and in the entire river, bream have become abundant.* Obviously, due to the numerous mills and new settlements, the limpid and unusually cold water of the river gradually grew murkier and warmer, and bream at last began to live in it, though the method for rearing them that I discussed in the section "On Fish in General" was being used.

Small bream are called "breamet." Some consider them a separate species of fish, but, in my opinion, this isn't so. In spring, the rivers have scarcely begun to run in their channels, and the waters to grow clear, when the most avid biting of the bream starts, because, like any fish, they are emaciated and hungry after excreting roe and milt, and there's little food. They take on dungworms and earthworms, but most avidly on the former. One can, however, groundbait them with bread and stewed grains. They take well on soaked peas. For angling, if it's done in rivers, deep and quiet swims are chosen— backwaters and coves are best. In ponds and lakes you can select any swim you like, but it should be a place that is deep, has a flat, sloping bottom, and a bank suitable for landing the catch. In certain waters they're so abundant and, starting in spring, bite so avidly and surely, that one can catch an incredible quantity of them. I have in mind here medium bream— the very large ones take very seldom. One has to fish on the bottom, and with two or three outfits. Bream take quietly and carry the float without immediately sinking it; you'll always have time to seize the rod and strike. It's best to use large fishing outfits and medium hooks, mounting one or several dungworms on each rig, for bream take on both baits without

---

*This change has taken place over the course of forty years.

ado. The bream's first rushes when hooked are very spirited, but he soon tires and floats to the top like a wooden sluice-gate. Then it's a simple matter to lead him to shore, net him, and even take him by hand. I'm speaking here of medium-sized bream, that is, of around four pounds. But the initial movements of a huge bream—that is, of around eight or nine pounds—are so violent and dogged that one needs a strong line, a very flexible rod, and a great deal of skill and dexterity in order to cope successfully. This is what fishing outfits of the large sort are for. I say this based on the accounts of others, for I myself have caught few bream, and none heavier than five pounds. Many sportsmen passionately love the bream's spring-time biting, which lasts about two weeks. Without the slight-est doubt, the larger the fish, the more flattering it is to catch him, and therefore huge bream, which rarely take, represent for the sportsman a seductive form of angling. But dragging in small bream, that is, breamet—which weigh a pound or two and take ceaselessly, with extraordinary sureness and monot-ony, then immediately float to the top, and are dragged onto the bank as motionless as woodchips—this, in my opinion, is no fun at all. I sampled such angling, and didn't care for it. I consider it much more pleasant to catch bream among many other fish over the course of the summer and in the beginning of autumn, when they've already started to take infrequently.

Bream tend to be very oily, and tasty if you please, but are somehow crudely cloying, while the big ones are tough as well. On the other hand, one can, from time to time, happily eat a flank of cooked bream, that is, the ribcage stuffed with cooked groats.[73] The remaining parts of his body are very bony.

# 13. RIVER CARP

I'm unable to furnish an etymology for the river carp's[74] name (*sazán*). For that matter, is it even a Russian word?[75] The river carp is a handsome fish that can reach thirty-six pounds. I always used to hear that river carp wouldn't inhabit rivers of medium size. In Orenburg, Simbirsk, and other southern provinces, they usually brought them during the winter in significant quantities from several large rivers, including the Ural, which is stuffed with them in such unbelievable abundance right down to the Caspian that it can seem like a fairy tale. But about twenty years ago in the Sviiaga River, which flows just outside Simbirsk itself, river carp suddenly appeared. At first they were of medium and large size, but later a multitude of small ones bred too. I can't claim it as a fact, but I've been told that in the upper reaches of this same river a landowner had a huge pond that hadn't been drained for forty years, in which he raised river carp (carpia) in abundance. But this pond was suddenly breached, and the river carp escaped and dispersed themselves along the entire river. Of course, the river carp would have had less distance to travel had they come from the Volga, into which the Sviiaga flows—but then why had they not appeared earlier? Whatever the means, the appearance of river carp opened a superb new fishery for Simbirsk sport-fishermen. After a few years, the river carp had already appeared in other small rivers of Simbirsk and Penza Provinces as well.

I myself have succeeded in catching several river carp running from three to four pounds. Without doubt, they're livelier on rod and line than any other fish. The river carp takes quietly and carries the float with ever-increasing speed without suddenly plunging it into the water. But as soon as you set the hook, he throws himself with incredible swiftness straight away from you, diagonally rising to the top and dragging the rod and line straight out. Not anticipating the commencement of such a maneuver, I've lost several river carp and hooks: fairly thick lines were snapped in a second. For the angling of large river carp, fishing outfits of the very largest size and especially strong lines are used. The river carp bites only on dungworms and earthworms. His best biting is in the spring.

The river carp is very handsome. He's covered with unusually large, dark yellow-gold scales. It seems as though on this golden field he's all bestrewn with dark-headed carnations, which are reminiscent of the chub's handsome scales. He's fairly broad, and at first glance bears a certain resemblance to the crucian carp, but is more hunchbacked and even longer than that fish. Near the borders of his mouth he has two thick, short, and soft whiskers that terminate in flat, roundish caps.

I definitely recognize the river carp as the same fish as the carpia because of their perfect all-around resemblance, though I'm discussing each separately. A large river carp has slightly crude flesh, but small river carp are very tasty.

# 14. POND CARP, OR CARPIA

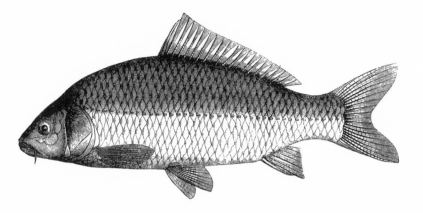

"Carp" is a foreign name, while "carpia" is a russified form of the word. In discussing the river carp, I said that he and the carpia are one and the same fish, with the only difference being that carpia in ponds lack bright color, have a dirty gray-ish hue, and don't reach such enormous size as river carp living in large rivers, especially at their mouths, where the rivers reach the sea. In Astrakhan', for example, the haul of river carp is incredibly huge and noteworthy as much for the number of fish as for their large size. In Moscow itself many carpia inhabited various ponds, especially in the Presnia River's ponds and in the ponds of the Palace Garden, which now belongs to the Cadet Corps.[76] In the environs of Moscow you'll rarely find a good pond—regardless of whether it's flowing or still, as long as it's fairly big—in which carpia aren't being raised. In ponds long left uncleaned, and choked with slime, carpia perish. They also frequently die off in ponds because, over the course of long winters, no one ensures that there's a sufficient quantity of holes made daily in the ice, and because of this the water stagnates and goes bad.

Carpia bite avidly on earthworms and dungworms. They're very bold and strong when taken on rod and line, and bite mainly on the bottom. I've heard nothing about carpia caught near Moscow in rivers, but those caught in ponds often smell like mud if the bottom is slimy. They can, however, like cru-cian carp, be put in perforated pens in flowing, clear water, where they'll soon lose the odor of mud and regain their usual pleasant flavor. Carpia raised in ponds are easily trained to take groundbait at an appointed hour and place. If one consistently rings a bell at feeding time, then they'll become so accustomed to it that they'll start to gather when they hear the bell's peal, even at a time other than the usual one. Other fish could probably be trained to do the same thing. In Moscow there are people who remember this little trick in the Pleasure Garden when it belonged to Prince Shakhovskoi.[77] Not very long ago, in the Presnia ponds, there was a multitude of very large carpia, and people used to enjoy feeding them kalaches.[78] This was an amusing spectacle indeed. As soon as a kalach had been thrown into the pond, several of the largest carpia (sometimes just one) would seize the kalach and plunge it into the water. Unable to bite bits off, the fish would soon release the booty from his mouth, and it would immediately float up to the water's surface. Other carpia, in larger numbers, would immediately appear behind it, and with greater greed and boldness seize the kalach from all sides, drag it, tug it, and dive with it. As soon as the bread became somewhat sodden, the fish would tear it into pieces and swallow the loaf in a minute. The people accompanied all these escapades with loud exclamations and hearty laughter.

I haven't managed to fish much for river carp, or the so-called carpia, but based on the accounts of sportsmen, I must conclude that this kind of fishing, especially in rivers or large ponds, is very pleasant, fruitful, and at the same time demands skill, circumspection, and a net, for large carpia are the boldest, strongest, and most tireless of fish.

## 15. TENCH

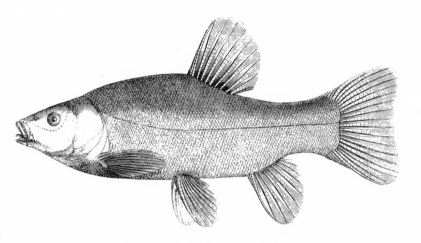

Although the tench's[79] name (*lin'*) could come from the verb "to cling" (*l'nut'*), because the tench, covered with a sticky slime, clings to one's hands, I strongly suspect that his name derives from the verb "to fade" (*liniát'*). This is because a caught tench, even in a pail of water or a keep-net, especially if it's too small for him, will immediately fade and large dark spots will appear along his whole body; even a tench taken straight from the water has a two-toned color prone to fading. People doubtless noticed this peculiarity of the tench and gave him a fitting name.[80]

In the cast of his body, the tench somewhat resembles the ide, but is a little wider and thicker than he, and somehow more foursquare. The tench is covered with very tiny scales of a dark green, golden color, and they're difficult to discern with the naked eye. He seems to be entirely coated in a thick slime. He has small, bright red eyes. His tail and fins are thick, soft, and dark, and his mouth is small. Tench attain considerable size. It's claimed that tench can weigh fourteen pounds, but I've never seen one of more than eight pounds. I have to say that I don't trust the large sizes and weights of fish that prompt so many stories from commercial fishermen and sportsmen. They frequently measure by eye and against their hands, and very often make mistakes. Tench serve as an example. If I've caught so many in my life, and seen so many caught by others or captured by various fishing rigs, then how could I not encounter at least one if not of fourteen pounds, then of only ten or twelve pounds?[81] The eight-pound tench that I saw and weighed on a steelyard was sixteen inches long, but, on the other hand, extraordinarily fat.

Tench bite on bread, earthworms and dungworms, crayfish tails, and on small molting crayfish, as they find it difficult to swallow large ones. The biting of tench in rivers (or, more precisely, in the coves of rivers, and then only in the very stillest ones and in early spring), lakes and ponds begins immediately after the spring floodwaters recede. In the summer tench bite only in ponds, that is, in their grassy flood-pools and upper reaches, and from time to time in the mainstream of the pond. But in a river that's undammed in summer you'll never catch a tench, try as you might. In Orenburg Province, I used to catch tench in September, and quite a few, even during weak frosts, in the deep reaches of a pond's flood-pools set about with weeds. Around Moscow, however, this biting doesn't exist: as soon as it grows cold, all the tench leave the coves and weeds, and they don't take while in the mainstream. Tench do well in quiet, muddy, weedy rivers. They don't like cold water, and reproduce best in flowing ponds, lakes, and even in small, stillwater ponds. Fishermen say that tench spawn twice a year, in March and August. While in no way making that claim, I'll nonetheless note that their best biting is in April and September, as if after spawning had taken place. Backwaters, coves, and flood-pools (only if overgrown with weeds) are the tench's favorite haunts.

One must bottom-fish for tench without fail, provided the bottom is clean. If the reverse is true, one must fish at intermediate depth and on several outfits. They take quietly and surely. For the most part the float will move from its place to one side or the other, even backward toward the bank, without the slightest trembling, and imperceptibly to the eye—this is the tench. He's taken the baited hook into his mouth and is quietly absconding with it. You seize the rod, strike, and the hook's point pierces some part of that soft, narrow, mouth, which seems to have swelled up within. The tench props himself with his head down, raises his tail, and in this position moves very slowly along the muddy bottom, but only if you start to pull. If not, then he's capable of lying like a stone in the selfsame place. When you feel that the tench is very large, you mustn't hurry and pull too hard. It's possible to break the hook if it's stuck in the roof of his mouth and forced to snap. Keep the line under gentle tension and wait until the tench makes up his mind to move. Then start to play him, and play him for a long time, because he's very strong and doesn't tire quickly. Beware of the weeds: he'll immediately rush into them and become fouled, and he's prepared to remain there for several hours. From then on, proceed as befits a big fish. The tench very rarely comes loose, unless the line snaps or the hook breaks. Tench-fishing in shallow swims, among thick aquatic weeds, which very often happens, demands particular deftness and skill: having become fouled or having wrapped the line around the weeds, a tench suddenly goes motionless, and it stands to reason that one mustn't pull. But if the fisherman, while waiting for the tench to move again, lowers the rod and holds the line too slack, then sometimes the fish will rush to the side with such speed that he'll pull the line taut and immediately break it (if it's a large tench, of course). I therefore recommend that among weeds you fish with the thickest, strongest lines, and use rods that aren't too flexible. Because of their softness and animation, little tench fry serve as excellent bait for predatory fish. Fish soup made from tench is thick, nutritious, and also has a peculiar, fairly pleasant, dulcet taste, but it's best to eat tench dried, with sour cream. Tench often smell of mud, which can easily be remedied by putting them into a wicker pen and leaving them in flowing water for a week or two. In the pen they must be fed baked bread, which will soon make them grow plump.

# 16. CRUCIAN CARP

A most prolific and ubiquitously abundant fish.[82] In cast he's wide and round. His figure represents a halfway point between rudd and bream; that is, he's wider than the rudd and narrower than the bream. The crucian carp is covered with scales of a silver or gold color. Sometimes both white and yellow crucian carp (as they are unceremoniously called by fishermen) live together in the same water. In small artificial ponds, crucian carp of a roseate color are caught in abundance. This middling color seems transitional from white to yellow, and probably indicates a cross-breed. The difference between them consists entirely in the fact that yellow crucian carp are somewhat rounder and have red fins, especially the lower ones, while white crucian carp have grayish, gray-blue ones. In general the crucian carp—especially the gold variety—is a well-built and handsome fish.

Many people have assured me that crucian carp can reach ten and even twelve pounds, but I've long been skeptical of this. Having caught a countless multitude of crucian carp in my life, I've never landed one heavier than two-and-a-half pounds. I remember in my childhood how they seined flood-lakes along the River Belaia (this was when Orenburg

Province was still called Ufa Province), how they laboriously dragged the *bunt*,* tightly packed with fish, out onto the green bank, and how they would shake from it a whole cartload of large pike, perch, crucian carp, and roach, which flopped about on all sides.[83] I remember that sometimes they'd be astounded at the size of crucian carp and then weigh them, and none were over five pounds. But one winter several years ago a friend of mine (F. I. Vas′kov)[84] sent me in Moscow several frozen crucian carp caught in Kostroma Province. They were all of unusual size, or, to put it better, thickness, because when crucian carp reach a little over fourteen inches in length, they start to grow only in thickness. One of these denizens of Lake Chukhloma weighed nine pounds! Catching such a giant crucian carp on rod and line would be merry sport indeed! While living in Orenburg Province, I never used to hear about angling for crucian carp. In the midst of an abundance of all kinds of large river fish, of course, no sportsman would give any thought to crucian carp. I became acquainted with them out of necessity, while passing the summer in the vicinity of Moscow one year. There, artificial ponds are everywhere, sometimes very large and deep ones, fed by sources springing from the bottom, which means they always have good water. Crucian carp are raised in abundance there almost everywhere, and I grew fond of this angling willy-nilly.

In the spring, crucian carp begin to take later than other fish. The warmth of the air and the vernal rays of the sun have to heat the water through and thereby raise crucian carp from the muddy bottom, out of the deep holes where they take refuge for the winter. If it's very cold, then in the beginning of September they stop taking, but if warm, they take until October. Crucian carp bite best on red dungworms, or gutworms, but they also take on earthworms and on bread. One can train them to feed on the latter by tossing in pieces of bread as groundbait. I once unexpectedly caught a yellow crucian carp on a crayfish tail intended for tench; crucian carp are thus capable of taking on crayfish as well. If both white and yellow crucian carp inhabit a pond, then the yellow ones will pre-

---

*Bunt* is the name given to a long, pointed net-bag located at the center of a seine.

dominantly take on bread, while the white ones will take on worms; exceptions are fairly rare. But if a white crucian carp takes on bread, then it will almost always be a large one. This oddity is inexplicable, since white crucian carp also eat bread groundbait, just as the yellow ones do. Though crucian carp for the most part inhabit lakes and artificial ponds, it's by no means possible to say that they never live in rivers. I've very often noticed that in rivers there seem to be no crucian carp, but they're ubiquitous in all the small lakes and backwaters flooded by the dammed waters of the selfsame river. They reproduce in unbelievable numbers in the filthiest waters and, like any fish, grow very rapidly the first few years.

Though they live in dirty, and therefore warm, waters, crucian carp can also live in the coldest water; here's some proof that I gathered myself. In the Mordvinian hamlet of Kivatskoe,[85] about a mile from Aksakovo, there was a breached mill-dam abandoned for over ten years. Opposite this place, where the flood-gate had formerly been, there always stood, filled to the brim, a deep pit of water, as cold as ice, out of which flowed a little brook, a sure sign that there was a source in the pit. Almost every day, while hunting, I rode past this place. Once, returning from a hunt at the end of June, I saw a crowd of people near the aforementioned pit. I walked up to see what they were doing. What was my astonishment when I saw that they were catching crucian carp in the pit with a few dragnets and had already landed more than a cartload. They were yellow crucian carp, all of the same medium size. Those who were fishing shivered with cold in spite of the hot weather. It had never entered anyone's head that there might be fish, least of all crucian carp, holding in this pit. Some little boys had seen dark swarms of some kind of fish swimming on the surface, and had told about it in the village.

The biting of crucian carp is extraordinarily varied. Sometimes they take unceasingly and very surely. The touched float makes one or several small circles and starts to the side, but is rarely sunk. There's enough time to seize the rod and strike. One can fish several outfits and comfortably lay out the rods on whatever surface is at hand. Sometimes, however, in the same pond, crucian carp will start to bite so cautiously, or, to put it better, uncertainly, that one has to fish a single outfit and hold the rod in hand, because it's necessary to sense the slightest dragging of the float amid all the touching and bumping. There will be more than a few missed strikes, but otherwise you'll catch nothing. In this instance it's much more reliable to fish with bread. Sometimes, though, crucian carp take only on bread, and sometimes only on worms. I explain this change in the character of their biting as follows. While crucian carp of equal, medium size are holding near your rigs, their bite continues to be certain. When, however, schools of small crucian carp turn up (and that's why it's improper to throw out a great deal of groundbait), the useless touching and bumping will begin, and a decent crucian carp must crowd through a throng of little ones and cannot take quietly and comfortably. Instead, he too takes by fits and starts, striking the worm at the tail, and therefore not confidently. On the other hand, one must also say that when a considerable quantity of crucian carp is caught in a small pond (and twice that number have had their lips torn or ripped off* or wounded), even the crucian carp, as unpretentious as he is, is forced to become circumspect.

One must use small fishing outfits for bread-bait, and medium ones for worms. Rising very early in the morning is unnecessary. On hot and fair summer days, as soon as the sun sets, crucian carp begin to move near the banks. At this time, the fishing outfits too must be cast as close to shore as possible. At midday, though, they rise to the top and, resembling large black spots—like spilled pitch, sometimes darker, sometimes lighter—they quietly move from place to place along the surface of the water. Then one must attach the floats as shallow as possible, for at this time crucian carp take at the bottom very little. When hooked, a large crucian carp—I have in mind a fish of close to two pounds—will rush fairly boldly to the side, twirling his head and whole body, and wagging his tail. I submit that with the largest crucian carp this maneuver can be dangerous, and therefore one has to try to turn the fish to the side immediately without allowing the line to go taut. The

*The lips of crucian carp (and of any small fish) are often torn off altogether by a forceful hook-set. Their lips, which look exactly like a little ring, are connected to the mouth by a pellicle, and are stretched out when necessary in the likeness of a small trunk.

crucian carp soon grows weary and floats up to the top on his side, like a bream. Crucian carp dried, and, especially, cooked in sour cream, make a most splendid dish, but since they live in ponds, their flavor depends on the quality of the water and they often smell of mud. But if such crucian carp are placed in a wicker pen and submerged in clean, flowing water, then after two (at most three) weeks, they will lose this unpleasant flavor and become very tasty. The crucian carp is a most lively fish, and therefore little ones serve as excellent bait for any large predatory fish.

The latter two species of fish—bream and crucian carp—have a peculiar trait, characteristic of them alone. They can be called "muddy," because only where the water is still and the bottom is covered with mud do they reproduce in abundance. Mud is their habitat. They take refuge in it for the winter without fail and remain alive even when, during cruel and snowless winters, all the water in small ponds and lakes freezes solid and the moist, muddy dirt on the bottom is all that remains.

I'll turn now to a description of predatory fish.

# 17. PERCH

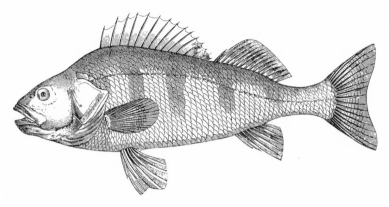

I don't actually know the origin of the perch's[86] name (*ókun'* ). Does it come from the verb "to plunge" (*okunát'* )? For the perch always plunges, that is, submerges the float, and he even does so more than once if the piece of bait he's swallowed is too big. . . . But I certainly won't insist on this etymology.[87]

After the roach, the perch is the most abundant species of fish. In rivers, lakes, flowing ponds, and even stillwater ponds, as long as the water is clean, the perch reproduces abundantly. He's fairly wide in cast, rather hunchbacked, and covered with scales of a greenish, somewhat golden color. On his back he has a crest with sharp spines and between it and the tail there's a fin. His tail, and especially the lower fins, are red, the belly white, and his eyes yellow with black pupils. Along the whole body lie five bands, which make him appear motley and generally very handsome. He has a single spine on each of his cheeks, which cover the gills, and you can be very painfully pricked if you grasp him carelessly. The perch's large mouth and wide throat bespeak his ability to swallow large pieces of food, even ones disproportionate to his size, and point to the predatory habits of his species. The perch reaches considerable size and, especially, weight. According to the accounts of trust-worthy people, there are perch of twelve pounds, but I've only seen fish of eight pounds, and these were frozen, brought from the Urals. I myself caught a three-and-a-half-pound perch, and have never seen live ones heavier than that. Perch don't grow much in length, which I've particularly noted in comparing an eight-pound perch (eighteen inches long and seven inches wide) with a perch of three and a half pounds: there wasn't as big a discrepancy in length as one should have expected. On the other hand, perch grow in thickness, which can reach over four inches through the back.

Perch begin to bite in spring as soon as the water becomes clear and they continue until the water is covered with ice, even taking through ice-holes in the winter, though I've never tried winter perch-fishing. At the end of April perch are full of roe, which they void in May. After spawning, they begin to take more eagerly. The perch's richest biting occurs in August and the beginning of September, when the water has been made clearer and cleaner by light frosts and it's not as easy for them to catch small fish.* Almost all sportsmen like perch-fishing very much, and many prefer it to all other kinds of angling. First, this is because perch bite often and, if a school of perch approaches (for they shoal in the autumn), very few of the fish will swim away without striking the food offered them. Second, because they take avidly and surely, for the most part even to the point of swallowing the bait altogether. Third, and finally, because angling for them doesn't require circumspection. The perch not only doesn't fear noise and motion in the water, but even rushes to investigate them, and therefore the water can be deliberately disturbed, on the bottom near the bank, with a stick or rod-butt, for this is similar to the murk stirred up by small fish. Medium perch more often take at intermediate depth, while the large ones take on the bottom, if it's clean. Starting in the spring, one must fish with worms, and in summer, with crayfish tails and molting crayfish—especially the large pincers of molting crayfish, which perch love. By autumn, however, right up until winter, it's best to angle with small baitfish. If there are none, then it often happens that one must catch a little roach or some kind of nonpredatory little fish, cut it up into pieces—large ones or

---

*It must be noted that this isn't so everywhere. Near Moscow, for example, the perch's biting declines considerably in the second half of August. Because of endless mills and factories, however, the streams here are always impounded in millponds and therefore lack the character of rivers that flow freely, that is, by their own mass of accumulated water.

small, depending on the fish that's taking and on the size of the fishing outfit—and bait your hooks with them. The perch, however, is not finicky and almost always bites on all the aforementioned baits, even on pieces of raw meat. Perch take very avidly on large earthworms at any time of year.*

The most profitable time of day for perch-fishing is, without doubt, the morning, but there's no need for early rising, before the sun is up. In the morning one must fish in swims that are clear, open, or *near* weeds. At midday, the reverse is true (I have in mind summer hot spells), and perch love to hold in the shade, among snags under bushes, under overhangs of grass, and beneath lily-pads. Consequently, one must fish *in* the weeds. When evening comes, perch once again move along clear and open places. If perch are taking infrequently, then one can even fish three outfits, of which one is large and put on the bottom with a sizable bait, while the other two are set at intermediate depth. If, on the other hand, perch are taking constantly, then it's hard to manage with two fishing outfits. In this case the problem isn't setting the hook in time, but ensuring that the perch don't start swallowing the hook too deeply and don't drag the rods into the water altogether. If the fish swallow the bait too far, this takes time away from recovering the hook and spoils the leader and fish, who will immediately die. As soon as the perch has carried the float or submerged it in the water, one must immediately land him. The perch never snatches or tears away bait from a running start, or with all his might, as many nonpredatory fish do. His bite is decisive, serious, and conscientious, never deceptive. I've had occasion many times to observe him in transparent waters. Having sighted his prey, a large perch rushes straight for it, quickly at first, but more slowly as he gets closer. Drawing near, he opens his mouth wide and, almost touching the piece of bait with his lips, suddenly stops, motionless, and, without making any movement with his mouth, seems to draw water into himself. The baited hook disappears, but the perch continues to swim as if nothing had happened, carrying along behind him the line, the float, and even the rod. When

---

*Near Moscow, no matter how I tried to fish with pieces of little fish or meat, I've never had perch bite.

going after live bait, he behaves differently, rushing headlong after it and striking it on the run. Perch almost never break loose, and missed strikes occur just as seldom. It's true that sometimes their bite can lead the inexperienced fisherman astray, for it can seem that some kind of fish is ceaselessly carrying off the float, and missed strikes endlessly follow, one after the other. Seeing that the end of the worm has been torn off each time, the sportsman at first considers this the mischief of dace or roach, even though the character of the biting is purely perchlike. Meanwhile, amid the multitude of missed strikes, he sometimes lands decent perch and convinces himself that perch too make mischief, deceive, and bite uncertainly from time to time. That accusation is unjust. All these pranks come from the very smallest perch, who sin without meaning to, for they can swallow neither a long worm nor the fat tail of a crayfish. As soon as a somewhat bigger perch comes up, then he immediately takes surely, and the fisherman will catch him. In order to verify this, one has only to take a small fishing outfit, bait a little worm, and immediately tiny perch fry will be caught. If the sportsman does not want to wait for the approach of larger perch to whom the little ones will concede their prey, then he must move to another swim, for the school of perch fry he's stumbled upon won't leave his fishing outfits alone all day.

Large perch are certainly great fun to catch—to say nothing of the huge ones—but I must confess that the frequent biting of small and medium perch is so monotonous, so sure, their float-dragging so simple, that all this together can sometimes be as dreary as the dragging about perpetrated by breamet. The art of angling practically disappears, and with it, all of angling's interest. I know that many sportsmen will rise up against me for saying this, for the biting of perch is considered the best, but I state my opinion openly. Large perch are very stubborn and strong and, until they're wearied, will on no account rise to the surface. Fishing outfits of large size are used for them, but regardless of this, one has to land them carefully. Though a huge perch doesn't fling himself swiftly in all directions, he does, on the other hand, turn so sharply while trying to dig his head into the bank or bottom that he can break even a strong line.

It's well known that perch constitute a superb and most nutritious foodstuff. Prepared cold, or, even better, baked unscaled, they have an excellent flavor and, what's more, they're not at all bony. Fish soup made from them is also very good.[88]

The perch's distinguishing characteristic is his greed, in which he's equaled perhaps only by the pike. *Lure-fishing,* which I'll discuss separately, serves as irrefutable evidence of this. I'll describe two convincing instances of this greed in which I was involved. One fine summer morning, on a large lake called "Kiishki"*[89] in Tatar, I was catching roach and breamet. Suddenly, I saw many small fry jumping out of the water at the sandbar, right next to the bank. I knew that this was the result of pursuit by predatory fish, but, seeing that the row was not stopping, I moved a bit closer to watch. What did I see? On the bar, which ran into the bank at a sharp angle, no deeper than four inches, a large school of decent perch were catching the small fish, which, because death was inevitable, even jumped out onto dry land. The perch pursued their prey so avidly that they too ended up on the sandbar, from which they made it to a bit deeper water by means of a few jumps. I even caught three of them with my hands. In spite of my presence, the perch never stopped chasing and catching fish. I ran off for my fishing outfit, baited it with the small fry that were lying on the bank, cast into the very center of the school, and caught thirty good perch. The next incident is more striking still. In inclement and windy weather, I came to angle for perch at a mill's wicket,**[90] among the piles that surrounded it. Scarcely had I cast out my medium outfit, baited with crayfish tail, than there started to fall a soaking rain from which I took refuge inside the sawmill. The rain cloud hadn't yet scudded past when I heard the miller's cry summoning me. I hurriedly rushed to him and saw that he was tinkering with

---

*Kiishki:* the name means "long." This lake is located twenty miles from the provincial capital Ufa and one-third of a mile from the River Belaia, with which it commingles in the springtime. Russians, of course, call it and the village sitting on its shore *Kishki.*

**I have already said that near Moscow a wicket is called a "palace" (*dvoréts*). Doesn't this term come from the word "door" (*dvértsa*), that is, a small door which is raised to allow a stream of water onto the wheel? Perhaps at first they used to say *dvérets,* and then, for ease of pronunciation, started to say *dvoréts.*

my fishing rig, and that there was a big fish on. But I didn't get there in time: the miller was standing with only the rod and the line, which was broken off above the float. . . . How annoying was his solicitude, which caused me to lose a large fish and beautifully appointed fishing outfit, but there was nothing for it. I unwound another large rig, baited it with a cluster of gutworms and a crayfish tail, and cast out. After a minute the float disappeared and I landed a splendid perch of about two pounds, from whose mouth dangled the other long line and float which he'd just broken off. When I sometimes relate them to people other than sportsmen or fishermen, the two incidents I've just described often elicit sly smiles that seem to express the opinion that my stories are fit for the famous little book entitled *Don't Listen If You Like, But Don't Interfere With My Lying.*[91] Sometimes, though, there's nothing more improbable than truth or stranger than reality.

Here's another story, no less dubious to nonsportsmen. I know a certain deep pond, in the Karsun district of Simbirsk Province,[92] which was formed solely by the damming of a strong source known as White Spring. The water was of such excellent quality that many transplanted chub and even sterlet[93] lived in it. Such a multitude of perch and gudgeon reproduced in the pond that the fishing turned out to be magnificent, even *miraculous:* a fisherman would cast his outfit baited with worms, and right away a gudgeon would swallow it, and in a short time the gudgeon would be swallowed by a perch. . . . At first this was a surprise for the sportsmen, but then we all took advantage of this convenience (that is, the spontaneous gudgeon-baiting), and whoever wanted to fish solely for perch would simply refrain from removing caught gudgeon from his hook. In my discussion of hooking live baitfish through the lip (page 33), I spoke of the advantages and disadvantages of such baiting. Anyone who has fished for only one hour in White Spring Pond would be completely convinced of the fairness of what I said regarding the disadvantages of such a method, for lip-baiting was being used there: though the perch took incessantly, less than half were landed. I therefore tried baiting through the back, and not a single perch broke loose.

Last year, in 1853, at the end of July, a perch bit for a certain fisherman who was using earthworms, but he failed to notice the strike, and the perch was then taken by a pike, which the fisherman landed. It's noteworthy that the pike could not swallow the perch, whose tail protruded from the pike's mouth.

# 18. PIKE

In spite of all my diligence, I haven't been able to find the source of the pike's[94] name (*shchúka*).[95] This fish is for the most part predatory. A long, bar-shaped form, wide tailfin for rapid movements, forward-slung mouth descending from the eyes like a weaver's shuttle, enormous jaws studded above and below with continuous, sharp, criss-crossing teeth*[96] from which no prey can tear itself away, and wide throat with which the pike swallows bait thicker than himself—all this combines to make him the rightful sovereign of those predatory fish that inhabit ordinary freshwater rivers and lakes. I have in mind here only those species of fish known as "white," as opposed to all the other species, namely, sturgeon, sevruga, sheefish, and so forth, which are called "redfish."[97]

The pike has large, dark, sharp-sighted eyes with which he spots his prey from afar. He's covered with scales and all mottled with spots and speckles of a dark green color. He has a white belly, and his tail and fins are greenish-gray with dark, sinuous little borders. I've heard that pike can live for a very long time, up to one hundred years (the same is said and even written about pond carp). This has supposedly been established by experiments in which small pike fry with markings on the tail or fins were released into clean, flowing ponds that never dwindle, and the date of their release was noted. I've also heard that pike supposedly grow to four-and-a-half feet in length and ninety pounds in weight. All this may

---

*The pike changes his teeth annually, in the month of May. To my amazement, I learned of this only very recently.

perhaps be true, but I won't assert what I don't know.[*][98] The largest pike I've managed to see weighed 49½ pounds; he was 39¼ inches long and 6¾ inches wide through the back and sides, but, on the other hand, he was of the same square thickness along almost his entire length.[99]

The pike feeds predominantly on fish and all sorts of aquatic vermin. In his greed the pike even swallows frogs, rats, and ducklings, which is why a large pike is called a "duck-eater." Pike inhabit only clean waters and appear in rivers together with roach and perch, and will perish with them if the water in a pond or lake is polluted somehow. Pike spawn at the very beginning of April, or, sometimes, if the spring is an early one, at the end of March. Wherever there are large numbers of any kind of little fish, there too the pike will multiply and be found in abundance. For the most part they're caught on trimmers, which I'll discuss later. The pike takes very avidly on a fishing outfit whose hook is baited with some kind of small fish. A metal leader or simple bass-instrument string, which was discussed above,[100] is used, but he also takes on crayfish and even on worms from time to time. The pike's bite is very swift, and as soon as he strikes the bait, the float momentarily disappears from sight, but it can happen that he'll strike the baitfish without having swallowed it, and quietly carry the float to the side without sinking it in the slightest. Pike often take on simple fishing outfits not cast out

---

[*]After the first edition of my little book came out, I chanced to read in Mr. Lëvshin's *Sportsman's Book*, printed in 1812 (part 4, page 487), some curious information on the longevity of pike. I cite it here with perfect exactitude: "When the ponds at Tsaritsyno, near Moscow, were cleaned, some twenty years since, during the transplantation of fish into pens, there was incidentally caught a pike of close to seven feet long and fourteen inches wide, with a gold ring, pierced through his cheekbone near the gills, bearing this inscription: 'Planted by Tsar Boris Fëdorovich.' According to their calculations at that time, this pike proved to be over two hundred years old. Lehmann claims that in 1497 in Heilbrock there was caught in a certain lake a pike of nineteen feet (over seven *arshins*), and, according to the inscription on a copper ring that was on him, it was found that he was planted in this lake by Kaiser Friedrich II in the year 1230; thus, he had lived in this water for two hundred sixty-seven years. His weight was three hundred fifteen pounds, and he had grown almost entirely white with age." I leave it to my readers to believe in the veracity of such stories as they see fit.

for them at all. They can of course bite through the thickest line or leader like a pair of scissors, which can be most vexing. There's only one way a pike can be landed on rod and line with an ordinary leader: if the hook lodges in the edge of his lip and he can't reach the line with his teeth, but such lucky occurrences are very rare. One need not bottom-fish for pike. On the contrary, the bait will be much more visible if the small fish mounted on the hook starts to move at a depth of two or three feet. In general, angling with baitfish is seldom undertaken on the bottom. Starting in the spring, pike rarely bite on trimmers, and in the summer they can be found near weeds, in which they usually hold, lying in wait for small fish, but it's best to fish for them in the autumn.*[101] In the first place, this is because the water becomes clearer and pike see the bait from afar, and, in the second place, because aquatic weeds are brought down by the frosts and it becomes less convenient for pike to conceal themselves and harder for them to catch small fish. At this time, therefore, they're hungry and greedy.

Fishermen describe the following ruse of the pike. He holds in the shallows with his head pointing downstream, and with his tail stirs up mud on the bottom, so that the turbid cloud

---

*The following is said about Orenburg Province: it's the greatest of rarities for pike there to take on white worms (greasers) even in the summer or autumn. Though it's rare, they sometimes take on crayfish tails, but never on earthworms or dungworms. Near Moscow, it's quite the reverse: especially early in the spring, after casting their roe (and particularly in the River Voria of the Dmitrov district), pike take very frequently not only on earthworms, but even on small dungworms. This would be easy to explain by the fact that streams around Moscow are too heavily fished, which leaves few small fish in them and consequently makes the pike hungry, but I must say that they take much more frequently hereabouts on worms than on trimmers or fishing outfits baited with small fish, predominantly in the spring. This question therefore cannot be answered unless we assume that the pike here have a special taste for worms. Last year, in 1853, the fishing started very early, and I succeeded in catching several small pike in the month of April, all on small outfits and all with worms. One of them I landed on a leader of *one strand of silk!* The bank was steep, I was fishing without a companion, and I found myself constrained to toss the pike (at a pound and a half) onto the fairly high bank. He'd swallowed the tiny hook, but the silk strand in his very jaws had become fastened to the bony extremity of his upper lip and therefore didn't end up on his teeth. The fish was landed sideways and seemed doubly heavy. Fishermen will understand that this is a very rare and lucky occurrence.

altogether conceals him from little fish swimming past, upon whom he rushes like a shot, but only when they swim up close. I myself have never seen such tricks. Pike-fishing is good fun because as soon as you cast the outfit and there's a pike in the vicinity, he won't be long in appearing, and also because very large pike will often take. Though they are very bold and swift in their movements when hooked, they are not stubborn, but quick and easily turned. Their bar-shaped, canoe-like figure is probably the reason for this. Small pike, up to three pounds, are fairly easy to toss onto the bank even without a net. It stands to reason that the line must be thick and the leader sound. A perch of equal weight will seem much heavier. The presence of pike can be easily guessed from the sudden cessation of feeding by roach and other small fish and still more surely from small fish leaping clear of the water. They spatter on all sides like rain when the pike flies past underwater with the swiftness of an arrow. After catching a pike, or perhaps two, in one swim, one has to move to another, and another, and so forth. The same must be done if more than half an hour goes by and the pike don't take—this is a sure sign that there are none in the vicinity. Certain sportsmen passionately love pike-fishing and prefer it to all other kinds of angling. Without sharing this opinion, I understand the reason for it. For anyone who doesn't find it tedious to move from place to place, but rather, on the contrary, finds it boring to sit at one and the same swim, waiting in vain for a decent fish to bite, pike-fishing, and angling for predatory fish in general, must in the main be pleasing, as it is for anyone who likes a quick resolution (either he bites or he doesn't) and enjoys playing a fish who is nimble, lively, and swift in his movements, and who sometimes tosses off unusual, unexpected leaps.

There is a strange trick for catching pike. When he doesn't have room to conceal himself, the pike can take up station near a bank, dam, tree-stump protruding into the water, piling, or pole stuck into the bottom, and he sometimes holds very close to the water's surface, motionless for hours, just as if he were sleeping or dead, so that you won't immediately notice him. Small fish even swim near him without apprehension. The pike's aim is obvious, but he carries this instinctive strategy to unwise excess. Pike and pickerel holding in such a spellbound state are not only shot with guns,* but also beaten, or, more accurately, stunned, with truncheons, as any fish may be stunned under thin ice.** They're even taken with horsehair snares tied to a long linden-staff, and then thrown out onto the bank. I had occasion to kill with my gun a nine-pound pike holding in such a position. Moreover, before my eyes a fisherman friend of mine who was sitting and fishing with me in a boat tied fast to stakes noticed a pike holding under the stern and seized him with his hand. . . . The fish weighed over two pounds.

The greediness of pike knows no bounds. They often attack fish or ducklings they can't possibly swallow, which makes for some extremely amusing scenes as the prey, being stronger than the foe who has seized hold, drags the fish about in the water. I myself have seen a fully fledged duckling, or, to put it better, a young duck, flapping its wings about the water with a terrible cry of fright and pain, even lifting off from the water, and struggling for a long time with a pike who had bitten the hind part of its body. I've also seen a large ide dragging a small pike who had seized him by the tail. But I'll relate two incidents that still further demonstrate the pike's excessive avarice. A fisherman who was standing next to me on the dam of a huge pond and landing a small fish suddenly felt such weight and resistance on his fishing rig that he almost dropped the rod, but, taking this for the unexpected movement of some kind of medium-sized fish, he began to pull with greater force and dragged a decent pike out onto the dam. What was our astonishment when we saw that the hook had been taken by an ordinary roach, and the pike had then seized him without touching the hook. The pike had plunged his teeth so far into

*Any fish holding shallow in the water can be shot with a gun. One has only to take into consideration the birdshot's angle of incidence and shoot not at the fish himself, but farther or closer. The birdshot's angle of reflection (always equal to the angle of incidence) will depend on the height of the bank upon which the sportsman is standing.

**As soon as the water in a lake or pond is covered with the first thin, transparent ice capable of supporting a man, shallow places are patroled with truncheons. When a fish holding high and close to the ice is spotted, the ice over his head is forcefully struck with the truncheon. The fish is stunned (falls into a faint) and turns belly-up. The thin ice is quickly broken and the fish taken by hand before he comes to.

the roach that it was necessary to pry open his mouth with a stick! The other incident took place not long ago, in mid-September 1845, to be precise. I'd come to fish for perch at about eight o'clock in the morning at my own mill. Near the dam, there were long weeds growing, and I cast my outfit through them into the deep mainstream, having baited the hook with earthworm. I'd only just set the rod upon the weeds and begun to prepare another outfit, when the float disappeared, and I barely managed to seize the rod. I lifted it—and the leader was chewed through. I knew that this had been a pike, and immediately cast the other outfit. After a few minutes the same story was repeated, but I succeeded in setting the hook and had already begun to play some kind of large fish, when suddenly the line flew up to the surface with a whistle—and the leader again proved to be chewed through. It was obvious that this too was a pike, and a big one, for I'd almost seen him. Not having a leader for pike with me, which was very annoying, I cast a third outfit, also baited with earthworm, but now held the rod in hand, ready to strike the pike at the first movement of the float. And so it happened: scarcely had the float begun to dip when I swiftly set the hook and easily landed a small pike, who also bit through my leader, but only when he was already lying on the dam. At home, when they started to clean this pike in order to cook it for the table, they found in his throat not only the last hook, but also the first one, with the chewed-off leader. This then was the pike who had taken my bait the first and third times, for the second fish, with which I'd busied myself for quite some time, had been twice as large as the landed pike. But such was his avarice that neither the pain from the hook in his throat, nor the clamor of my troubling over the second pike, could drive off the first one! I know very well that the detailed description of such occurrences can be of interest only to true and passionate sportsmen, but it's precisely for them that I write. For them I must also say that in the same year I caught a pike of three-and-a-half pounds on one strand of the Indian plant, or silkworm gut. I had no net, because I was angling for small fish, and I should have sent home for it. So, for nearly half an hour, the pike who had deeply swallowed my hook struggled and rushed about on one little strand and could not chew through it. Though I'm not keen on this imported gut, I'm nonetheless obliged to acknowledge its quality in this regard. Pike of medium size, caught in the spring (when they are called "bluefin pike") and even in the summer, make a decent dish if cooked straight from the water (not dead) and served cold.

Pike sometimes take very late in the autumn, at night, on the bottom, on boulters set out for burbot and, it stands to reason, baited with small fish.

In discussing ide, I described how a five-pound specimen had been caught by the dorsal fin.[102] But that same sportsman caught a pike of eighteen pounds by the tailfin, which had been pierced by his hook. Though the line was thick and strong, when the fisherman saw that he had an enormous fish, that it was impossible to turn him, and that the line was being stretched tight, he threw his rod into the water. The pike wandered about the wide pond with it, even plunging the rod into the water completely. The fisherman went after him in a boat. As soon as the fish stopped, he would take the rod in his hands and begin to play the fish. As soon as the line was pulled taut, he would throw the rod. By wearying the fish in this manner *for several hours* running, the fisherman brought him—as if sleepy or stupefied—up to the surface and captured him with a net. For a long time the angler hadn't known what kind of fish he was fighting, and saw that it was a pike only when his quarry swam to the top for the first time. Honor and glory to the sportsman's art and patience!

# 19. ASP

In all the southern provinces, this predatory fish[103] is called *zhérikh*, but, in Moscow, he's known as *sherespër*. The first name probably comes from the verb "to gambol" (*zhirovát'*); that is, to play, to jump, which suits well the character of this fish, for he very much loves to jump out of the water and splash on its surface solely for pleasure, and not for the pursuit of prey. The second name, however, must come from the fact that the asp, when leaping out of the water, spreads wide his fins (*pér'ia*) and crest, which are already very wide (*shirókie*). I've also heard that this fish is called "steed," a fitting term thanks to his gallops. I'll employ the first name for its ease of pronunciation and because it's much more widely used.[104]

The asp is long, and similar in shape to the ide, but the color of the asp's large scales is much whiter and more silvery, except for his back, which is darker than the ide's. He has the peculiarity that his mouth's lower lip is longer than the upper one. The upper lip has something like a groove, while the lower is formed like a bird's bill turned upward, and it fits into the grove of the mouth's upper part. In this way the asp's mouth rather has the appearance of a raptor's beak, but upside-down. His tail and upper fin are very stiff and wide, gray in color, while the lower fins are reddish. The asp's eyes are gray, with dark pupils, and his mouth is fairly big, but not huge. The lower part of his body is white.

The asp doesn't inhabit small streams, but likes big rivers or at least rivers that are full, deep, and swift. He also lives in large, clean lakes, feeding on all kinds of aquatic insects and small fish. Only on the latter will he take on rod and line. His bite is extraordinarily quick, and he fights with unusual spirit when hooked. He grows to twenty-seven inches in length and can weigh eighteen pounds. Fishermen say that there are asp of thirty pounds, but I can't confirm this.[105] They spawn at the end of April and beginning of May. Without doubt, asp-fishing is one of the best and most interesting for the sportsman. Unfortunately, though, I'm very little acquainted with it and can report no further details of these remarkable fish. I've seen fishermen angling for them with baitfish, in swift waters, at intermediate depth, about a yard deep. The asp's favorite swims are the deep tailwaters below flood-gates and sluices, where the water endlessly roils and swirls, when two or three sluice-gates are raised, which is constantly done on strong rivers. In the foam, roar, and spray, these "aquatic steeds" leap upward and fall with a plop, and this is where the fisherman throws his sturdily constructed fishing outfit with a heavy sinker. Asp, when prepared straight from the water as a cold dish, is splendid.

## 20. ZANDER

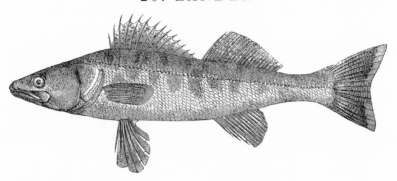

I'm even less well acquainted as a fisherman with this superb table-fish,[106] but I know that he takes on rod and line. Zander grow to enormous size, weighing up to eighteen pounds and more. They live in large rivers and flowing lakes and ponds, but they prefer the fresh, swift water of the river. The zander has a long, extended mouth, and teeth that are sparse but thick and strong. His tongue is fairly large, which, in my opinion, gives him the right to be counted as a kind of trout.[107] In form he's bar-shaped and similar to, but somewhat wider than, the pike. The lower half of his body and his belly are silvery-white, while his back and the upper halves of his sides are grayish. Banding the length of his entire body are twelve faint stripes of a faded dark-blue color. His eyes are fairly large and yellowish, with dark pupils. In rivers where there are many zander, they take avidly on outfits baited with small fish. The zander, obviously, is a predatory fish. Like the pike, he's caught on trimmers and boulters, but predominantly at night, from spring until the middle of summer. Live zander that haven't been exhausted by long confinement in slit-pens make a tasty and nourishing dish. They're essential to a fine repast, and as a result zander are sometimes very expensive. On the other hand, frozen zander are carted to Moscow and its vicinity in such abundance that by the end of winter they're very inexpensive, that is, about one ruble in assignats for six pounds. For people observing the fast, this is a precious fish: the meat is tasty even when refrozen, nutritious, not bony, goes well with everything, does not pall upon its eaters, and is inexpensive. In a word, zander is Lenten beef.

# 21. TAIMEN, OR REDLING

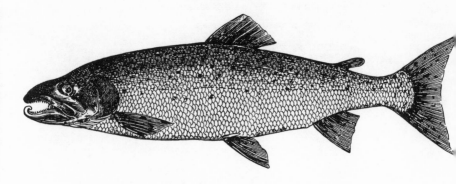

This utterly splendid fish[108] deserves his second name, "red-ling," by which he's known in Orenburg Province. Sometimes the name "red fish" is also employed, probably because of the yellowish-pink color of his body and, perhaps, because of the red spots with which he's speckled, but one mustn't confuse redling with the so-called "redfish," or Atlantic salmon. The latter is distinguished from the former by his wider torso, the grayish-white color of his scales and the more extensive red-ness of his body. He lives primarily in large rivers. The redling is a kind of trout[109] and is found with the trout only in clean, cold and swift rivers, in small streams or brooks, or in ponds constructed on them that haven't been polluted by manure, though only if the ponds are deep and clear. His figure is long and bar-shaped, but wider than the pike's. He's very hand-some. Like the trout, the taimen is completely covered by large and small black, red and white spots. He has blue-gray fins, the lower half of his body is whitish-pink in color, and his mouth is rather big. He feeds on small fish, worms, and vari-ous insects that fall into the water from without, as well as on those that live in it. The redling reaches enormous size. Once I was brought a redling caught in a little stream he'd entered by means of the turbid spring run-off: the fish weighed twenty-seven pounds and was somewhat fat-bellied.[110]

While one is trout-fishing, usually with red worms, redling will sometimes be caught, but this seldom occurs, because they take chiefly on baitfish. For the most part anglers catch them with odd fishing methods, and take them at night with spears or even shoot them with guns, lying in wait for redling as they make their way from one pool to another along shallow, stony riffles on fine summer days, always near midday. This last unusual method is used especially by the Orenburg Tatars who live on the banks of the Great Zai and Little Zai, which flow and merge into one river in the Bugul'ma district.[111] Once, when I was driving from Bugul'ma to Kazan', a Tatar coachman of my acquaintance asked me at a station for several powder cartridges and some large shot. I gladly gave him both, and asked him what fowl he was after. The Tatar replied that he was shooting fish, namely, taimen. I of course questioned him on the particulars of this unusual sport and even went down myself to examine the places along the Little Zai where he was shooting the redling which inhabited this river in great abundance. The banks were high and well-suited for concealing sportsmen, and the water was so shallow that it wasn't difficult to shoot even small fish. In my entire life I caught only one redling, on a small dungworm, only about three pounds in weight, but he put up an extraordinarily spirited fight. One can suppose that it would be very difficult to play a large one. The taimen's flavor is superb. He has quite a big tongue, like all three species of trout.

# 22. TROUT, OR SPOTTIE

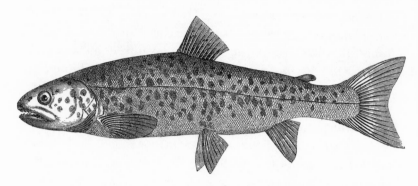

In Orenburg Province, trout[112] were found in exceptional abundance in all the brooks and streams, for in the summer they were all cold as ice and clear as crystal. But the various races and tribes of the human population that have invaded from everywhere—but that still haven't come close to settling this wondrous region—have trampled the province's luxuriant meadows and muddied its bright waters. Now far fewer trout are to be found, but they're still abundant. In certain streams I know, they've remained in the upper reaches, down to the first mill.

The simple folk don't even know the word *trout*,[113] but call this delightful fish *spot*, or *spottie*—a most appropriate name, for he is speckled with black, red, and white spots. In his figure, shape, and speckling of the skin—simply put, in every way—the trout is so similar to the redling that it's possible to take them for one and the same fish. The spottie, however, appears wider and flatter than the redling, and is much more speckled. People say he can reach enormous size, weighing up to fifteen pounds, but I scarcely believe this and think that they must be confusing the trout with the redling, small specimens of which I've never encountered. I confess, though, that I'm not entirely without doubt as to whether the spottie and redling are different sizes of the same fish. I myself once saw a spottie of seven pounds, killed by spear.

This method of slaughtering all species of trout—which, like any fish-bagging by odd methods, is repugnant to the true angler—is accomplished in the following manner. On a dark autumn night, two sportsmen set out, one with a bundle of lit kindling and carrying a supply of it on his back, the other with a spear. They walk the length of the stream and painstakingly examine every small pool or deep place, illuminating it with the flaming torch. The fish usually hold tight to the bank, leaning against it or against some tree roots. Having located a redling, spottie, grayling or burbot, the sportsman with the spear approaches from the opposite side, while his companion provides him with light, for when one stands on the bank under which the sleeping fish have taken cover, spearing them is awkward and visibility poor. The spear-fisherman, maintaining all possible silence, little by little submerges his neptunian trident, and, bringing it to within a few feet of the fish's back, deftly plunges the barbed points of the spear into his prey. In precisely this fashion they also spear all kinds of fish in ponds, lakes, and river coves while floating about in a boat, with the difference that the fire is carried on an iron grate made fast to the bow with an iron shaft. They sometimes get and keep pike of greater size this way than with any other fishing gear. In the pike's case I'm willing to allow the spear.[114]

I discussed stream-fishing for trout above.[115] I repeat that I was never very keen on trout-fishing in streams, but I've also caught many trout and grayling, and with great pleasure, in the upper reaches of clean ponds where the water, without flooding the bank-tops, stands even with them, forming a mainstream that is sometimes very deep and consequently not quite transparent. There one can bottom-fish with two outfits and lay the rods on the bank without being especially cautious or quiet. The spottie take without their typical swiftness and one has time to seize the rod when the float begins to tremble and bob. This is a most diverting and alluring form of angling, especially if there's reason to hope for a large trout or grayling. The largest spottie I've caught weighed almost three pounds, but they were spirited fighters and a net was indispensable. I especially like this method of fishing. There's no need to change swims often, and one can quietly sit in the same place for an entire morning with all the amenities, and a pipe or cigar. In hot summer weather one must fish early, but, in cold weather, one may fish all day. I've always used medium outfits with ordinary dungworms or earthworms, on the bottom for the most part, but many sportsmen fish shallow and with live bait. Perhaps the latter bait is best, for little fish are often found in the trout's belly. Unfortunately, I haven't had occasion to verify this.

The spottie is so delicate that in summer he won't live five minutes in a bucket of cold water. While you fish, it's possible to keep him alive in a *keep-net,* but you often get him home dead even though the swim may have been very close by. Because of this he loses a great deal of that delicate taste characteristic of trout alone. The spottie is often cooked dead and his flavor still can't be overpraised, but the gastronome who wishes to appreciate the trout's merits fully should try soup at the riverside made from freshly caught trout, or at home from trout transported back in a barrel with ice.*[116] The spottie is as excellent prepared as a cold dish as fried or dried, with sour cream.

The spottie may be well taken with muzzle-traps when he runs in late autumn. He's also caught in winter on rod and line through ice-holes, and even taken at night by lantern-light when the flame's ray is directed straight into the ice-hole. I myself have seen peasant boys catching small spottie by piercing thin autumn ice with truncheons and lowering into the broken opening a thread and hook baited with dungworm. The thread is tied to the middle of a small stick that is laid across the opening so that the fish, when hooked, is unable to drag the stick into the water. Having placed many such outfits along the river's whirlpools, the boys would walk back and forth along the stream and examine their fishing rigs, removing hooked fish and replacing stolen worms with new ones.

Though the spottie is the most skittish and watchful of fish and the swiftest in his movements, he can be taken by hand (as can grayling and burbot), for he likes to squeeze himself in between snags and tree roots, and to get under rocks or even into holes. I've already discussed catching any kind of fish by hand, which is widely practiced near Moscow.[117]

---

*If it's impossible to get the trout to the kitchen alive, then the best way to preserve his flavor is to clean the fish, wrap him in grass and rinse him in the shade with cold water (better still, cover him with ice). Any fish loses his flavor when he expires because he wears himself out dying in the pail, and, probably, vents some bile.

## 23. GRAYLING

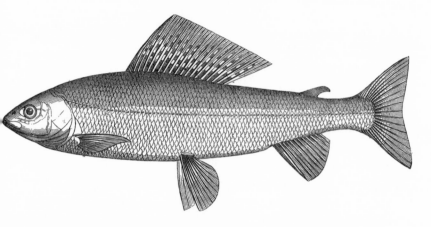

I haven't seen this fish[118] anywhere but in Orenburg Province. Though his name (*kutemá*) sounds Russian, I've heard that the word is Chuvash and means "bright," "shining."[119] I definitely count the grayling as a species of trout.[120] First, because without fail the grayling lives wherever the trout is found, and in greater numbers; second, because he has a tongue; and third, because he perfectly resembles the trout in the structure of his bones, all his habits, and his superb flavor.

In the cast of his body he's just a little wider than the trout, though a good deal thicker through the back. In color he's entirely a grayish-blue silver. His fins and tail are the same gray-blue color with a tint of pinkish-violet. This hue is perceptible if you look at him with the light on his fins and his back, which is somewhat darker than the perfectly white lower half of his body. Grayling, according to the unanimous opinion of people who live in his range, and to my own personal observation, do not grow to more than fourteen inches long or weigh more than two and a half or three pounds at most. Although he also likes clean and cold water, the grayling is somewhat less outspoken in this regard than the spottie. When the first mill is built on a wild, clean, free river, and the water is impounded with a dam of fresh brushwood and earth, topped with several layers of turf turned up by the plow, then spottie, redling, and grayling will live in this clean pond, which is clear as glass during the dam's first few years. Such a pond can be wondrously handsome! This is especially so in calm weather, at sunrise and sunset, when the flashing mirror of the water lies still, like an enormous piece of ice, between its green, darkened banks. Bending toward the sunrise, you see spottie and grayling, seemingly pinkish-silver in the brilliance of dawn, leaping on the flat surface of the water. They're catching various midges and other winged insects knocking about above the quiet water and often falling into it. In such a pond, far from human habitation, where it's too far to cart dung and the dam is supported only by turf and soil, these three splendid species of trout may live for a long time. But the brushwood will rot through, the dam will settle, and dung will accumulate in the mill-yard because the plowed fields are not being fertilized and there's nowhere else to put it. At that time, dung (even from the village if the dam isn't too remote) will start being dumped onto the dam, which will communicate its odor to the water. Spottie will cease to live in the pond, and will move upriver, while grayling will remain in the pond for a while. But when the water becomes even more polluted, the grayling too will disappear. The grayling takes on rod and line more avidly than the spottie, so you'll always catch twice as many. Angling for grayling is absolutely identical to trout-fishing, and therefore I won't discuss it separately.

———

Those are all the species of fish that take on rod and line and inhabit the waters of provinces where I've chanced to live, and therefore to fish. This is a tiny fragment in relation to the endless expanse of our Russia, and many are the species of fish unknown to me even by name, and many the methods of angling unfamiliar to my experience. My notes are therefore very incomplete. I leave it to others to make up for this deficiency. I believe, however, that it would not be out of place to discuss two species of fish that, though they don't take on rod and line during regular daytime angling, are nonetheless caught on ordinary fishing outfits when these are set out at night. It's also impossible to pass over crayfish in silence, since they fully deserve the fisherman's attention. Crayfish play an important role in angling, and the sportsman has to know where, when and how to get them. Something must also be said about those methods of fish-bagging that it's impossible to call "angling," but that are closer to angling than to catching fish by other means. I have in mind lures, boulters, and trimmers. The fish I wish to discuss are called "burbot" and "sheatfish."

# BURBOT

The burbot[121] inhabits small spring-fed streams and all large rivers, flowing ponds and lakes that have good, clean water.[122] He too belongs to the race of predatory fish, for he primarily feeds on small fish. His shape is quite peculiar, and altogether unpleasant. From the burbot's head, with its fairly large and wide mouth and single whisker protruding from beneath the lower lip, the fish's whitish belly, which can be big and round in large burbot, immediately begins. From his belly, the burbot's shape flattens and ends in a long, flat, sinuous train, trimmed with a continuous, soft fin down to his small, roundish tail. The burbot has no scales, but is covered with slime, which makes him difficult to hold in one's hands. He's completely marmoreal, speckled with black spots against a dark green, yellowish background. He has dark eyes. Some burbot are quite dark, while others are very yellow. I've never seen burbot over fifteen pounds, but it's said they can reach thirty pounds.

Although I've only spoken to one fisherman who angled for burbot, nonetheless, based on this, I can relate that burbot take at the bottom on ordinary fishing outfits baited with small fish or a piece of fish and set out near the banks for the night in late autumn and the beginning of winter. You can do very well if you fish for burbot at night, but no one is going to start night-fishing at that time of year.* Soup made just from bur-

---

*I recently became convinced that burbot can take on rod and line during the day. While I was present, a fisherman caught a burbot of two pounds on bot (even without ruff bouillon), only if the fish are alive, and especially if you put in a little extra liver and milk, is so good that, in my opinion, it can rival our celebrated sterlet soup.[123] Because of my esteem for food of such high quality and because of the impossibility of angling for burbot, I allow and even enjoy catching them with *muzzle-traps,* as they are called on the left bank of the Volga, or *mouth-traps,* as they are called in Moscow.[124] This is done in the following manner.

In the riffles of a river inhabited by burbot, *weirs* are built, that is, the entire width of the river, or only that side which is deeper, is intercepted by thin, continuous stakes protruding from the water by about fourteen inches, such that the water's current can freely flow through them but a decent-sized fish cannot pass. In this barrier a gate or clear place is left, and a muzzle-trap* (or mouth-trap) is put in, tied fast in the middle to a long stake. If its open end is square, then the muzzle-trap can be inserted between the stakes very securely, but if it's round (which, in my view, is very foolish), then the holes must be stopped up with pine or fir boughs or, if these are not available, with some kind of twigs. The most crucial thing is that the muzzle-trap lie squarely on the bottom. In the winter, especially during hard frosts, primarily around Christmastide, burbot come out of the deep whirlpools in which they hold all year, and move up the river along the very bottom, searching for hard, gravelly or even stony patches against which they rub themselves to expel roe and milt. Thus, when they encounter a barrier they can't crawl through, they're inevitably caught in the muzzle-trap's throat as they seek an opening to provide free passage. Sometimes such enormous burbot stumble in that it's incomprehensible how they could have crawled into the narrow aperture, being twice as wide as it is. This is explained by the fact that the burbot's entire thickness consists of his belly, which, because of its softness, contracts easily, and

---

earthworms, in the spring, in a drained pond. Burbot also take on boulters in the spring, immediately after the flood-waters recede.

*Muzzle-trap* is the name given to a round bag woven of withes. Its rear end is tied shut, while in the front end, which has the appearance of an open purse, a throat resembling a funnel is constructed, so that fish can enter freely but can't get out.

the fact that the burbot is covered with an unusual slime. It's best to set up weirs at the mouths of streams flowing into the main river. Burbot always move at night and are never caught in muzzle-traps in the daytime. During our long, cruel winters, the weather can be very fine after a blizzard which has raged for several days, especially, sometimes, after an Orenburg snowstorm, when the blizzard grows still and the snowy plains it's plowed up create the appearance of a sea suddenly frozen in the midst of its agitation.[125] It's great fun in the sun's bright splendor to force one's way along the snowbound path to the similarly snowbound weirs, which you'll often fail to find right away under the drifts of snow, to shovel them off with spades, to break up the ice with ice-axes and hatchets, to throw it out with a flat landing-net or spade and drag up the muzzle-trap, sometimes half stuffed with burbot.[126] From time to time, especially by Lent, perch, roach, and crayfish are also caught.

Burbot take in the autumn on hooks tied to a thick line or lace, without a float, mounted with whole baitfish or a piece of fresh fish. Such boulters are set out overnight. The bait is lowered to the very bottom right next to the bank, sometimes in the middle of the river, and the lace is tied to a peg or tree-knot, but I'll discuss this in greater detail in its turn.[127] Burbot large enough to break thick laces are caught. Obviously, it's best to fasten these to a bush or tree-knot (but not an alder, for it will immediately break or be torn out at the trunk) that has some bend. Burbot soup, burbot-liver pie . . . these are dishes whose superb flavor is known to all.

# SHEATFISH

In shape the sheatfish[128] is very similar to the burbot, but his mouth, or, more accurately, his maw, is wider, uglier. His head blends even more into his torso, that is, his belly. He's much more repulsive than the burbot and somehow resembles a huge tadpole. I've heard that sheatfish can reach monstrous, fabulous size, and that they swallow not only children, but also adults.[129] They inhabit only large rivers, primarily slow, muddy, and deep ones. The flavor of the sheatfish is coarse and unpleasant, but his train, or tail, which consists entirely of backbone and fat, has a superb taste. Coulibiac with some kind of red, freshly salted fish and a good filling made of slices of fresh sheatfish fat laid along the inside, which then all melts in the oven and permeates both stuffing and crust—now that's what I call eating![130] Sheatfish are caught on huge hooks or boulters no smaller than firehooks, with commensurately large barbs, tied to strong ropes and baited with big fish, enormous pieces of meat, half-plucked chickens, ducks and even small piglets. Cow and sheep entrails are also used as bait, but sheatfish take more avidly on a bait of pure meat. I've also heard that where there are many sheatfish, they angle for them with huge fishing outfits, using fish and large frogs as bait.

# CRAYFISH

Though crayfish[131] is neither fish nor flesh, it's better than either. The saying "Even crayfish is fish when you're fishless" is unjust. Besides their own high gastronomic value, crayfish, as I've already said, play a very important role in angling, for they serve as the best bait for all species of fish.[132] This is especially true of molting crayfish, which are irreplaceable during that season. Crayfish are found in almost all rivers, in flowing ponds, and sometimes even in lakes, but they can't bear water that's too cold, or too warm, especially if it's stagnant or dirty. In large and sandy rivers, crayfish tend to be very big but not tasty and are found in small numbers. In small streams, though, especially in the black-earth provinces, they're found in such multitudes that they may even hamper fishing, especially after molting, when they tend to be thin and hungry. No matter what you put on your hooks, even crayfish tails, no sooner do they touch bottom than crayfish attack from all sides, seize the prey with their pincers and mouths, and crawl with it into a hole. At first you'll mistake this for the strike of a large fish, and you'll begin to give him freedom to bite. As a result it will occasionally be quite some time before you extricate your hook from the crayfish's hole. You'll soon come to recognize their biting and no longer let them drag your hooks about. As soon as a crayfish carries the float, you must lift the rod gently right away. Sometimes you'll pull out the crayfish as well. But is the fishing any good if you have to pull up your rigs constantly? When you fish at intermediate depth and not too close to the bank, then crayfish will take less often. They attack baitfish, dungworms, earthworms, and bread most greedily of all. There's one trustworthy salvation from crayfish: flood-pools and the overflows of ponds, where crayfish are few and where they won't touch any bait, probably because they don't crawl about on mud. Nonetheless, they don't strike fishing outfits everywhere. I've chanced to angle in many rivers where there were crayfish, and sometimes not one of them touched my rigs.

They're caught with rings and crayfishers. The first is nothing more than a wooden or iron hoop sewn across with netting. In the middle of it a stone is attached for weight, as well as a piece of meat, fish, or bread for bait: the more noisome the meat, the better. Such a ring is fastened to three small ropes of equal length at equal distance from one another, and all three are then tied to one rather thick rope (the ring has the appearance of a chandelier hung from the ceiling). The length of this rope depends on the depth of the water. That rope in its turn is tied to a long stick. Several such crayfish traps are cast into deep swims where there are always multitudes of crayfish holes. After half an hour, there will be several crayfish sitting in each ring, eating the bait. It only remains to pull out the rings gently and gather up the catch. The construction of *crayfishers*, as they're called in Orenburg Province, is exactly the same as that of the rings, with the difference that old bast shoes (called *osmëtki* hereabouts) are used instead of a hoop and netting. This is simpler and more convenient. It's easy to fashion about three dozen such crayfishers. Inside every bast shoe (with a stone attached to it or packed with clay for faster sinking) one must attach with bast a piece of any kind of meat, or fish, if you happen to have it, or, if neither the one nor the other is available, then a crust of bread. Scatter the crayfishers along the river about thirty-five feet from one another. When the crayfisherman has cast the last crayfisher, he then returns to the first and after half an hour starts to pull up the crayfishers in order. Two or three crayfish will be sitting in each one. It's necessary to pull the trap to the surface of the water carefully and quietly and then to throw it out onto the bank swiftly. In rivers abounding with crayfish, one can catch more than a hundred of them this way.

In very swift or small rivers, this method is awkward, and crayfish are therefore caught by hand after they're sought out in holes, and under snags and stones.

In muddy ponds or lakes crayfish live not in holes (because firm soil is required for the construction of holes), but in the mud. They won't enter rings or crayfishers, and therefore there's no other means of catching them than with a small, close-woven dragnet or burlap net; haul out onto shore as much mud as possible, and, together with it, the crayfish.

At night crayfish crawl along bars right next to banks, and even crawl up on shore (probably to search for food). One may catch crayfish by hand by walking along such places with a burning torch.

Finally, there's another method, and a rather amusing one, of getting crayfish, but it's essential that the water be very transparent. One must take a fairly long stick (not a dry one), split it at one end and insert into the split a little wedge so that the stick's edges are separated no more than about three inches. Supplied with such an implement, one must choose a moderately deep swim where the most crayfish live, and throw onto the bottom right next to the bank any kind of meat, guts, offal or at least some compacted bread. Crayfish will immediately crawl to the food from all sides. Then cautiously put the split stick into the water and, taking careful aim at the crayfish, as close to him as possible, suddenly drive the forks into the bottom. The crayfish will be caught between them and get stuck in the top of the split. It seems a simple thing, but it's necessary to practice a great deal, and at first there will be many missed strikes. If the crayfish in the river are numerous, then even with this method you'll be able to catch enough of them.

In June and in July, male crayfish molt and convalesce in holes, while females, also in holes, deposit their roe. Both the one and the other must be taken by hand. Females molt later than males. Hoping to catch molting crayfish, small burbot enter their holes, and village boys after crayfish thus often catch burbot with their hands.

# BOULTERS AND TRIMMERS

Setting out boulters and trimmers,[133] which I've mentioned more than once, is done in the following way. *Boulters* of the large variety, or even medium ones, are made with thick lines or strong laces (with sinkers, if the water is swift) and baited with small fish. They're lowered to the bottom of a river, pond, or lake, preferably along the bank near roots and snags, and then attached to a stake planted in the bank, or to a bush or fishing rod. Fish are caught on boulters at night. They're first set out in autumn, when it gets cold and the frosts begin. This kind of fishing continues all winter on rivers that don't freeze over, or that are only covered by thin ice.* Burbot, chub, zander, and pike are caught. As a precaution, it's not a bad idea to use boulters with leaders of wire or instrument-string, for pike will chew through the thickest lace. Pike do take on boulters at the bottom, though rarely.

*Trimmers* are set out solely for pike. They're the same as boulters, but the baitfish must be mounted live, through the back (the best baiting method is to thread the baitfish onto the hook sideways) and the bait is put down no deeper than a yard. A long string or lace, always with a metal leader, is wound around a forked stick, then jammed into a deliberately made split in one of the fork's horns. The stick itself is tied fast with a short line to a long pole whose other, sharpened end is planted at an angle in the bank or shallow bottom. For large pike, the rig is usually baited with good-sized perch. The pike, having swallowed the bait, unwinds the lace up to its full length from the forked stick, and, if he's well hooked, will stay on all day and not break free for any reason at all. Trimmers are set primarily in ponds and lakes, in shallow places near weeds and rushes. A boat is required for placing and retrieving trimmers because it's best to set them in the overflows of

---

*I've only heard tell of winter boulter-fishing, for my own attempts have always been unsuccessful. If there's a frost, the very best catch is around 1 October; if not, then later.

ponds. Pike can bite on trimmers during the day, but they're more often caught at night. Ordinary strong hooks are no good for large pike because they're too slender and small. A huge pike is so strong, and will thrash and writhe so much, that the hook will certainly tear through him and he'll leap away, even if the hook has lodged in his stomach, or *bladder*, as fishermen call it. For this kind of fish-bagging, special, thick hooks are prepared, and they too are called "trimmers." I've chanced more than once to pull up pike with their bladders, or stomachs, turned inside-out like stockings, though the fish were still lively and fought with spirit. Huge perch are also caught on such trimmers, and even burbot from time to time (in late autumn, it stands to reason), but only if the lace is unwound from the forked stick and the bait lowered to the bottom, or if it rests in the water against the bank, for burbot will on no account take at intermediate depth. The best time for catching pike on trimmers is the end of summer and first half of autumn. In spring and late autumn they seldom take. Double trimmers, that is, with two hooks, have always proved inconvenient in my experience.

I'm not a very keen trimmer-fisherman. Is it worth spending your time on pike alone when any fish will take on rod and line, without trimmers? But I used to love, and still do love, setting out boulters in autumn for burbot, and so will discuss this method in greater detail. Besides the fact that burbot are precious for their flavor, and that there's no other way of getting them at this time of year, setting boulters is pleasant because it begins when rod-and-line fishing ends. By replacing angling in some way, it can serve as the only joy for a passionate fisherman aggrieved at being deprived of his favorite amusement for a whole six months! Boulters have a considerable advantage because they can be set secretly, so that no one other than their owner will see or find them. And this circumstance is very important if the sport is undertaken in bustling places where many people are lounging about. Rarely will someone not be curious enough to examine a set rig, if he sees it, and there will be many such people who will come and pull out your catch deliberately. And the man who has looked out of mere curiosity will always cast the line back out idiotically, to the wrong place and in the wrong way. If the baitfish has somehow thrashed his way under the bank, gone behind a stump, or snagged on a root, then, when the uninvited guest pulls up the rig without the slightest care, he'll probably snag or pull off the bait sideways or tear it off altogether. To avoid such hindrances, one can attach the lace to a peg (which is driven firmly into the river bottom by the bank and covered by a yard or more of water), or even to a snag or willow switch, for the willow often grows over water and is very strong. This can be so cunningly set up that even a thief who knows the probable location of the boulters won't find them. In places secure from visitors, one can set the boulters on fishing rods, and with floats. The latter method is pleasant because when the fisherman approaches, he can already see from a distance whether or not a fish has taken on the boulter or where the float has been dragged, and also because it's more fun to play and land fish on the rod. One mustn't set the lines over deep places, but near them, as well as close to snags, roots, and steep banks, or "on timberworks," as the fishermen say. Burbot, though, sometimes take in the middle of the river, on clean and smooth bottom, and therefore the rigs must be set in various ways. For bait one can use any small fish other than ruff, perch, and pickerel. For burbot, it makes no difference if the bait is alive or dead. I even believe that a dead baitfish is better, for a live one can dive beneath the weeds and wiggle under snags, and the burbot won't see him. Because of their whiteness, I prefer small roach over all other baits, but fishermen reckon that little crucian carp are best, claiming that they're softer and sweeter than other fish, as well as *hardier*. The latter is perfectly true, but, according to my observation, burbot and other predatory fish don't take on them as avidly. One can bait the boulters with pieces of meat, half-peeled crayfish, and small frogs. Where there are many burbot, they'll take on anything. The biggest threat to any bait is live crayfish. Where they're to be found in abundance, they seriously hamper the fishing by eating the bait and dragging the hook into a hole from which you'll be long in extricating it. Crayfish attack their prey more during the day, for which reason boulters must be removed for the day very early in the morning and set out as late in the evening as possible. The hooks required aren't so much large as thick, for where huge burbot are to be found, some fish of twenty pounds can turn up. A thin hook can tear through the stomach of such a fish since he can wrap the *string* or lace (a strong one, of course) around a snag and strain so hard that he sometimes turns his bladder inside out, just as the pike does.

# LURES

Fishing with *lures* resembles regular angling most closely of all. This is real angling, if you please, with the difference that the sportsman's hand, in which he holds the line with the lure, serves as a rod. Nevertheless, I'm puzzled: why not just use a very short rod? With a rod it would also be easy to tug and shake the bait.

Lures are used in the following way. To a normal line is fastened a small, shiny, metal fish to which a hook has been soldered on one side. Sometimes there's a hook on both sides, and sometimes a hook protrudes from the mouth of the man-made fish. The fisherman sits in a boat, and, as he directs his craft downstream, throws out one or two lure-rigs, on which the artificial baitfish appear to be swimming. Greedy perch, and sometimes pike, strike the lures trailing behind the boat with all their might and are caught on the hooks. This kind of fishing is done in the autumn, when the water becomes clear. I've never fished lures, but have seen how others fish them. I've met passionate devotees of this sort of angling, but I've never cared for it myself, perhaps because I'm not keen on fishing from a boat floating over deep places. . . . I have to confess that I love dry land, the shore, and dread using the waterways.[134]

One can nonetheless catch fish with lures, or "lure-fish," as sportsmen say, through ice-holes in the winter, and in the autumn from shore at deep places, right next to the bank. Moreover, one must frequently shake and tug the line to make the artificial baitfish resemble a real one as much as possible. Lure-fishing from shore and in ice-holes is quite inconvenient, and, as regards hibernal angling, fishing loses its attraction for me in the severe cold of winter.

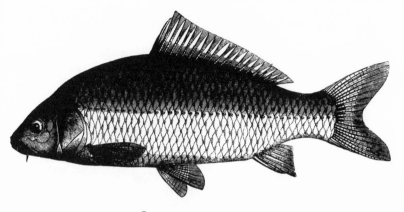

# Appendix 1

## Selected Fishing Prose by Aksakov

# FLOODWATER AND FISHING THE SPRING RUNOFF

One of the favorite amusements of the Russian people is to watch floodwater as it starts to flow.[135] "The river's breaking up" is passed from mouth to mouth, and the whole village, young and old, surges out onto the bank, regardless of the weather. For a long, long time, the motley crowds stand, dressed any which way, watching, admiring, accompanying every movement of the ice with their observations or merry shouts. Even in the cities, as, for example, in Moscow, all the banks and bridges of the shallow Moscow River are strewn with people. They're replaced by others, and all day crowds of spectators, who lean through the bridge railings and embankment grates, can't gaze long enough at their swelling Moscow River, which, during the runoff, really does resemble a decent river. Indeed, the appearance of a river that has broken up is, at that time of year, not only a majestic spectacle, but also a strange and striking one.

For about six months, it's as though the river didn't exist. It was an extension of the snowbanks, and of the roads constructed on their surface. People walked, rode, and galloped on top of the river as they would on dry land, almost forgetting about its existence, when suddenly, a wide bank of this firm, unmoving, snowy expanse stirred, broke away, and was set in motion . . . in motion with everything to be found upon it at the time: frozen-over ice-holes, heaps of dung, landmarks and blackened roads, cattle that had accidentally wandered across it, and sometimes even people! Quietly, solidly, at first accompanied by a muffled but terrible and ominous rumbling and creaking, the huge, snowy, icy, endless snake sets off. Soon it begins to crack and break, and the bulging, blue blocks of ice rear up, as if doing battle with one another, cracking, shattering one another, and still they float on. Then the ice-floes become smaller and less frequent, and finally disappear altogether . . . the river has passed! . . . The turbid water, freed from its half-year captivity and now gradually rising, over-flows the edges of the banks and floods into the meadows. Such is the spectacle presented by large rivers. Small ones, purged of ice down their entire length, "pass" imperceptibly. Only at full flood do they excite the gazes of village dwellers for a time, when these little rivers have been enriched by the water of neighboring ravines and woods, and submerge the land downstream, forming islands and channels where there had been none before. On the other hand, flowing mill-ponds and releases of floodwater through flood-gates resemble artifi-cial waterfalls, and they make up for meagerness of volume with the swiftness, roar, and foam of their falling waters.

The opening of a river, the overflow of water, the release of a pond or dam are all events in country life of which city dwellers have no conception. In the capitals, where ice on the streets is still chopped and carted away in March, and in several degrees of frost the high roads have dried out and clouds of dust are repulsively borne aloft by the north wind, many city people realize that spring has arrived in the country only because morels, which they've not yet contrived to raise in greenhouses, appear at dinnertime in the clubs . . . but that's a separate article and doesn't concern us here.[136]

Fishing along large rivers during the spring runoff is ac-complished in the particular fashion I now intend to discuss. As soon as a river has passed, but before it's overflowed the banks, the *first* fishing with a "pole-net" immediately begins. This is nothing but the familiar landing net with a bunt, that is, a net-bag of fine mesh resembling a stretched-out pointed cap. The net isn't round, but sewn to a triangular wooden frame which is then made fast to a long pole.[137] It's well known that fish move upstream as the floodwater rises. They hold near the banks until the river overflows, and when the water pours into flood-lands, the fish disperse about the flood-pools as well. Thus, pole-netting along the bank continues in spring only until the river overflows its banks, and is then repeated when the water starts to draw back between them. This kind of fishing is repeated any time the river rises to stand level with the bank-tops because of pouring rains. The murkier and muddier the water, the better. Pole-nets can be *single* (a little smaller) or *double* (a little bigger). One strong man can manage a single, while two men are definitely needed for a double.

Swift current hinders the movements of fish and carries them downstream; they therefore prefer to hold to those places along the bank where the water moves more placidly. Pole-netting exploits this tendency. The fisherman, standing on the bank, casts his pole-net (whose bag is immediately inflated by the water) as far as possible, lowers it carefully to the bottom, gently directs it toward the bank and, pressing it firmly to the bank but not snagging it on uneven surfaces, drags it straight up toward himself, pulling up the pole with both hands more quickly as the net-bag draws closer. For this kind of fishing, a great deal of strength, as well as agility, is obviously required. The swift current carries the pole-net downstream, which sometimes makes it necessary to place the end of the pole on one's shoulder for support to make it easier to submerge, for the pole-net must move straight across stream and all three sides of the net-frame must lightly touch the vertical surface of the bank at the same time in order to bag the fish holding against it. If the current somehow turns the pole-net and it strikes the bank sideways or with its edge, then the fish rush from the bank to the other side, frightening and carrying along behind them all the other fish who were holding nearby, even though they never saw the source of the disturbance. If this happens, it's impossible to catch anything. The water's turbidity prevents the fish from seeing the fishing-rig draw near, and the pole-net gathers into its purse, so to speak, any fish holding at the bank in that place. Pickerel, perch, ruff, and roach are usually caught—small ones, for the most part—but sometimes other species are bagged, and fairly big ones. In narrow, steep-banked rivers as well, and in streams teeming with fish, especially in the upper reaches of large ponds, a multitude of fish can also be caught during spring runoff with a pole-net. It's great fun to shake the heavy pole-net, its bag loaded with fish of especially fascinating variety, out onto the snow or thawed-out bank. Here one encounters the blue-finned pike, banded perch, and motley ruff, who is so hideously full of roe that it's just as if her belly and sides were stuffed with sharp pebbles. There are many others, too—golden, silvery, swift and beautiful—dwellers of the underwater kingdom long unseen by the sportsman!

But over there a dark summer cloud has turned blue on the southwest edge of the horizon, and raindrops have begun to sprinkle . . . thunder rumbles . . . and rain has begun to pour down. . . . The time has come to cleanse the soil which is emerging from beneath the snow, entangled by cobwebs, or spiderwebs—time to thaw and drive away the last iced-over snowbanks! The big ravines have broken up, the forest streams have risen, rivulets are running, brooks are purling into the river from all sides. The river is overflowing its banks and submerging the land downstream, while fish, quitting the useless banks, rush into flood-pools. The pole-net is no longer of any use; the time has come to employ other fishing rigs: muzzle-traps (or top-traps), withe-traps,* and tail-traps. The muzzle-trap (called "mouth-trap" or "gullet-trap" in Moscow, and "top-trap" in Tula) is nothing but a rounded, oblong sack, or small barrel, woven from willow twigs, whose shape is similar to that of a pointed cap opened wide. Its rear end is roundish and tied up securely, and to its very tail a stone is fastened, while the front, shaped like a four-sided frame and about two feet or even a yard square,** is wide open. Inside this open end there is a funnel-shaped throat, also woven of willow twigs, which allows fish to enter easily but makes it impossible for them to get out.

For setting muzzle-traps in floodwater, swims are prepared ahead of time at "low water," as they say. It's well known which low-lying places will be flooded by the water, and therefore at narrows, little dells, and shallow gullies, always in the fish's run, stakes are driven in and wattle fencing woven onto them, from seven to fifteen feet or more in width, depending on the location. Water passes over the top and through the barrier, but fish, except for fry, that is, the smallest ones, can't pass through. In the middle of this wattle barrier,

---

*Or "osier-traps," which in the Mozhaisk district are called "knaves."
**Near Moscow, round mouth-traps are woven, but they're no good. They don't lie squarely on the bottom or fit snugly into weirs, and their holes must be plugged with conifer boughs, that is, the branches of a fir.

one or sometimes two gates, or doors, are left (two feet to a yard in width), in which muzzle traps are placed and fastened to poles. Two passages, or openings, are sometimes left so that one muzzle trap can be set with the current, and the other against it. Fish first move upstream and then, reaching the upper extreme of the flood, return downstream and in both instances are caught in the muzzle-traps. But when the water recedes, all the muzzle-traps and other rigs of this kind are set against the falling water, that is, against the current. Swims in flood-pools among bushes, brook mouths, waterless valleys, and, generally, any depression in the ground relative to the surrounding area, are considered best. In such muzzle-traps with barriers, all fish without exception are caught, and not only large ones, but also small ones, because even a tiny roach cannot get through a wattle mouth-trap. Muzzle-traps, or mouth-traps, are also set without wattle fencing, even without stakes, on ropes alone, but this is not the method used in springtime.

The "withe-trap" or "osier-trap" (or "wing-trap," as it is called in the southern provinces), is shaped very much like a long muzzle-trap, but instead of being constructed of osiers on a foundation of wooden hoops, it's covered with fine netting. Moreover, along both sides of the open forward part, it has wings, or walls, of the same mesh, and is sewn at its end to stakes. The rear part or tail of the withe-trap is connected to a stake as well, and, on these three main stakes, which are driven firmly into the ground, the wing-trap is stretched to its full width and length. It's set in places inundated with water, preferably quiet swims that have an even bottom. The name "wing-trap" is very apt, because the mesh side-walls that re-place the wattle around the muzzle-trap have the appearance of unfurled wings. The overall shape of the rig resembles a horse-shoe bent wide open. Wing-traps have the advantage of not requiring staking, wattle-weaving, or that a swim be pre-pared ahead of time. They can be set anywhere and moved from place to place every day, for if no fish are caught in the space of twenty-four hours, then the chosen swim is obviously not in their run. On the other hand, the withe-trap, or wing-trap, can't be set in swims where the water flows deeply and swiftly, because it may be washed away by strong current or breached, if any snags, large boughs, or tree-roots washed in from the bank are floating in the water. Muzzle-traps can be set in a narrow and fairly deep swim (prepared ahead of time) because the fish move along the bottom. Wing-traps, though, are set no deeper than a yard, and sometimes even much shallower, in swims that are gently sloping and wide, where its wings can be unfurled. Both muzzle-traps and wing-traps can be set from a boat, but this is rather awkward. Russians, however, are not afraid of the cold (for which they often pay dearly) and usually set their fish-traps while wading about in the water, sometimes up to their necks. The muzzle-trap is secured on the outside, that is, tied fast, at two places to a pole that runs across the middle of the open end and, being longer than the lower edge of the muzzle by about two feet, is firmly driven into the bottom. The wing-trap is attached to the three main stakes and also to two auxiliary ones, so to speak, which are located in the middle of the wings, each of which is up to five feet or more in length. The two auxiliary stakes, somewhat smaller than the main ones, serve to support the wings for the best possible unfolding and opposition to the current. All five stakes are firmly planted in soft bottom.

Any fish can be caught in wing-traps, as well as in muzzle-traps, and sometimes in such numbers and of such size that the netting tears or the stakes on which the wing-trap is secured may even get pulled out. During the spring runoff, it's very easy to intercept a considerable expanse of water with several withe-traps set at river narrows. Wing-traps are set securely one alongside the other, wing to wing. One must make sure that one wing-trap stands with the current, or flow, of the water, while the other stands against it, obviously with the aim of catching fish in the arranged traps whether they swim upstream or downstream.

The *tail-trap*'s very name suggests that it ought to have a long tail. It's a kind of muzzle-trap, also woven from osiers, but isn't shaped like a little barrel, which is wider at the middle, as the muzzle-trap is. From the front opening itself—which is made round, oval, or square—the tail-trap gets narrower toward the tail and is bound up at the bottom where the osiers, whose ends are not lopped off, terminate. At three or four places, depending on its length, the tail-trap's sides are woven around with transverse bands made of the same flexible osiers in order to bind more sturdily the sticks lying lengthwise and to prevent the fish from moving them apart and escaping. The tail-trap is always longer than the muzzle-trap, and the osiers used for it are thicker. To its tail, as well as to the two ends of the lower side, are attached fairly heavy stones to keep the tail-trap submerged and lying firmly on the bottom, since it's not secured anywhere by anything else. Moreover, it's always set in the water that flows swiftest, or, to put it better, falls swiftest, because only these currents are capable of overwhelming the fish and ramming them into the narrow part, or tail, of this rig. There, because of the trap's tightness, a fish cannot turn and swim back out, and the swiftness of the current prevents him from turning around. I've chanced to see tail-traps so filled with fish that the ones in back (the last ones in) couldn't fit and were half-protruding from the trap. The best place for setting tail-traps is where the water flows down a steep slope. The best time is during the release of millponds, when they are overfilled with spring runoff, especially if the channel along which the heavy flow is rushing tends to slope.

I vividly recall this kind of fishing in my youth.[138] There was such an abundance of fish in the river on which I lived that now it seems incredible, even to me. They'd not yet built a flood-gate with locks, which would have made it possible to raise one lock after the other and thus let out the accumulated water gradually. The flood-gate used to be dammed up tight when the floodwater ran, and in spring, when the pond would fill up like a cup running over and threaten to submerge and break through the dam, they'd dig out the plugged gate. The water would rush out furiously and wash away the previous year's millpond to the very bottom, to the mainstream. The strong slope of the location multiplied the water's swiftness, and there I used to see such catches with tail-traps as I've never seen anywhere since. Along the entire width of the current, at various places, strong stakes would be planted in advance. A tail trap would be attached to each stake, on a fairly long rope, so that it could be dragged to the bank without being unfastened. Sometimes, though, the rope would end in a tight loop and be put around a stake. Fish initially moving upstream would reach the steep drop of the river and be beaten back by the opposing flow, and fish would also run downstream out of the pond (which tended for the most part to happen at night); both would be caught in the tail-traps, which, though not set in an unbroken row, would nonetheless fence off almost the entire current. Such an incredible abundance of fish would tumble in, and so quickly, that the men wouldn't leave after casting their rigs, but would stand on the bank and, from time to time, after half an hour or, at most, an hour, enter the river up to their belts and drag out the tail-traps half-stuffed with various fish, shake them out onto the bank, and once again cast their simple rigs. There was a veritable carnival on the bank—shouts, noise, conversations and running about. A crowd of women, old men, and little boys would drag all sorts of fish home in baskets, sacks, and shirt-tails. There were, of course, quite a few mere spectators who would offer advice and assistance, and they made a good deal more noise than the actual fishermen. All this was accomplished amid the roar of falling water, with the torrents, foam, and spray crashing about the sturdy bottom and the stakes with tail-traps attached. Many very large fish were caught: chub, ide, perch, tench (at seven pounds), and particularly large pike. I myself saw a peasant with the help of his companion haul out a tail-trap from which a pike's tail protruded: the fish weighed forty-one pounds. I can't understand how such a huge, strong fish failed to throw himself back out. One must assume that the speed of the water drove his head into the narrow end of the tail-trap, where it got stuck between the connected osiers, and he was beaten to death by the water. Furthermore, the fish crammed in around the sides of the pike prevented him from turning around. Tail-traps left overnight, that is, for about six hours, would only be stuffed with fish up to seven inches from the brim, and at the top there would usually be small roach; the large fish were probably jumping out.

Just when the floodwater overflows, pike cast their roe and expel their milt. During the course of this operation they move on top of one another, sometimes several at a time. Having noted the swims where they hang about—always in weeds or bushes along flood-pools—the sportsman enters the water quietly and stands still, facing the fish's run, with a spear at the ready. When the pike swim up close to him, he strikes them with his neptunian trident, which has, however, not three, but five or more barbed prongs, or spikes. At this same time, pike are shot with guns loaded with large shot, because a pike swims shallow and not only his dorsal fin, but also part of his back is visible on the surface. Such enormous pike are sometimes bagged, with both spear and gun, that the catches of fishermen using ordinary fishing rigs rarely match them in size, and, when they do, their rigs don't bear up.

# SPEAR-FISHING

Spear-fishing[139] can afford a great deal of pleasure, especially because it's done in late autumn, when the fish have already ceased to bite, which means that the first and best kind of sportfishing no longer exists, and catching fish at this time of year by other means is bothersome. Another advantage of this sport is that large fish can be speared, namely: pike, sheatfish, asp, zander, and so forth, which sometimes reach such great size that the usual fishing rigs—here I have in mind drag-nets, small seines, nets and withe-traps—won't hold them. It must be added that this sport takes place at night, leaving the entire short autumn day free for the sportsman, and he can engage in all the other kinds of hunting available in late autumn. Spear-fishing possesses much that is poetic, and though the men who undertake it might seem incapable of accepting poetic impressions, they nonetheless perceive and understand them unconsciously, while saying only, "It's good fun to go spear-fishing!"

Spear-fishing demands three conditions: a dark night, clear water, and absolutely calm weather. Autumn satisfies the first two conditions; that is, the nights get long and dark, while the water becomes perfectly clear because of the frost. The third condition—calm weather—has to be waited for. Spear-fishing is not done in a large boat, but neither in a small one. The vessel must be light, fast, and fairly deep, but not wobbly or prone to tipping. To its stern, on a sturdy iron shaft, is attached a four-sided grate, around two feet square, on which there must constantly burn a bright but calm fire, and one must therefore have in the boat a decent supply of dry, finely split birchwood. The grate, held aloft by the upward-curved shaft, must be higher than the stern so that it illuminates the water well to the bottom.

Spear-fishing must be undertaken in calm or still waters—ponds, lakes, and the large backwaters, or coves, of rivers that are of decent size but not swift-flowing. On a dark autumn night (the darker the better), but a calm and rainless one, two sportsmen board the boat—one astern with an oar, and the other with the spear almost amidships, a bit closer to the bow. Two extra spears are put into the boat, one of ordinary size or somewhat bigger, while the other is very large, for the biggest fish, with a long, thin but strong length of string attached to an iron ring at the spear's butt end. As probably everyone knows, the spear is shaped like a dinner fork, but with short prongs that can number from five to seven. Each prong or point is no shorter than seven inches and ends in a barb exactly like the kind made at the end of a fishhook, which ensures that a fish impaled by the spear cannot tear itself away. The iron spearhead is fastened very securely to a wooden pole that is strong, smooth, dry, light, and seven to ten feet long, but never longer, because one has to strike the fish in no more than seven feet of water, and more often in four feet or less. The fire can't clearly illuminate water to a depth of seven feet; moreover, the deeper the water the more cumbersome and difficult it becomes to use a spear, as both eye and hand begin to falter. Spearing a fish, it would seem, is no cunning affair, but not everyone is capable of it. Besides a steady eye and a strong, steady hand, one must have a great deal of shrewdness and dexterity. Even a man who has all these qualities and has received detailed instructions from an experienced spearman will err at first. Without hitting the proper spot, he'll strike near the tail, or at the end of the fish's head, or he'll miss completely. The most important thing is reckoning the distance to the point beyond which a calm, slow lowering of the spear should turn into a swift thrust. This distance ranges from about ten to fourteen inches away from the fish. The spear isn't lowered into the water directly above the fish, not vertically, because in that position the spear's pole and man's hand would obscure the fish, and taking good aim would be impossible. Thus, the spear is at first lowered to one side of the fish and, when it gets close enough to permit a strike, carefully moved over toward the target and directed against the fish's back. The very best thrust is considered that which hits the fish's back no farther than about three fingers from the head. Such a blow prevents a large fish from thrashing forcefully and flopping about on the spear, which will happen without fail if the spear strikes near the tail or the end of the snout. In both of these instances a large fish can easily break free and, regardless of the cruel wounds from which he'll later die, he can swim away and deprive the sportsman of a splendid catch. Even a blow to his very forehead, which happens quite seldom, allows him to wriggle about and get off the spear if it doesn't kill the fish outright.

The oarsman must also be a master of his craft because steering a boat while pursuing fish with a spear is altogether different from guiding a boat the usual way. Even a different oar is required, one that's a little wider, similar to a wooden spade, but at the same time as light and handy as possible. The boat must move forward stably, quietly, and without the least agitation of the water's surface. The oar is never raised out of the water, and all turns and maneuvers are executed underwater, similar to the way in which geese, swans, and waterfowl accomplish them with their oar-like feet. In order to give a clearer and fuller idea of this sport, I'll describe, with all the particulars, one of my most amazing and fruitful forays with a spear, in which, because of my tender years, I was only a spectator, not an active participant.

The autumn nights were growing long and dark. Frosts penetrated and chilled the water, precipitating aquatic vegetation to the bottom: duckweed, mold, and all the scum that floats on the surface. The water had settled and become clear in the flood-pools and coves of our wide pond. For some time the sportsmen had been saying, "Time to go spear-fishing." They'd been planning to meet, and, finally, they did meet— and they took me along with them. The weather was most favorable; that is, it was dark, somewhat frosty, and absolutely calm. A fire was started on the grate, and everything we needed was put into the boat. We took our seats, pushed off from shore, and floated about the flood-pools. The fire brightly lit but a small, roundish expanse around the grate, and even the bow of the boat was weakly illuminated. Our ring of light was soon swallowed up by the encircling murk, and still darker and blacker seemed the night that closed in from all sides. It was as if a limitless expanse of water surrounded us. In the dense gloom, no reeds, no dam, no banks were visible—the boat sailed alone in its bright circle. I sat with my back to the fire. The face and whole form of the spear-fisherman—a young, strong man who sat facing me—were vividly illuminated. But when I would look at the old fisherman with the oar, lit and warmed from behind, he seemed a black shape, a faceless image silhouetted in the fiery circle. Whenever the boat turned or the oarsman moved, light would pour over him, sometimes from the left, sometimes from the right, and seem to peep in at his face. The bankside view of a boat moving across the water by firelight was also very impressive. How the enchanted, brightly half-lit boat moved noiselessly, and, it seemed, motionlessly, as if commanded by the flame, with no help from the phantoms seated within!

Soon we began to encounter small fish holding, or, to put it better, lying on the bottom, along small holes and hollows. The sportsmen paid them no heed, and I alone was taken with inspecting the muddy pond-bottom lit up by the fire. Suddenly, a shroud appeared from some other, unknown world, with its diverse soils, uneven surfaces, plants, and sleeping inhabitants! . . . I'd been ordered in advance to sit quietly and not to speak loudly, so I only pointed out with a whisper or my finger the fish that we passed and that seemed to me to be fairly large and deserving of a spear-thrust. But I was mistaken, for fish in the water, especially at night, when lit by firelight, seem much bigger than they actually are. The young fisherman who was holding the spear in his hands as it lay across the gunwales wasn't listening to me. He replied to my gestures and words only by shaking his head, or with a curt whisper: "This is all rubbish—now sit quietly!"

At last we were floating along the channel. Such was the name given to the long, meandering stretch that cut diagonally across almost the entire pond without ever getting overgrown with weeds. This was probably the river's mainstream at one time—the "old bed," as they call it when it's not flooded with water. Perhaps this had been a little ravine through which a brook once ran. The depth of the channel sometimes reached seven feet, but for the most part it ranged from three to five feet in depth, and was nonetheless twice as deep as the flood-pools surrounding it. The channel had its own underwater banks, which were set about in the summertime with dense aquatic weeds that would spread out along the water's surface. Beaten back from above by frosts, they had receded and now lay in beds along the bottom, bending to one side. It was in this channel that we started to encounter large fish.

"Hold!" whispered the chief fisherman. The boat came to a stop, and his spear slid into the water, at first moving slowly, then swiftly plunging in. After several seconds a huge ide of at least six pounds was carefully pulled out, stuck in the teeth of the spear. The second catch was made: a perch bigger than any caught in our pond before or since. Unfortunately, they weren't weighing their fish in those days, so I can't positively say how much this perch weighed, but he was certainly more than five pounds. After that they started to catch medium ide and perch, of which they bagged about fifteen. Several very large roach were also landed. From time to time we sailed into pike from three to seven or ten pounds (approximately), of which about five were killed, not counting the little ones; pike were shown no mercy, and the fisherman struck any pickerel his spear's prongs could reach. Such malice was directed at pike because they'd reproduced too much and were doubtless eating large numbers of little fish. We began to hit pike more frequently around the coves, near bulrushes, and, preferably, in little lakes set about by rushes, as well as in sloping hollows that terminated at the river's mainstream. One mustn't assume that the fisherman was able to kill every fish we encountered. On the contrary, several were so quick that they swam off as soon as the boat drew near, while others would usually flee when the spear was directed toward them. One must also note that when landing a decent fish it was impossible to manage without a certain amount of noise and disturbance of the water, which caused many fish that held and slept nearby to swim away.

Finally, we floated out onto the mainstream and, ascending fairly far upstream, turned by way of a narrow but deep cove into the bulrushes once again. We had just started to enter a round, wide lake, when the fisherman sighted a pike of enormous size holding between two flooded hummocks not far from a dense reed-bed. My heart stopped beating when he laid down his spear and picked up the very biggest one from the bottom of the boat. I understood what this meant. With whispers and signals he showed his companion the place toward which the boat should be directed. We quietly floated to the sleeping fish, who looked to me like a long, fat, wooden block or the tip of a log that was lying on the bottom. With redoubled caution, the fisherman moved his trident—or, more accurately, septident—into position. For a long time he pointed it and took aim. Finally, he struck with all his might, nimbly jumped to his feet, pressed down with might and main on the spear, and then pushed it away from himself. . . . The water veritably boiled beneath us, and the boat began rocking from the shove and agitation, and I became very frightened even though the depth there was no more than five feet and though I feared water less at that time than later.[140] Having turned and vigorously disturbed the water, the pike at first rushed like a shot, but then moved more quietly. The spear's shaft protruded from the water at an angle, and its own weight and the strong twine attached to its upper end turned him onto his side. The pike moved straight from the lake into the river's mainstream. Holding the end of the twine, the young fisherman said in a loud and merry voice, "You're mine, duck-eater! I've been after you for a long time now!" But the other fisherman responded, almost angrily, "Save the celebration for later—and hang onto that string." And so it was that the string started to go taut. The fisherman wound it around his hand, and we sailed after the pike, carried along by him. When he first went down into the mainstream, the pike submerged the entire shaft, which was more than nine feet long, more than once, but then began to tire. He rushed about, swam to the top, and tried to throw himself into the bulrushes in order to tear the spear loose, but it was no use. The fish was growing visibly exhausted. After some time, at least half an hour, the fisherman pulled the shaft's upper end toward himself with the string, took it in both hands, stood up and again pressed his fish. But the pike no longer rushed so quickly as the first time, and made a small lunge forward of about twenty feet, writhed, stopped, and went absolutely quiet.

Having dragged the pike some thirty-five feet on the string, the fishermen decided to lift him up and put him in the boat. We entered the channel (now familiar to the reader), whose mouth was a dozen or so feet away from us. With no small effort, both fishermen joined forces to drag out the enormous fish and heaved him into the boat without removing the spear. He was still alive and his mouth was wide open, but he didn't stir. They put the spear-shaft on my shoulder, and I held onto it with both hands to keep it from falling into the water and hampering our progress. The young fisherman took up an oar as well, sat down on the bow, and we flew like a shot to the mill's wicket. There we summoned the miller and, with his help and his mate's, disembarked on the dam.

In the meantime, grain-haulers came running from the mill-barn, spied the glorious catch by torchlight, and loud exclamations of pleasure and astonishment rang out. Among the haulers there happened to be one very short man, and jokes immediately came raining down on him.

"Well, Grishka," one very tall fellow was saying, "It's a good thing this pike never got a look at you. Back when you were swimming here in the summertime, he'd've swallowed you up just like a duckling. You'd've vanished, disappeared without a trace!"

"No, no, the fish would've choked on him," objected another. "Grishka's feet would've stuck out! And why're you giving him such a hard time—he's stronger than a duckling, though only just ..."

And noisy laughter drowned for a time the roar of falling water and mill-wheels. Meanwhile, the spear was pulled out of the pike and we triumphantly carried the whole fish home. Next day the miller told me that it was a long time before the grain-haulers went to sleep, for they wondered, laughed, and talked about the extraordinary pike, which, lit by a burning torch, simply seemed to them to be some kind of monster.

As for me, from the very first minute the fight with the pike began, I was in some sort of half-conscious state, combined (I must admit) with a certain amount of fear. Only at home, when the pike was brought indoors, put on a bast mat and surrounded with candles so that it could be examined, did I fully come to and abandon myself to the noisy joy of a young fisherman. Those truly responsible for the triumph were taciturn, though they did drink up a goodly glass of wine. I, however, long and loudly related for them all the smallest details of the just-concluded event, repeating their words and making them corroborate my own. How poorly I slept that night! The impressions were so vivid and contradictory that they excited my blood with great force. The pike, with all the circumstances of his killing, appeared ceaselessly in my dreams, for such an adventure was indeed something to be excited about! If this had happened to me in adulthood, when the passion for fishing was fully developed in me, if this had happened to me now—I think the impression would have been even stronger. Because of my youth, I couldn't then adequately appreciate the importance of such a noteworthy event in the history of fishing, especially if one takes into account that a pike reaching such size over many decades, or perhaps even centuries,[141] is extraordinarily seldom found in such insignificant waters as our pond and river, and still more seldom falls prey to fishermen. This was the only time it happened at our place, and the feat has to this day never been repeated. One has only to imagine the first runs and fits of that terrible fish! Until he went out into the mainstream, where he could dive deep, he was producing such turbulence in the water that, had we not been a few dozen feet away, the boat could have capsized. Sportsmen know from experience that at night, even if you're standing on the bank, you involuntarily shudder when an ordinary large fish turns or splashes nearby, a fish that can't even be compared with the pike I've described. But in a small boat, loaded down fairly heavily, over a decent depth, on a seemingly limitless expanse of water, in impenetrable darkness aside from our small circle of light, while we awaited the desperate rushes of an aquatic monster who was pulling and turning our boat in all directions . . . I confess, my heart skips a beat from the recollection alone, and in old age one ought to be able to keep from being carried away once again by such a poetically piscatorial scene! . . .

I examined the pike carefully the next day. He measured over forty-one inches without the tailfin and was very fat. Everyone was astonished by the width of his forehead, on which there appeared some kind of silvery mottling that seemed protuberant and gray. Fishermen said that he was very old and that his forehead had "grown moss." When his jaws were pried open, it was truly frightening to look at his sharp, double teeth, large ones and small ones. His throat was so wide that he could have swallowed a mature duck without any difficulty. His presence in our pond had been noted for many years, and, of course, many ducklings, both wild and domesticated, had been swallowed by him in the course of his life. Unfortunately, this rare pike was not put on the scale, so I can't speak conclusively about his weight, but, if we judge from a comparison with the 49½-pound pike that I saw several years afterward,* the speared pike must have weighed close to 72 pounds.

Afterward I chanced more than once to go spear-fishing and strike fish myself, but we caught no remarkable prey, and I must confess that I never mastered the technique. Only once did that same sportsman bring in from Lower Sokolov Pond (also on the Buguruslan, some five miles downstream) a huge burbot he'd also killed with a spear, in the mainstream beneath some snags. The fish was holding so deep that he was barely able to reach him with the largest spear. He weighed close to thirty pounds, and his livers were too big to be served on an ordinary plate. This happened in the very latest autumn, when the small flood-pools were already covered with ice.

Pike and other large fish are speared when they cast, or *thrash*, their roe, as fishermen put it.[142] When in this special condition, the fish move in schools and often come up so shallow that their upper fins are visible on the water's surface. A fisherman standing motionless in the rushes, in water up to his knees or even his belt, or concealing himself on the bank behind some kind of bush, lies in wait for his quarry and plunges the spear into any fish that swim near. In deep holes, below flood-gates, a large fish likes to move against the falling water, sometimes swimming up fairly shallow and holding stubbornly in a fixed position, having buried his head in brushwood or any of the timber that usually covers the bottom by the millrace or below its floor or platform. The fisherman (usually a miller because such fishing is convenient for him), after lying in wait for or simply having noticed a shallow-holding fish, sneaks up with a spear and sometimes pulls out glorious ide, chub, perch, or asp. This sort of incidental bagging can be very pleasant, but can't be called real *spear-fishing*.

*I mentioned this in my *Notes on Fishing*, p. 125. That pike was caught in a tail-trap during the spring flood.

# FROM "A FEW WORDS ON SPORTSMEN'S SUPERSTITIONS AND SIGNS"

Everyone knows that all sportsmen who come from the simple folk, without exception, are superstitious—much more superstitious than other people.[143] The explanation and reason for this, it seems to me, are not hard to find. The constant, usually solitary, presence of sportsmen when various natural phenomena occur must certainly dispose the sportsman's soul toward a belief in the miraculous and supernatural; such phenomena are mysterious and often inexplicable even for educated people and scientists. People dislike being left in uncertainty. Upon seeing or hearing something not readily explicable, they create fantastic explanations for themselves and pass them on to others with considerable certitude. Those others, in taking these explanations on heartfelt faith, add their own observations and conclusions, and so a multitude of myths arises. These are sometimes very witty, graceful, and poetic, and sometimes ridiculous and ugly, but they're always original. I'm certain that hunters were the first to begin creating the world of myth that exists among all peoples. The first rumor of a wood-spirit was probably started by the forest hunter; water-maidens, or she-devils,*[144] were marked by the fisherman; and werewolves were discovered by the trapper. . . .

In the late twilight, early dawn, and especially at night, water—mainly large bodies of it—produces the same effect on people that a dense forest does. A sudden commotion and splash in the water, when the fish or beast that made them can't be properly descried through the darkness, could scare any fisherman sitting on the bank with his rod and line, or in a boat with his net. In bulrushes or sedge, the noise and movement produced by a duck with her ducklings, or even by

---

*In Orenburg Province, just as in Kazan' and Simbirsk Provinces, the simple folk don't know the word *mermaid.*

jumping frogs, could seem, to the fevered mind, to be something like the movement of a creature of far greater bulk. An otter who has jumped out of the water onto the bank, or from the bank into the water, glimpsed fleetingly as a dark, indistinct phantom, could be reflected in the sportsman's imagination as something resembling human form. "Fear has big eyes," as the proverb says. Why couldn't the sheatfish's round, blunt snout—which has thrust itself onto the water's surface and then been quickly submerged—be taken for a human head that's floated up for a single moment? Why couldn't the pointed nose and head of a pike or asp seem to be an elbow or some other human limb? Just as the forest hunter would tell of his nocturnal frights and visions in the forest, so too the fisherman would tell his family of what he'd seen on the water. He would have met with the same faith in his stories and the same inflamed imagination would conjure up mysterious inhabitants of the water, calling them mermaids, water-maidens, or she-devils, supplementing and embellishing their images and assigning them a legitimate place in the world of folk mythology. But as the water-dwellers themselves—the fish, that is—are mute, so too the lovely water-maidens have no voice.* Isn't it possible to explain in this way the origin of other folk beliefs as well? Investigation of this interesting subject, however, doesn't concern me. I mention it only to explain why sportsmen are more superstitious than other people. . . .

The belief that certain persons—mainly old women and old men—possess the evil eye, and the belief in their ability to "cast the evil eye," or to "curse," are deeply rooted in sportsmen. They believe in this power absolutely, and not only are they themselves afraid of encounters with such people, especially when setting out on the hunt, but they also protect their dogs and hawks from them and even hide their guns and all sorts of trapping and fishing equipment from view.

Independent of the belief in sorcery, sportsmen have many signs that can be general and, sometimes, exclusive—belonging personally to one particular sportsman. The following are considered bad signs of the general kind:

*At least this is what the people of Orenburg Province claim.

1. An encounter with malevolent people, for the most part those who supposedly possess the *evil eye;* with derisive people (mischief-makers); and with women in general, especially old ones. Regardless of the kind of sport, the sportsman, when departing, carefully looks ahead. If he catches sight of what might be an evil encounter, he turns off the road and takes a roundabout way, or waits it out, having concealed himself somewhere outside so that the old crone who is afoot, or the evil or untrustworthy man, won't see him. If any kind of woman who goes unnoticed by the sportsman suddenly cuts across his path, he abandons hope of a successful day, often returning home and, after some time, setting out in an altogether different direction, on a different road. Women know about this sportsman's sign, and therefore when the decorous among them catch sight of a sportsman walking, under no circumstances will they cross his path, but will wait until he walks or rides by. It's noteworthy that this sign does not apply to maidens.

2. An encounter with empty carts or wood-sledges also portends unsuccessful sport, while, on the contrary, a wagon that's filled—with bread, hay, straw, or whatever it may be—is considered a good omen.

3. The cry of a raven, eagle owl, or owl, if a sportsman hears them while in the field, presages failure.

4. If someone says "Bring back a wing" to a hunter who's going shooting, or "Bring back some fur or a tail" to a trapper, or "Bring back a fish-scale" to a fisherman, then the sportsman reckons that the day will be unsuccessful. Sportsmen are often deliberately teased with the aforementioned words as a joke. They may get very angry, and it often ends badly for the jokers.

   There's a fairly trustworthy means of counteracting ill encounters and omens: the sportsman takes a bath, the dog is bathed, or the hawk is sprinkled with water.

5. There's also a sign among certain anglers: water must not be poured into a bucket intended for keeping one's catch until the first fish is caught. This sign, however, is far from universal. . . .

# FROM "STRANGE SPORTING
# OCCURRENCES"

. . . I've already discussed in my *Notes on Fishing* the extraordinary greed of pike and told of several true occurrences
confirming my opinion. Here are two more incidents of the
same kind.[145]

The first of these is so unbelievable and like a fabrication
that it's impossible to keep from smiling when hearing it
described. I wouldn't even have decided to relate it in print if
the incident had not had a witness, I. S. Turgenev—a sportsman with no interest in fishing—who at that time was with
me in the country. At the end of May in 1854, some ordinary
fishing outfits with strong lines and hooks, baited with small
fish or earthworms, were set out overnight, because the perch
were taking very little during the day, while at night fairly
large ones were being caught. On one of these outfits, baited
with a worm, a small perch took and swallowed the hook
down to his bladder. The perch was then taken and swallowed
in the same way by a small pike, or pickerel. The pickerel in
turn was seized across his middle by a large pike, over five
pounds, who has sunk his teeth so far into the prey that the
fisherman dragged him out of the water without the slightest
caution, never suspecting that the hook hadn't penetrated the
large pike's gills. But when he caught sight of this remarkable
trick, the fisherman hurried to bring us the pike. The fish,
dangling in the air, did not unclamp his teeth during the
journey (the distance was a third of a mile), and Turgenev and
I pried open the fish's mouth ourselves and conducted an
investigation into the perch and pickerel, who, having taken
the perch like a bait, had in turn become a bait himself. The
leader was an ordinary one, of silk, that is, and the pickerel
could easily have chewed through it, but one must assume that
the perch, who was a little big for him, had so distended the
pickerel's jaws or throat that he couldn't close his mouth, and
that in precisely this position was bitten around the middle by

the large pike, because of which the pickerel's mouth gaped still wider. When this triple catch was brought to us, the pickerel seemed long moribund and even stunned. The large pike was perfectly healthy and not even scratched.

After this adventure it's barely worth mentioning that in the same year a pike took a gudgeon who'd been placed, together with other small fish, in a keep-net,*[146] which was about nine paces from me. The fish vigorously seized hold of the net with his teeth and made such a splash that the boy who was fishing with me, when he heard it, approached the keep-net and dragged it and the pike onto the bank when he saw the fish's escapade. Again we were forced to pry open his mouth with a stick to make him let go of the net. The pike weighed nearly three pounds, and the net turned out to be bitten through.

That the mesh of a keep-net had been chewed through by a pike explained an incident that befell me about two years ago which I hardly understood at the time and which I now relate in passing for sportfishermen as a caution against similar misfortunes. I don't well and truly remember the month, but it was probably at the beginning of August, because the weather was still hot. I'd gone to fish in the upper reaches of Repekhovo Pond on the River Voria.[147] My devoted fishing companion rose earlier than I and had already been long on the river. When I arrived, he showed me five glorious perch and a just-caught pickerel swimming in his keep-net. Half an hour later it was necessary to put in a perch I had caught. But what were our surprise and vexation when, having pulled up the keep-net, we saw that there remained within it only one dead perch—a small one, as if on purpose—while the four big perch and the pickerel were no longer in the net. Upon examining it closely, we found the hole through which all the live fish had escaped. The keep-net was new, and we didn't know how to explain what had happened. We thought that either some rotten threads had turned up or that the pickerel had chewed through the mesh. They were biting unusually well, however, and large perch were taking, so we made up for our loss. Nonetheless, my companion was very sorry about his big

*A mesh bag of special construction that I discussed in my *Notes on Fishing.*

perch. Now, however, after the attack on a keep-net by a pike that I described above, it makes sense that it was not the pickerel that chewed his way out through the mesh, but probably a big pike who had seized one of the perch from the outside, ripped through a few knots, and, without snagging his teeth on them, departed, frightened by the noisy and violent splashing of the remaining fish, which we'd heard but which didn't prompt us to check the keep-net. The perch and pickerel then exploited the tear to return once more to the Voria. The moral of this story is that it's best not to put pike in a keep-net (though I used to do this often without any dire consequences), and that if a keep-net containing caught fish is put into the water, it must be carefully examined every time a fish splashes hard.

# FROM "NEW NOTES ON SPORT"

In the spring of 1855, after the appearance of this little book's first edition, I chanced to see something with my own eyes about which I'd never even heard before, and which commercial fishermen, because of their profession, should certainly know.[148] I learned that pike change their teeth annually, in May.[149] It was a sportsman who occupied himself solely with pike-fishing on trimmers who told me this news. He showed me several pike he'd caught whose old teeth, weakened at the roots, had lost all their stiffness and become soft. They drooped and lay there like hairs when I gently rubbed the inside of the pike's mouth while wearing an ordinary glove. From beneath the old teeth, which hadn't yet fallen out, new ones—thin and sharp, but still soft—were emerging. At this time, when pike bite a fish, they often merely damage it, and, because of the weakness of their teeth, are unable to hold their prey. This is precisely the reason that fishermen in that season often chance to see fish that have been bitten by pike. It stands to reason that this is the case with fish that are somewhat bigger, since pike can swallow the small ones without the aid of teeth at all. Baitfish on trimmers at this time of year are often rumpled up, but not even bitten through to the point of bleeding.

---

Though I knew that cats ate fish, I'd nonetheless never heard or seen how they went about this sport. On 3 May 1855, I was sitting very quietly on the bank of a small flowing pond where perch and tench were feeding. Near the opposite bank, which was already set about with weeds, roach were thrashing their roe and to this end were throwing themselves into the weeds at the very bank. Suddenly I saw a large tabby cat cautiously sneaking up, crawling and hiding, having stretched herself out in the grass hard by the bankside. This is always the way cats approach as they wait out their prey. I started watching intently. The roach continued to cast their spawn and toss themselves into the weeds, when the cat pounced, seized one little roach and carried the fish away in her mouth. I pointed out this trick to the gardener who was digging in his beds not far from me. He wasn't in the least surprised; on the contrary, he told me that early in the morning, when there aren't yet any people about, some six or more cats go out to hunt, take up position at suitable swims, and catch fish.

———————

Not long ago, I learned from a certain reliable person that in Kaluga Province, on the River Oka, the following kind of angling is undertaken with great success. In June, a great multitude of white butterflies (I've forgotten their name) appears for only a week along the banks of the Oka. The fishermen build small, smooth "clearings" on the sand and light small straw-fires on them. The butterflies rush into the fire, are scorched, and fall. They're then swept together into piles and gathered up by the peck. The burnt butterflies are forcefully mashed together with bread or dough, and then hooks are baited with little balls of this mixture. Fish take on this bait with unusual eagerness, and big ones, at that: ide, chub, bream, and even perch and zander. Thus, for the shortest time, a glorious and productive form of angling emerges. One must note that perch and zander never take on bread, which means the sole enticement is contained in the butterflies. . . .[150]

# A FEW WORDS ON ANGLING IN
# EARLY SPRING AND LATE AUTUMN

In the old days, that is, the days of my youth and early adult-hood, I knew nothing of early-spring and late-autumn angling.[151] By "late" I mean not only September, but the whole of October and beginning of November—in a word, the entire season that lasts until the ponds and rivers are covered with thick ice. Being a passionate hunter, by the end of August—at the very peak of perch season—I'd usually laid aside my fishing rod until the next spring. Only in my country house near Moscow, on the banks of the little River Voria (which, because it's dammed, seems at first glance to be a river of decent size), only on those picturesque banks did I become familiar with and fully appreciate both early-spring and late-autumn angling. I value them highly, for this is the sole sport to which I can devote myself here, thanks to the insufficiency of game near Moscow, but chiefly because illness and weak vision long ago forced me to give up shooting, which is, of course, incomparable sport.

Not long ago I stayed at my country house for five years running, and it was then that angling attained its full development for me. When I lived in Orenburg Province, I didn't fish in spring during the arrival of wildfowl or in autumn during their departure. But here, at the house outside Moscow, things are altogether different.

I thus wish to inform sportfishermen of my experiences and observations while angling early and late in the season.

In the spring, as soon as the river had begun to flow between its banks once more, I began to give it a try, despite the current's swiftness and water's turbidity, and without the slightest hope of success. An outfit with the ordinary sinker was impossible to cast at that time of year, since it would be carried away by the swiftness of the current and the baited hook would rise too high. I therefore used a sinker perhaps ten times heavier than usual and attached it about twenty inches above the hook. The float rose so high that half the line would lie on the bottom (I of course knew the depth of the spring floodwater quite well). Having thus assembled my outfit, chosen a swim where the water was spinning near the bank, and baited a large or small worm (depending on the size of the hook and thickness of the line), I would cast across stream and plant the rod in the bank, having inclined the rod-tip almost to the water's surface. The bait didn't come to rest immediately on the bottom, despite the heaviness of the sinker. The fast current carried it off and washed it toward shore. The line stretched out diagonally, but the sinker probably touched bottom at times, while the baited hook ceaselessly rushed about, which could be dependably discerned from the various movements and plunges of the float. Knowing that at this season fish hold close to the bank and swim deep (regardless of whether they're moving upstream or down), and hoping that the water's cloudiness wouldn't keep the fish from making out my worm at a short distance, I patiently awaited the results of my endeavor.

I sat for three hours in various swims, and only once did the float's movement seem suspicious, like a fish's bite, and when I lifted the rod, the worm seemed to have been somewhat dragged about. Both the one and the other could have occurred because of the water's swift movement and the bait's getting snagged on the bank or bottom. Next day, I repeated the experiment, increasing the sinker's weight and, to my great joy, very soon caught a small chub and then several perch. From that day on I angled with constant success, even though the water continued to be turbid and too fast. In this fashion I gained two or three extra weeks of fishing. As the river's current became calmer, I removed weight from the sinker bit by bit. For four years in a row I fished earlier in the spring than I ever had before. The best bait turned out to be red dungworm (or gutworm). On a big worm the fish would take uncertainly, probably because it was awkward to swallow a large piece on the run while it moved constantly. The fish wouldn't take on bread until the water became clearer. I must also note that at this time of year the fish weren't biting in particular "swims"—that is, not in deep whirlpools—but everywhere, and preferably in shallow places with a sandy bottom. All species of fish would bite except for tench and pike. Why the tench wouldn't take, I don't know, but the pike probably refused because in this season they're casting their spawn and swimming shallow. In rainy years, especially last year (1857), when the river rose level with the bank-tops three times over the course of the summer due to a sudden abundance of falling rain, and even overflowed the banks and was therefore swift and turbid—in short, during "spates"—I'd reconfigure my fishing outfits in the springtime fashion I've just described and continue to fish, at times with great success. Large ruff and ide, which at the middle and end of summer take very rarely, would bite especially frequently.

I've caught fish with rod and line many times in rivers that rushed along level with the bank-tops at terrible speed and resembled expanses of liquid clay. Without having tried it myself, I'd never have believed someone who told me that it was possible to catch any fish at such a time.

I turn now to fishing in autumn. I love even the latest autumn, but not that part of it everyone else likes. I love not the frosty, fine days that are windy almost from dawn to dusk, but the days that are warm, gray, calm, and perhaps rainy. The harshness of dry, irritating air disgusts me, while gentle moisture in the atmosphere, even dampness, I find most pleasant. And you can always defend yourself against the rain (as long as it's not torrential) with waterproof clothing, an umbrella, or the boughs of a bush or tree. It's at this time of year that I love to fish, and I do so with even greater zeal and delight than in the spring. Spring promises much ahead, and signals the beginning of warm weather, the commencement of fishing. In the autumn, fishing is coming to an end, and each day you are parting with it—for a long time, for a whole six months. For sportsmen who love autumn I wish to say a few words about it, for I know many of them who feel the same way.

O autumn, late autumn! The gray sky, and low, heavy, moist clouds; naked and transparent grow the gardens, groves, and woods. One can see right through the densest thicket that no human eye could penetrate all summer. The old trees have shed their foliage and only a few young birches still keep their withered, yellowish leaves, which shine gold when touched by the slanting rays of the low-lying autumnal sun. The evergreen firs and pines, as though grown younger, freshened by the cold air and rains as fine as steam, and by the moist nocturnal mists, stand out vividly through the reddish netting of birch-boughs. The ground is paved with dry leaves of various kinds and colors, so soft and downy in damp weather that no rustling is produced by the feet of a carefully stepping hunter, and so hard and brittle in the frost that far-off birds and beasts leap away at the stirring of human footfalls. If the air is still, the cautious leaps of hare, squirrel, and all small forest game are audible at great distance and easily distinguished by the trapper's keen and practiced ear.

The overwintering tits of all kinds—except the roadside tit, who has concealed herself long before—have moved toward human habitation, especially the Moscow tit, called "Novgorod tit" in Petersburg, and "sprite" in Orenburg Province.[152] Her ringing, piercing call is often heard in the house through closed windows. Bullfinches too have emerged from the forest thicket and appeared in gardens and kitchen-gardens, and their creaking song, not wholly bereft of pleasant melody, quietly echoes among the naked bushes and trees.

The as yet undeparted thrushes, chucking and squealing, have gathered in large flocks and are flying into gardens and river-woods, lured there by the berries of elder, honeysuckle, and especially the red bunches of rowan- and guelder-rose berries. The fruit of the bird-cherry—their favorite berries— have long since dried up and dropped off, but they've not run their course in vain, for they'll all be picked up from the ground by eager guests.

There goes a flock of blackbirds heading straight to the park. Some arrange themselves in the trees, while others descend to the ground and hop about on all sides. At first they'll be silent for two hours or so, as they surreptitiously satisfy their hunger, but then, having eaten their fill and stuffed their craws, they'll gather into a group, alight in several trees, and start to sing, because these are singing thrushes. They don't all sing well, probably just the old ones. The others only squeal, but the chorus as a whole is very pleasant. Their singing astounds and delights someone hearing it for the first time because the voices of other birds have long since gone silent, and this late in autumn you don't hear the earlier diversity of song, but only the cries of birds, for the most part wood-peckers, bullfinches, and sprites.

The river has taken on a particular appearance, as though it's changed, straightened its bends, and become much wider, because the water is visible now through the naked twigs of stooping black-poplar boughs and the leafless switches of river bushes, but still more because the cold has killed the aquatic blooms and because the bankside aquatic weeds, beaten back by frost, have withered and retreated to the bottom. In rivers, lakes, and ponds that have clayey and, especially, sandy bottoms, the water has grown clear and become as transparent as glass. But dammed rivers and streams, which flow slowly, turn a light bluish-green color that's unpleasant and seems murky, though this is an optical illusion. Their water is perfectly clear, but the bottom is covered with settled duckweed,* tiny green moss, or short water-silk, and the water acquires a greenish color from the lining of its bottom, just as crystal or glass lined with green foil appears green. In spring (this is imperceptible in summer), the water is murky on its own, and the spring flood covers the bottom with new layers of mud and soil, on the surface of which no moss has yet formed. But when ponds are dammed after the floodwater has receded, the sleepy waters of such rivers bloom continually, and the blossoming vegetation, floating in masses and tufts along the water's surface, at the same time fills the water with its tiny particles (by the process of blossoming) and makes it thick and murky, which is why the bottom's own green color is imperceptible.

Such is the autumn I love not just as a sportsman, but as a passionate lover of nature in all her various transformations.

The same causes (that is, uninterrupted life in the country and the impossibility of hunting with a gun) that have forced me to try fishing so early in the spring have also made me continue my rod-sport in the autumn up to the last possible day, regardless of the weather. At first, before the hard frosts and the arrival of cold inclement weather, fish would take in the same deep and safe swims as they had all summer. Little by little the biting in whirlpools moved to the bankside; that is, it started close to shore. After that, small fish, of medium

*"Duckweed": a green plant, an aquatic blossom.

size, began to move upstream into the pond's upper reaches*
and held more toward the middle of the river, which made it
necessary to cast the fishing outfit far from the bank. I kept up
this kind of fishing until the frosts were so hard that my whole
river, despite its springwater sources, was covered with fairly
sturdy ice. But weak ice over places where fish were holding I
would break with a long pole, then push the little blocks of ice
through downstream or throw them out. At places cleared in
this manner I continued to fish, catching for the most part
medium perch and various small fish. Often I'd go fishing in
several degrees of frost, kneeling in the snow and keeping the
worm-box hidden in my bosom because the worms would
freeze even while they were being mounted on the hook.
Obviously, I had to do my baiting expeditiously, although several times I saw a worm that was frozen stiff immediately
thaw in the water and start to wriggle. While my river was
frozen only at the margins and there still stretched along its
middle a long, clear lead, it was possible to fish anywhere
there was open water, provided one only took care that the line
not touch the edges of the ice, because it would immediately
freeze to them and could break off at the first hook-set. It was
also necessary to be careful when landing fish by cautiously
pulling them out onto the ice and then throwing them onto
the bank. This kind of twofold method for landing the precious catch was necessary to keep the sharp edges of the ice at
the bank from cutting through the line.

When the frosts became harder, the only places on the river
that didn't freeze up were those where large springs were
more numerous and where all kinds of small fish continually
congregated. For the most part perch would bite, but the takes
lost their decisiveness and boldness, and the fish themselves,
dragged from the water as if not resisting, seemed rather limp
and sleepy.

*I remind my readers that I was fishing in the River Voria, which consists
entirely either of ponds or the upper reaches of ponds. There's practically no
actual, free-flowing water in the river, or, put more precisely, in the brook. The
free current continues no more than about two hundred yards from the mills, so
my observations can't be applied to an undammed river flowing freely by its
own mass of water.

Perhaps many will object: "Where's the sport in bagging a few half-dead fish, and by such difficult means?" To this I'll reply that "sport outcompels coercion," that any sport possesses its own relative worth.[153] I think that in this instance all sportsmen will agree with me. Of course, where there's a great deal of noble game or large fish of the best species, no one will give a second thought to the lowliest game or to little fish. But where that's all there is, and not much of it at that, there is it precious.

3 January 1858
Moscow

# LETTER TO THE EDITOR OF
## *SPORTING JOURNAL*

Moscow

23 October 1858

Dear Sir,

Permit me on the pages of your fine journal[154] to relate an incident that befell a certain venerable sportsman, N. T. Aksakov, in early September of the present year (1858).[155] He was fishing on the River Inza, which serves as a living border between Simbirsk and Penza Provinces. After he had cast out several fishing outfits baited with small fish, one of the floats quietly began to stir, turn, and, at last, sink altogether. The sportsman set the hook and felt unusual weight. He played the fish to the surface of the water and saw that a decent pike, of about six pounds, had taken on the outfit and that he in turn had been half-swallowed by an enormous pike. He began to play the fish back and forth, led them to the bank, and scooped them into the net. The large pike then released the other pike, who had actually been caught by the hook. Taking advantage of his freedom, he swiftly rushed sideways and tore free from the rod and line, but the enormous pike, a twelve-pounder, remained in the net and the sportsman landed him. The greediness of pike is well known to me and I have more than once seen a pike who has lodged his teeth in a fish get caught on a fishing outfit without in the least touching the hook, and thereby permit himself to be dragged to shore. Nonetheless, in the incident I have related I find it curious that the pike who had swallowed the hook was saved by the fact that a second pike, twice as big, had taken it into his head to swallow the first. Here is fresh proof that pike eat other pike.

With true esteem, I have the honor to be

A zealous reader and admirer of your journal,

S. Aksakov

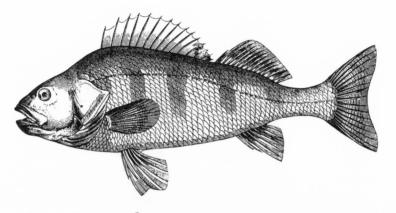

# Appendix 2

## Selected Fishing Poetry by Aksakov

There is my homeland. . . . There the untamed
    wilderness! . . .[156]
And there the land so grateful to the plowman!
Woods of oak, and grassy vales,
And fields all crowned with fertile harvest!

There the mountains raising brows to heaven,
Youthful branches of the ancient Rhipean range,[157]
And rivers foaming amid the precipices,
Enthralling our gaze as they flood about the fields!

There are the clear and bottomless lakes,
Surrounded by the Bashkirs' nomad camps,
And sportive steeds, countless in their herds,
Admire themselves reflected from the hills therein! . . .

I greet you, blessed country!
O land of plenty and all worldly riches!
Not forever will you be forgotten in contempt,
Not forever will you serve for flocks alone.

# THE FISHERMAN'S WOE

## A Russian Idyll

*Younger Fisherman*
Friend, why so glum? Are you in good health, dear fellow?[158]
Is your wife well, and well the little children?

*Elder Fisherman*
                    Thank you,
My friend, for your sympathy and your cordial words.
I am in good health, by God's mercy, and so too is my family.
But only yesterday a vexation befell me
Which, it seems, will haunt me forever . . .

*Younger*
                    Tell me the story now;
First we will be vexed together, and then we will forget.

*Elder*
Yesterday morning, just at break of dawn,
I was at the dam with all my fishing gear:
Three rigs, a sack of wheat, a box of worms,
And bread sliced thick, and ten molting crayfish or so
(Bought for a penny from little village lads),*
And hooks to spare, and lines, and sinkers too,
And a net for ide (borrowed from a neighbor—for my sins).
The mist churned like smoke! . . . In water knee-deep,
Across the flood, I somehow reached the point.**
I groundbaited fast and cast all the rods,
One with molting crayfish, one with crustless bread,
And one with white eel[159] and the usual worms.
I filled and lit a pipe, then sat down upon a board.
The misty damp sank deep into my bones,
And only against the dawn, and stooping, could I see my floats.

*Crayfish, when molting (i.e., sloughing their shells), hide in holes, which
makes obtaining them very difficult, but fish especially love them.
**Point: a place not entirely surrounded by water.

I love, dear companion, the golden hours of sunrise!
I know not why, but morning seems a holiday!
The sunrise blazed. A stream of fugitive breeze
(Which, before the sun's arising, flies down from heaven)
Disturbed the mist and reed, with ripples coating
The misty waters . . . and the smallish noise, whisper-like,
Ran about me and fell silent, leaving no trace.
Only now and again a big fish splashed, like a billet,*
And the circle, widening, imperceptibly merged with the
    water.
Well, friend, how sad and merry it was for me then! . . .
Harder from the pipe I puffed out my smoke, and it mingled
With gray mist, flying off into air,
And, one after another, through my head ran thoughts
That I shall never find words to convey, though they were
    many.
And then it was time for the fish to bite:
Sensing the groundbait, they took both above and below—
The ide, chub, tench, and roach-rudd,
The insatiable perch and simpleton bream.
Releasing bubbles along the bottom, they begurgled the river,
And my heart, as if doused in roiling water, started
    beating. . . . Hardly had
I taken a quiet breath, when my hand lowered, holding the
    pipe.
Avidly gazing at my motionless floats,
I expected them to be seized and plunged to the bottom any
    minute—
But in vain. He rustled the first float a bit, then the other,
And that was all. You know I am patient, not easily bored,
So I took up the outfits, one after another, fixed up
The bait, and cast out, then smoked my forgotten pipe again,
And awaited the lucky hour once more.
All was the same: ide played tricks but did not take as they
    should.
Hope beckoned, more than once, but all was for naught.
Is it not the same in life for us, my friend?

*_Billet:_ slab of fish meat; a technical term among fishermen.

## Younger

Of course: who has lived his whole life undeceived?
I am always in awe, though, of your patience!
Laugh if you like, but catching roach is better fun.

## Elder

Dear friend, without patience you will never bag the ide.
To me, dragging in little roach, as you do, is dreary.
Already the sun had risen high, but still no luck.
The line baited with white eel
Three times was taken and tugged hard.
With great care I took up the rod—and the worm had been
    taken.
The worm was large—"Perhaps," thought I, "he can't
    swallow it,"
And I chose one a bit smaller, baited and cast out.
Scarcely had it left my hands, when suddenly the float
Was dragged off to the bottom . . . and I struck.* What then?
    A little chub,
Though small, still not a roach, still better than that.
"Aha!" thought I, "If you're up to mischief here,
Then I'll show you" . . . and I tossed aside the big outfit,
Seized the medium one, baited a young worm,
Cast out, held the rod in hand, and, of course,
The bait had not reached bottom before the float took a turn
And was quietly taken to the reeds. . . . I struck gently. . . .
There was a terrible tug, as if I were fouled on some roots. . . .
The rod was bent double . . . I jumped up, and my heart was
    aflutter.
"Got you, my darling!" I cried, and withdrew all the rods.
I played him very gently to the left of the point,
To a clearing, but the fish was enormous, I felt,
And he moved heavily, as though the water gave purchase.
Barely had half the line appeared, and in a twinkling,
Like lightning, a yard-long fish leapt to the surface . . .
What sort I could not descry though, and my hands trembled.
Fear that I could not manage the fish had me seeing stars:
The hook was small and my line of only six little hairs!

---

*To strike: to pull up the fishing outfit suddenly.

To and fro I played him . . . and he grew quiet.

I looked and finally made him out: a terrible giant of a chub!

I had never seen nor even heard of such a fish.

With trembling hand I seized the net, and saw it wouldn't do:

It was small, had no ruffle,* and could not contain the fish.

As soon as I started to lead him in, my chub

Leapt like a shot from the water . . . and I discarded the
    accursed net.

I led the chub upstream, just to the first backwater,**

For I would succeed in taking him by hand in the shallows

(In a millpond, the river is level with the banks, you know).

I had only started to play him in and—might of heaven!—

The chub leapt onto the bank, of his own accord, like a bird.

I grew more timid, and I, a sinner, purposing how best to bag
    him—

By hand or by falling upon the fish—went mad,

Forgot the warning of old men, and seized the line with my
    hand. . . .

The line snapped, the chub went over the bank—and into the
    water!

And I? I stood, as if turned to stone,

Holding in my hands the end of a broken line,

Fixing my gaze on the damp spot,

The green bank, where the silvery chub had lain . . .

And long I stood rooted there, as if doused with water,

Until my chub, feeling the hook's sharp point

Piercing his lip, and wishing to free himself,

Swam twenty yards away and jumped.

I came to, as disappointment gripped me,

And in a rage abandoned all the rods and tackle,

Then went home, whence I have still not ventured to set foot.

I am ashamed to show my face. Where is my contentment,

If I could not master such a catch?

Perhaps I had left at an ill-omened hour, or some ominous
    encounter

Cursed me with uncharacteristic foolishness.

---

*Net with no ruffle:* name given to a net if the mesh sewn to it is short. It does
not ruffle like a sack.

**Backwater:* a narrow cove in the river.

As if I had never landed huge ide
On light lines, and there are no bolder fish than they!
Believe me, friend, from despair I have been unable to eat
And I find no slumber at night.

*Younger*
Dear companion,
Forget your failure. Who does not make mistakes,
Or experience misfortune while fishing at an evil hour?
Come along with me—the weather now is golden.
After thunder and foulness all the fish are about
And biting eagerly. Let us go, and try our luck a little.
Friend, you are older than I, and wise sayings
Have I often heard from you; where have they gone?
Have you not always told me, "Fair weather follows foul,
And twofold fortune trails misfortune"?

*Elder*
Quite right, but I cannot reproach bad fortune,
And must blame myself for my impatience,
For avarice, impulsiveness, still more for stupid timidity.

*Younger*
Friend, was it not you who said, "We cannot gain wit
Without losses, failures, deprivation and assorted sorrows"?
Was it not you who said, "Patience assures success,"
And, "Joy without woe would be no joy at all"?

*Elder*
Of course these words are true—thank you, dear sir!
You have restored me to life with your kindhearted speech.
O, a kind companion is the most precious thing on earth:
Sorrow seems easier with him, and joy so much the sweeter!

1824

## TO GRISHA

Bestir yourself, my fisherman,[160]
Hasten, hasten,
Hurry off to catch
Stone loach and gudgeon!

With welcoming waves
The spreading pond awaits you;
Beneath green shrubs
Go set about your merry work!

Bogorodskoe<br>1832

Believe me, there's no greater torment
Than to look for a country place near Moscow.[161]
Vexation, boredom and impatience
One has no choice but to endure.
This one has a little garden, but not enough shade;
That one has a big garden, but there's no water;
This little pond's a knee-deep puddle,
And the house is good for nothing.

That one has groves for strolling,
But no manor house at all;
This one's house is good, but has no swimming:
There's not a drop of springwater.
There the whole structure's in ruins,
While here cattle recently roamed;
This location's good,
But Kostia will call it a hummock.[162]

In that place the peasants live well,
But there's a whole regiment of house-serfs;
In this one the whole forest was logged out before—
What would be the point?
There the peasants know nothing of plowing,
While here the soil's no good.
That one has all the household customs,
But not a farthing's worth of income.

That place has summer front-rooms,
A fruit orchard and kitchen garden,
Orangeries and greenhouses,
But all the people have just died off.
This one's an estate without a flaw,
There is no obstacle at all:
All's well there for my pocketbook,
But—there's not a single fish to be found!

August 1843

"Swim forth with caution
To catch wiggling worms,"
Said the Ruffian Empress
To gather her ruffs.

$1843^{163}$

There at last, for all our patience,
Fate has richly rewarded us:
At last we've found an estate
Precisely to our taste.[164]
The location is lovely,
On a hill overlooking a swift river;
The village is hidden from view
By a thick, green grove.

There's a park as well, and lots of shade,
And an abundance of all kinds of water.
A pond is there—not a knee-deep puddle,
And the house is good for everything.
There's wondrous strolling all around,
A well with springwater,
And in the pond and river there's bathing everywhere,
Both on the hill and beneath it.[165]

The peasants are not impoverished;
Of house-serfs there are only three;
Though the little wood was logged out before,
Fine groves have remained.
The peasants there are always plowing—
There are no varlets on the Voria;
It has all the household customs,
And white mushrooms in abundance.

A varied natural setting,
A secluded hideaway!
Of course there's not much income,
But income's not the point.
The fishing here is free and easy
For ide, and roach, and perch,
And plenty of crayfish can be found,
And burbot, pike and chub.

Moscow 1844

Fisherman, fisherman, stern is your fate:
Impatient, you awaited dawn,
And at the East's first light,
You leapt from bed in haste.

Dark and misty are the heavens,
Heavy rain pours as through a sieve,
Wind shakes the woods about—
So back to bed, o hapless fisherman.[166]

# EPISTLE TO M. A. DMITRIEV

I promised to write some verses . . .\*[167]
But I'm no longer glad of life.
How can I turn out rhymes to parade
In rhythmical step?
My poetry is my heart's expression,
The cry of passion and wail of the soul . . .
In it there's disquiet and worry—
And my verses are no good.

You and I are old and sick
And we sit each in our own corner.
We conduct our conversations
In letters, not in spoken words!
Old age can be so good
That there's no regret for youth:
It's quiet now, and joy is tranquil,
And sorrow is tranquil now too.
Euphonious is the general pitch
Of mental and bodily forces . . .
Many are the joys in old age
Unknown even to youth itself!
But such is not my lot:
Neither illness, nor passing years,
Nor life's captivity,
Nor crushing calamity
Have thus far been able
To cool my passionate nature,
And no tranquil visage shines
As a bright facade!
My spirit as before is troubled
And there is no peace in my heart;
Spiritual peace is impossible
Amid these worldly waves!

\*Dmitriev has written verses to me three times, and I promised.

And I am no longer free within myself.
By turns I'm angry, sick,
Dissatisfied with myself,
And attacking others—
Both strangers and my very own!
My spirit in a weakened body
Has grown annoyed and restless,
And it's painful that my
Heart's keen hearing is so delicate.
And in tranquil moments
I see clearly, though it doesn't make me glad,
The repulsive discord
Of my bodily and spiritual forces.
There is, though, a conciliator,
Eternally young and alive,
A miracle-worker and healer—
I go to him sometimes.
I venture into nature's world,
The world of serenity and freedom,
The kingdom of fish and sandpipers,
To my own native waters,
To the expanse of steppe meadows,
Into the cool shade of forests
And—back to the years of my youth!

Moscow
March 1851

Farewell, my quiet country home![168]
Your summer tenant flees you.
My deserted abode
Is covered with snow;
The ponds have frozen,
And ice gently blankets the river.

I have disputed enough with nature,
Wrestled with snow and foul weather,
Wandered along the river's banks,
Casting my hooks deep within her.
A blizzard seethed around me,
And the water cooled and congealed,
While I, using frozen worms,
Fished for sleepy perch.

Farewell, my seclusion!
I thank you for the enjoyment
Of your modest natural world,
For the crucian carp, the gudgeon,
For those joyous moments
When visions of the past
Would quietly arise before me,
Imparting their poignant delight.

# 17 OCTOBER (TO A. N. MAIKOV)

Again the rains, again the mists,[169]
And falling leaves, and naked woods,
And glades grown dark,
And low gray vault of heaven.
Once more the autumn weather!
And, filled with gentle moisture,
It gladdens my heart:
I love this time of year.

I love the tit's ringing whistle,
The squeak of bullfinches in my shrubs,
And the white flocks of geese
On winter crops of emerald green.
Protected by an umbrella, I love
To sit at the river's bend,
Beneath a bush, sheltered from the wind,
Warmed by a cozy homespun coat—
To sit and wait with fervent patience,
Having cast my rods and lines
Into the greenish waters,
Deep in the quiet, murky Voria.*
I fix my gaze upon the float,
Though it lies unchanged;
And suddenly—a barely perceptible motion,
And the fisherman's heart is ashudder!

And there he is, a noble perch,
Tempted by an enormous worm,
He swam up brave and free,
With wide and gaping mouth
And, boldly swallowing the bait,
Dragged it all down to the river's bottom . . .
Here's where the fisherman's business starts,
And I, with a motion of the hand,

*The name of a stream.

Nimbly strike the fish,
Draw him from the river-depth
And onto the bank I throw him,
Quite far behind my back.

But perch are no great marvel here!
I love the autumn bite of ruff:
They do not take at once, not boldly,
But I am ready to wait unwearied.
The float trembles . . . patience!
It's making rings . . . never mind!
Let it sink! I find pleasure
In dragging ruff from the river's bottom:
All spread out wide and angry,
He stubbornly crawls from the water,
Covered with thick slime,
Raising his defensive spines—
But there's no salvation from his misfortune!

But now it's all wrong. A sudden ailment
Has made me its victim. What is our significance?
I gaze upon the Voria's banks
Through a window, like a captive from his prison.
The warm, wet weather has passed,
Frost has bound the waters' surface,
And I am sad. Already Moscow
Calls me to her.
Farewell again, my dear seclusion!
Fruitless was my summer rest,
And unattained my inspiration.
I'm not grumbling: I hate to whine.
Farewell, you hills and gullies,
O beauty of water and woods,
And farewell to you, my "snags,"*
And to you, my "ruffy places"!

Village of Abramtsevo<br>1857

*The name of a place where big fish bite.

# TRANSLATOR'S NOTES

1. *Kniga glagolemaia Uriadnik: Novoe ulozhenie i ustroenie china sokol'nich'ia puti* [The book called ordainer: a new rule and establishment of order for the falconer's way] was written by an anonymous author in 1656 by decree of Tsar Aleksei Mikhailovich Romanov (1629–76; reigned from 1645), an avid hunter. Aksakov, who published a short article on the work (in *Sobranie pisem Tsaria Alekseia Mikhailovicha s prilozheniem Ulozheniia sokol'nich'ia puti*, ed. P. I. Bartenev [Moscow, 1856], 139–46) and believed Aleksei wrote or dictated much of the treatise, elsewhere called the tsar, "A true patriarch, and royal representative of Russian hunters, who fully sensed all the poetry of sport and viewed with artistry not only sport itself, but all the details and intricacies of its environment" (*Sobranie sochinenii v chetyrëkh tomakh* [Moscow: Gosudarstvennoe izdatel'stvo khudozhestvennoi literatury, 1956], 4:610). This epigraph for *Notes on Fishing* is taken from a famous passage in the *New Rule* actually written in Aleksei's own hand: "An addition of my own to the book, here is a lesson for the body and the soul: Do not forget truth and justice, benevolent love and martial order. There is a time for business and an hour for amusement" (Bartenev, *Sobranie pisem*, 92; N. S. Ashukin and M. G. Ashukina, *Krylatye slova*, 4th ed. [Moscow: Khudozhestvennaia literatura, 1988], 97). See also Serge A. Zenkovsky, ed., *Medieval Russia's Epics, Chronicles and Tales*, rev. ed. (New York: Dutton, 1974), 520–22.

2. Outside the context of sporting activities, these two well-known Russian adages, "Okhotu teshit'—ne bedu platit'" and "Okhota pushche nevoli," carry the everyday meanings of "Indulging one's pastime is no calamity" and "Willingness to do something is more powerful than being forced to do it," respectively. In the context of Aksakov's fishing treatise, I have chosen to render Russian *okhóta* as "sport." *Okhóta* can denote either "willingness, desire, pastime," or "sport, hunt, hunting" and Aksakov is clearly playing on these proverbs' secondary meanings at the outset of his treatise on fishing—itself a form of "sport" (*okhóta*). My admittedly unusual rendering of "Okhota pushche nevoli" clarifies the maxim's relevance to Aksakov's comments in his preface to *Notes on Fishing* and in Appendix 1, "A Few Words on Angling in Early Spring and Late Autumn." See Andrew R. Durkin's discussion of the term in *Sergei Aksakov and Russian Pastoral* (New Brunswick: Rutgers University Press), 72–73.

3. Sergei's brothers, Nikolai Timofeevich Aksakov (1797–1882) and Arkadii Timofeevich Aksakov (1803–60), were also the dedicatees of *Notes of an Orenburg-Province Hunter* (see Translator's Introduction).

4. For the full text, and the history of the poem's publication, see Appendix 2, "Epistle to M. A. Dmitriev."

5. In "First Spring in the Country," *Childhood Years of a Bagrov Grandson*, the narrator—who acts as Aksakov's alter ego throughout the work—relates the following exchange with his mother: "She answered that no one was forbidding him [her husband] from shooting or fishing, but at the same time she spoke contemptuously of these sports, especially of fishing, which she called the amusement of idle and empty-headed people with nothing better to do, an amusement suitable only for children. I started to feel a little ashamed that I so loved to fish." Aksakov began writing *Childhood Years* seven or eight years after the first edition of *Notes on Fishing*, preface already in place, had appeared.

6. In "School (First Period)," in *Memoirs*, Aksakov reports that his own sickly condition was described by rumormongers as "epilepsy," or, literally, "the black sickness"—the same term he employs here in *Notes on Fishing*.

7. Count Pëtr Aleksandrovich Rumiantsev-Zadunaiskii (1725–96): one of Catherine the Great's finest generals. Rumiantsev first distinguished himself in the Seven Years' War (1756–63), then went on to earn accolades for his tactics in the First Turkish War (1768–74).

8. Jean Victor Moreau (1761–1813): French general trained under Napoleon who went to America in 1805, then returned to fight against him on the Russian side in 1813.

9. Neuilly-sur-Seine, a northwestern suburb of Paris, was Louis Philippe's favorite residence. His eighteenth-century castle there, where most of his children were born, and where he was offered the French crown in 1830, was destroyed by a mob in 1848.

10. At the end of the initial, "technical part" of *Notes of an Orenburg-Province Hunter*, Aksakov wrote, "In conclusion, I must repeat in part what I said in the preface to *Notes on Fishing: my little book is neither a treatise on hunting nor a natural history of all species of game. My little book is neither more nor less than the simple notes of a passionate sportsman:* sometimes quite detailed and complete, sometimes superficial and one-sided, but always conscientious" (Aksakov, *Sobranie sochinenii*, 4:167).

11. In "A Year in the Country," *Memoirs*, Aksakov provides the following footnote for a boyhood fishing adventure: "For the successful angling of big fish, a flexible rod is generally beneficial, while a rigid one is very bad. But, since this ide was landed in violation of all the rules of angling—straight over the shoulder—that rigid rod, which barely flexed, turned out to be useful, for the line, thanks to its strength, was capable of holding the fish." The ide in question was Aksakov's first big fish: "This initial success turned me into an ardent fisherman once and for all."

12. Aksakov also describes these line-making techniques in "The Road to Parashino," in *Childhood Years of a Bagrov Grandson*.

13. Assignats: Russian paper currency circulated from 1769 to 1849. Though the paper ruble was supposed to have the same value as the silver ruble, it eventually came to be worth roughly three times less.

14. Aksakov refers to the traditional scale of hook sizes promulgated by the manufacturers of Redditch, Worcestershire, who dominated the world

market through the first half of the nineteenth century, but then faced competition from such companies as Norway's O. Mustad and Son, founded in 1832.

15. Here Aksakov uses the word *glistá*, which normally denotes several kinds of intestinal parasites infecting humans and animals. Dal' classifies the word's fishing usage as a regionalism from Saratov and Astrakhan' Provinces (V. I. Dal', *Tolkovyi slovar' zhivogo velikorusskogo iazyka*, 3d ed. [Saint Petersburg: Tovarishchestvo M. O. Vol'f, 1903–9], 1:877).

16. The Dëma River rises ninety miles north of Orenburg and joins the Belaia at Ufa in modern-day Bashkortostan. Aksakov's first attempt at fishing was on the Dëma; he describes the event in "The Road to Parashino," in *Childhood Years of a Bagrov Grandson*. Chvanov has justly called the Dëma Aksakov's "favorite river" (Mikhail Chvanov, *Aksakovskie mesta v Bashkirii* [Ufa: Bashkirskoe knizhnoe izdatel'stvo, 1976], 29–30).

17. See Appendix 1, "Floodwater and Fishing the Spring Runoff," and "A Few Words on Angling in Early Spring and Late Autumn."

18. See Appendix 1, "A Few Words on Angling in Early Spring and Late Autumn."

19. See "On Fishing Skill" and "Trout, or Spottie."

20. These are regions boasting the dark, fertile, humus-laden soil found predominantly in the steppe country of Southern Russia, the Northern Caucasus, the Volga basin, Kazakhstan, and Western Siberia.

21. *Kvas* is a traditional Russian beerlike beverage made by fermenting rye bread or rye flour with malt; see Joyce Toomre, *Classic Russian Cooking*, Indiana-Michigan Series in Russian and East European Studies (Bloomington: Indiana University Press, 1992), 468 n.

22. Aksakov's notion of "fishing skill" (*umen'e udit'*) also plays an important role in his *Memoirs* (written 1853–55). In "A Year in the Country," he remarks that his servant, Efrem Evseich, lacked "fishing skill" and preferred to play his quarry roughly and toss it over his shoulder to the bank. (Aksakov's father, who clearly possessed "fishing skill," consistently landed twice as many fish as Evseich.) In the same chapter, Aksakov describes late-spring fishing on the Buguruslan: "It stands to reason that, in spite of our stout lines and hooks, the largest fish often got away, and broke our rods, hooks and lines, because we lacked fishing skill and had no landing-nets." To convey the rationality and meticulousness of Aksakov's techniques, J. D. Duff renders *umen'e udit'* as "scientific fishing" and "scientific angling" in his translation of Aksakov's *Memoirs* (*A Russian Schoolboy* [New York: Oxford University Press, 1983], 60, 73).

23. Aksakov refers to *The Perfect Huntsman, or Knowledge of all the Appurtenances of Field Sport with Guns and Other Means* (Saint Petersburg, 1779), translated and adapted into Russian from several German originals by Vasilii Alekseevich Lëvshin (1746–1826). On Lëvshin, see the Translator's Introduction, and Viktor Shklovskii, *Chulkov i Lëvshin* (Leningrad: Izdatel'stvo pisatelei v Leningrade, 1933), 137–51, 249–62; see also note 98. At the outset of *The Perfect Huntsman*, twenty-one ideal qualities

are named, ranging from "fear of God" (to which Aksakov had also referred in the 1847 edition of *Notes on Fishing*, 47) to "lack of envy." "Healthy and straight teeth" (10) appears fifteenth on the list. "Good teeth are necessary," the appended explanation goes, "because a hunter must always eat his fill quickly, without much chewing, unlike cows . . . for if he does not have a mouth full of strong teeth, he will waste valuable time and be like an old grandmother, who must chew at considerable length. But, first and foremost, good teeth are necessary for sounding the horn, since, without them, it is not possible to grip the horn's mouthpiece, blow hard into it, and sound the horn loudly, which is sometimes necessary in the forest" (20–21).

24. For the incident that no doubt inspired this advice, see "Chub."

25. These words playfully mock Turgenev's laudatory description of Aksakov's style ("he does not act the sage, use cunning, or add extraneous motives and goals") in Turgenev's well-known review of *Notes of an Orenburg-Province Hunter*. The review originally appeared in Nekrasov's *Sovremennik*, no. 1 (1853); see I. S. Turgenev, *Polnoe sobranie sochinenii i pisem v dvadtsati vos'mi tomakh: Sochineniia* (Moscow: Izdatel'stvo Nauka, 1963), 5:416. Aksakov's italicized phrase first appears in the second edition of *Notes on Fishing* (1854), 96; he considered Turgenev's published praise excessive (Turgenev, *Polnoe sobranie sochinenii i pisem v dvadtsati vos'mi tomakh: Sochineniia*, 5:644). See Translator's Introduction.

26. Aksakov is responding to V. A. Lëvshin's dubious contentions in *Kniga dlia okhotnikov do zverinoi i ptichei lovli, takzhe do ruzheinoi strel'by i soderzhaniia pevchikh ptits . . .* (Moscow: V Tipografii S. Selivanovskogo, 1814), 4:409: "females always pursue males. Eight or more of the former follow one male, hang about him, and chase him into shore up to the weeds, into the shallows. The male repulses them, but is finally forced to clamber onto the weeds, in which he lies upon his belly, protruding almost completely out of the water. He starts to release some milt, into which each female hastens to expel her roe. After approximately twelve to fourteen days, a single fry emerges from each grain of this roe."

27. See Aksakov's description of these woven willow fish traps in "Burbot" and in Appendix 1, "Flood Water and Fishing the Spring Runoff."

28. These are wild exaggerations. Carp live up to twenty-five years in the wild and forty-seven years in captivity (A. J. McClane, ed., *McClane's New Standard Fishing Encyclopedia and International Angling Guide*, rev. ed. [New York: Holt, Rinehart and Winston, 1974], 198); on the longevity of pike, see note 98.

29. Aksakov's "minute green worms" could be leeches, while the "large, green, aquatic worms" are clearly the larvae of some species of caddisfly (Order *Trichoptera*), actually a nonparasitic insect. The "water-lizard" is probably a predacious salamander or newt.

30. Il'inskoe lies east of Moscow, just north of Odintsovo. Somynka Brook, a tributary of the Moscow River, is now known as "Saminka," and Oborvikho is now called "Barvikha."

31. In the third edition of *Notes on Fishing*, this phenomena was analyzed at length by K. F. Rul'e in an appended article, "Khod ryby protiv techeniia vody" [The fish's upstream journey], 326–45.

32. See Aksakov's detailed description of these devices in Appendix 1, "Floodwater and Fishing the Spring Runoff."

33. The Belaia (White), a tributary of the Kama, is a large river rising in the Southern Ural mountains between Ufa and Cheliabinsk. Aksakov was born and spent much of his boyhood in Ufa, on the banks of the Belaia.

34. Mikhail Vasil'evich Avdeev (1821–76), remembered chiefly as a writer of Lermontovian and, later, Turgenevian prose fiction, retired in 1852 to his native village of Burunovka in the Sterlitamak district. His literary impressions of the region were published in the 1850s ("Poezdka na kumys," *Otechestvennye zapiski*, nos. 10–12 [1852]; "Dorozhnye zametki: 1854," *Biblioteka dlia chteniia* 144 [1857]). When Aksakov was a boy, his mother took a cure of *kumiss* (fermented mare's-milk) among the Bashkirs near Lake Kieshki, which afforded him a great deal of excellent fishing; see "Sergeevka," in *Childhood Years of a Bagrov Grandson*.

35. Another tributary of the Kama River, the Ik rises a few miles from Nadëzhdino, an Aksakov estate near Belebei (in modern Bashkortostan) where Sergei and his family lived from 1821 to 1826. Aksakov gives a detailed description of fishing on the Ik in "The Road from Parashino to Bagrovo," in *Childhood Years of a Bagrov Grandson*.

36. See Aksakov's comments on pike-stunning in "Pike."

37. Aksakov's friend, the great Ukrainian-born prosaist Nikolai Gogol' (1809–41), published this story in part 1 of *Evenings on a Farm Near Dikan'ka* (Saint Petersburg: Tipografiia Departamenta narodnogo prosveshcheniia, 1831), a collection of colorful Ukrainian tales. Aksakov slightly misquotes the passage ("Peep out at me" for "Peep out a moment"), which is taken from the story's first chapter. Use of the now-archaic term "Little Russian" as a synonym for "Ukrainian" was common in nineteenth-century Russian writing.

38. *Phoxinus phoxinus* is normally called *gol'ián* in Russian, or "minnow" in English, though Aksakov always uses a rare regional term (*loshók*) derived from his equally regional term (*lokh*) for the taimen (see note 108). "Because of its fine scales, motley colors, bar-shaped body, and range," writes Sabaneev, "this little fish is very reminiscent of the trout, which is why in some places, as in Ufa Province, it is called 'little taimen' [*loshók*], the diminutive of 'taimen' [*lokh*], while in Moscow Province it is called 'troutlet' [*forél'ka*]" (L. P. Sabaneev, *Ryby Rossii: Zhizn' i lovlia (uzhen'e) nashikh presnovodnykh ryb* [Moscow: Terra, 1992], 2:381); see also L. S. Berg, *Ryby presnykh vod SSSR i sopredel'nykh stran*, 4th ed. (Moscow: Izdatel'stvo Akademii nauk, 1949), 2:588–90. Due to the impossibility of deriving a satisfactory English diminutive from "taimen," and to the actual unrelatedness of the minnow and taimen, I have chosen to render Aksakov's *loshók* consistently as "minnow."

39. For an excellent overview of contemporaneous Russian fish cookery, see the notes and recipes of Elena Ivanovna Molokhovets (b. 1831) in Toomre, *Classic Russian Cooking*, 256–72, 548–49, 564–69. This is an abridged, annotated translation of Molokhovets's *Podarok molodym khoziakam*, which was first published in Kursk (where Aksakov's wife, Ol'ga Semënovna Zaplatina, was raised) in 1861 and had gone through at least twenty-nine editions by 1917.

40. *Leucaspius delineatus,* called *verkhóvka* by Aksakov, and also known in Russian as *ovsiánka* (literally "oatmeal," but which also carries the ornithological meaning of "bunting"). Berg (*Ryby presnykh vod,* 2:610) gives *ovsiánka* first, then *verkhóvka,* but Sabaneev (*Ryby Rossii,* 2:370) claims that the former term is used in Kazan' Province and Ukraine, while the latter is employed around Moscow. Lacking a standard English name, this species is often referred to with the German *Moderlieschen,* or simply called "verkhovka" in transliteration. "Toppie" is my literal rendering of *verkhóvka,* which is a diminutive form of Russian *verkh* (top).

41. *Nemachilus barbatulus;* see Sabaneev, *Ryby Rossii,* 2:389–94, and Berg, *Ryby presnykh vod,* 2:868–72. In Russian, this fish is commonly called *goléts,* which, as Aksakov correctly points out, is derived from *gólyi* (naked); see M. Fasmer, *Etimologicheskii slovar' russkogo iazyka* [O. N. Trubachëv's Russian translation of Max Vasmer's *Russisches etymologisches Wörterbuch*] (Moscow: Izdatel'stvo Progress, 1964), 1:428. Confusingly, *goléts* is also the standard Russian name for the unrelated *Salvelinus alpinus,* or arctic char, no doubt due to the very fine scales of that salmonid, which can also give the impression of "nakedness."

42. See Molokhovets's notes on fish soup (*ukhá*) (in Toomre, *Classic Russian Cooking,* 143–44, 548).

43. *Gobio gobio;* see Sabaneev, *Ryby Rossii,* 2:129–41, and Berg, *Ryby presnykh vod,* 2:640–43.

44. Russian *pisk* is used to describe the high-pitched sound emitted by small animals (mice, birds, and so forth), and is normally translated into English as "peep," "chirp," "squeak," or "cheep." Most linguistic authorities agree that the gudgeon's Russian name, *peskár',* is derived from *pesók* (sand), as Aksakov explains above. Chernykh, however, grants that the name might be related to the same Indo-European root as Latin *piscis* (fish) (P. Ia. Chernykh, *Istoriko-etimologicheskii slovar' sovremennogo russkogo iazyka,* 2d ed. [Moscow: Russkii iazyk, 1994], 2:26).

45. "Cooking in sour cream" (*zharit' v smetane*) is Aksakov's favorite way of preparing fish in *Notes on Fishing.* Unfortunately, it is difficult to know precisely what he has in mind, since *zhárit'* can mean "roast," "broil," "fry," or "grill," depending on the context. In "The Young Couple at Bagrovo," in *A Family Chronicle,* Aksakov seems to refer to the same process: "the fish [perch, rudd, ide] were meanwhile boiled, and cooked in sour cream in a skillet, while the largest of the perch were baked unskinned and unscaled." See Toomre's discussion of *zhárit',* which she calls

"the single most troublesome word for the translator of a Russian cook-book" (*Classic Russian Cooking*, 67).

46. *Alburnus alburnus;* see Sabaneev, *Ryby Rossii,* 2:354–63, and Berg, *Ryby presnykh vod,* 2:746–49.

47. Bleak are most widely known in Russia as *ukléika* or *ukléia,* and close cognates of these terms exist in several Slavic and East-European languages (see Fasmer, *Etimologicheskii slovar' russkogo iazyka,* 4:156, and 2:246).

48. See Molokhovets on Russian methods of fish-smoking (Toomre, *Classic Russian Cooking,* 537).

49. *Leuciscus leuciscus;* see Sabaneev, *Ryby Rossii,* 2:276–88, and Berg, *Ryby presnykh vod,* 2:545–46.

50. The city of Elets, whose river is now called the Sosna (Pine), lies two hundred miles south of Moscow. Aksakov's etymological theory linking the fish with this geographic name is erroneous. Cognates of *eléts* exist in many Slavic languages, and these words probably derive from terms for the color white; cf. Latin *albus* and German *Alant* (ide). See Fasmer, *Etimolog-icheskii slovar' russkogo iazyka,* 2:14–15.

51. *Acerina cernua;* see Sabaneev, *Ryby Rossii,* 1:71–89, and Berg, *Ryby presnykh vod,* 3:1046–48.

52. The Russian term for this fish—*ërsh*—can mean "brush," "spike," or "cowlick," and is also the name of a rapidly intoxicating mixture of beer and vodka. Derivations abound: *ershístyi* (bristling, obstinate), *ershóvyi* (brushy, spiky), *ershít' sia* (to stick up, to lose one's temper), *eróshit'* (to dishevel), *eróshit' sia* (to stick up); Aksakov even employs a form of *eróshit'* in the phrase "to flare his spiny crest." Vasmer confirms that the fish-name is the source of these other words, and Vinogradov suggests that they belong to a rich group of Russian terms derived from animal characteristics (Fasmer, *Etimologicheskii slovar' russkogo iazyka,* 2:27; V. V. Vinogradov, *Istoriia slov* [Moscow: Tolk, 1994], 819, 964). Thus, when Aksakov suggests that "the name ruff [*ërsh*] was given to him the moment he was first seen by man," he erroneously reverses the actual etymology, perhaps for comic effect, since it obviously contradicts the order of linguistic derivation he then goes on to espouse. The English term "ruff," attested from the early fifteenth century, is thought to be a special use of "rough," and is thus an excellent equivalent for Russian *ërsh;* cf. English "ruffian." *Acerina cernua* is also known in England as "pope."

53. Aksakov refers to the well-known *lubok* (a popular, cheaply printed picture with captions, short narrative, and dialogue; chapbook) called "Po-vest' o Ershe Ershove syne Shchetinnikove," which might be translated into English as "The Tale of Ruff Ruffian, Son of Mr. Bristleman." This fairy tale, which originated in the sixteenth or seventeenth century, pre-sents a parody of the pre-Petrine legal system: a bream lodges a number of complaints against the actions of a domineering ruff in Lake Rostov; after several charges from piscine witnesses are heard, the ruff is sentenced by

the judges (a sturgeon and a beluga) to being caught and salted. Depending on the variant, the cast of characters can include the whitefish, herring, perch, sheatfish, ide, smelt, zander, crucian carp, loach, tench, burbot, chub, roach, and crayfish. The typical illustration depicts a school of litigious fish in the lake surrounded by a few dozen men on the shore, each of whom has a witty verse caption describing the terrible treatment he metes out to the ruff. See D. A. Rovinskii, *Russkie narodnye kartinki* (Saint Petersburg: Tipografiia Imperatorskoi Akademii nauk, 1881), 1:402–5, 4:271–80, 5:148–54; and Alla Sytova, ed., *The Lubok: Russian Folk Pictures (17th to 19th Century)* (Leningrad: 1984), plate 57. Aksakov himself composed some fairy-tale verses on the ruff: see Appendix 2, "Swim forth with caution." In his "Karas'-idealist" (The idealistic crucian carp; 1884), M. E. Saltykov ("Shchedrin") drew on the chapbook tradition of the ruff's dispute. Saltykov's fable, which showcases his extensive knowledge of fishing terminology, depicts a debate between a crucian carp and a vicious ruff, with a pike joining in at the end; see M. E. Saltykov-Shchedrin, *Polnoe sobranie sochinenii v dvadtsati tomakh* (Moscow: Izdatel'stvo Khudozhestvennaia literatura, 1974), vol. 16, no. 1:79–89.

54. Molokhovets offers an appetizing recipe for this soup (in Toomre, *Classic Russian Cooking*, 548–49); see also her "Puréed mushroom soup with ruff" (ibid., 139), and her recipes for cold fish with jelly or aspic (ibid., 296–98, 571).

55. *Rutilus rutilus;* see Sabaneev, *Ryby Rossii,* 2:203–30, and Berg, *Ryby presnykh vod,* 2:493–97.

56. The standard Russian name for roach is *plotvá,* though Aksakov always uses the common variant *plotítsa.* Both are indeed probably derived from a source meaning "flat"; cf. Polish *płoć,* and German *Plötze* (Fasmer, *Etimologicheskii slovar' russkogo iazyka,* 3:285). According to Berg (Berg, *Ryby presnykh vod,* 2:493 n), *soróga* is employed in northern Russia and is a pleophonic russification of *särgi,* a name used for the roach by the Izhors (a small, non-Slavic, Finnic-speaking group inhabiting the region of present-day Saint Petersburg); cf. Estonian *särg,* and Finnish *särki.* Vasmer supports this contention (Fasmer, *Etimologicheskii slovar' russkogo iazyka,* 3:721–22). Aksakov's *sorozhniák,* also attested in Sabaneev, *Ryby Rossii,* 2:203, is simply a Russian variant of *soróga.*

57. I have been unable to identify "S. Ia. A." This footnote first appeared in the second edition of *Notes on Fishing* (1854), 167.

58. *Scardinius erythrophthalmus;* see Sabaneev, *Ryby Rossii,* 2:195–203, and Berg, *Ryby presnykh vod,* 2:593–96.

59. This fish's Russian name, *krasnopërka,* literally means "red-fin." The English term "rudd," attested from the early seventeenth century, is also thought to derive from a special use of "ruddy."

60. Vasmer primarily supports an etymology linking the term with Lithuanian, Latvian, and Indic roots meaning "goat," "because of the fish's whiskers" (Fasmer, *Etimologicheskii slovar' russkogo iazyka,* 4:551). This seems unlikely, however, since *Leuciscus idus* and all its subspecies lack

barbels. Vasmer's second choice is an argument linking *iaz'* with Russian *ëzh* (hedgehog). In English, this fish is also known as "id" and "orfe" (see W. E. Ricker, *Russian-English Dictionary for Students of Fisheries and Aquatic Biology,* Bulletin 183 of the Fisheries Research Board of Canada [Ottawa: Fisheries Research Board of Canada, 1973], 296, and Leo S. Berg, *Freshwater Fishes of the U.S.S.R. and Adjacent Countries* [Omry Ronen's English translation of Berg's *Ryby presnykh vod SSSR i sopredel'nykh stran,* 4th ed.] (Jerusalem: S. Monson, 1964), 2:96.

61. *Leuciscus idus;* see Sabaneev, *Ryby Rossii,* 2:288–354, and Berg, *Ryby presnykh vod,* 2:564–66.

62. Aksakov refers to the Orenburg Province river known today as the Great Buguruslanka, which runs south to join the Mochegai a few miles before the latter flows into the Great Kinel' at the town of Buguruslan. In 1797, Sergei Aksakov's parents moved to the family estate of Novo-Aksakovo (also called simply Aksakovo) on the banks of the Great Buguruslanka. Here Sergei spent most of his time between the ages of five and ten, as well as the first five years of his marriage (1816–21). See Translator's Introduction.

63. See "Pike."

64. *Leuciscus cephalus;* see Sabaneev, *Ryby Rossii,* 2:238–76, and Berg, *Ryby presnykh vod,* 2:555–57.

65. Aksakov employs *golóvl'*, a variant of standard Russian *golávl'*. As he correctly suggests, the name is derived from *golová* (head); cf. German *Grosskopf* (see Fasmer, *Etimologicheskii slovar' russkogo iazyka,* 1:429).

66. See "On Fishing Skill."

67. Ibid.

68. See "The Rod."

69. See the entire text of this poem, which Aksakov dated 1824, in Appendix 2, "The Fisherman's Woe." The phrase "though afterward I consoled myself by writing the idyll 'The Fisherman's Woe'" first appeared in the second edition of *Notes on Fishing* (1854), 185.

70. *Abramis brama;* see Sabaneev, *Ryby Rossii,* 2:141–76, and Berg, *Ryby presnykh vod,* 2:768–74.

71. Vasmer does not support Aksakov's hypothesis; see Fasmer, *Etimologicheskii slovar' russkogo iazyka,* 2:490–91.

72. The Nasiagai of Aksakov's boyhood is known today as the "Mochegai."

73. See Molokhovets's recipe for precisely this dish (Toomre, *Classic Russian Cooking,* 267–68).

74. The riverine form of *Cyprinus carpio;* see Sabaneev, *Ryby Rossii,* 2:8–63, and Berg, *Ryby presnykh vod,* 2:831–42. Aksakov discusses stillwater carp in the next chapter.

75. Sazán is a loanword from Turkish and Kazakh (see Fasmer, *Etimologicheskii slovar' russkogo iazyka,* 3:545). Berg asserts that *sazán* is used on the Volga, in Turkestan, and on the Amur (Berg, *Ryby presnykh vod,* 2:831 n).

76. The Presnia was diverted underground in 1908, and its industrial neighborhood became known as "Red Presnia" (*Krasnaia Presnia*) after the workers' uprising there in 1905. Aksakov also refers to the ponds located in the garden (on the left bank of Moscow's Iauza River) of the Catherine Palace, built in the late eighteenth century and later housing the First and Second Cadet Corps. In the twentieth century, the palace has been used as the Stalin Tank Academy and Malinovskii Tank Academy.

77. A friend of Aksakov, Prince Aleksandr Aleksandrovich Shakhovskoi (1777–1846) was a prolific dramatist and theatrical bureaucrat. Remembered today chiefly for his verse comedies and conservative literary and political views, Shakhovskoi died when Aksakov was hard at work on the first edition of *Notes on Fishing*. The Pleasure Garden (*Neskuchnyi sad*), now part of Gor'kii Park, was considered one of prerevolutionary Moscow's finest parks. See also note 91.

78. *Kalách:* Russian white wheatmeal bread baked in a knotted loaf bearing a handle. Intended to be carried as a portable meal, the main part of the loaf can be safely eaten, while the handle, which has been gripped by dirty hands, is normally fed to pets or discarded.

79. *Tinca tinca;* see Sabaneev, *Ryby Rossii*, 2:107–29, and Berg, *Ryby presnykh vod*, 2:614–16.

80. According to Vasmer, both of Aksakov's etymological theories are false (Fasmer, *Etimologicheskii slovar' russkogo iazyka*, 2:498–99, 543).

81. The largest tench mentioned by Berg is a 16½-pound specimen taken near Kiev in 1857 (Berg, *Ryby presnykh vod*, 2:616), but such size is extremely rare for this species.

82. *Carassius carassius;* see Sabaneev, *Ryby Rossii*, 2:93–107, and Berg, *Ryby presnykh vod*, 2:821–26.

83. In "Sergeevka," in *Childhood Years of a Bagrov Grandson*, Aksakov provides the following footnote: " 'Bunt': the center of a seine, having the shape of a long bag narrow at the end." It is in "Sergeevka" that Aksakov gives a detailed description of seining Kieshki, one of the Belaia's flood-lakes: "I was sorry," he wrote, "that they had so emptied the lake of fish, and I sorrowfully told Evseich that now there would no longer be the kind of biting there used to be." On Lake Kieshki, see note 89.

84. Aksakov remembered his old friend, the hunter and fisherman Fëdor Ivanovich Vas'kov (1790–1855), as an amusingly garrulous man disliked by Gogol'. Aksakov wrote a short verse epistle to Vas'kov in the 1820s (*Sobranie sochinenii*, 3:179–81, 649, 772), and inscribed the following in a copy of *Notes of an Orenburg-Province Hunter:* "To my dear old friend, Fëdor Ivanovich Vas'kov, from the author. 9 February 1853, Abramtsevo" (S. T. Aksakov, *Istoriia moega znakomstva s Gogolem*, Literaturnye pamiatniki [Moscow: Izdatel'stvo Nauka, 1960], 256).

85. This village's name is given as "Kivatskaia" in the second edition of *Notes on Fishing* (1854), 207.

86. *Perca fluviatilis;* see Sabaneev, *Ryby Rossii*, 1:20–49, and Berg, *Ryby presnykh vod*, 3:1032–39.

87. Aksakov's lack of confidence here is wise. According to Vasmer, *ókun'*, which has cognates in many Slavic languages, is most likely derived from *óko* (eye), in reference to the perch's large-eyed appearance. The verb *okunát'* is utterly unrelated; see Fasmer, *Etimologicheskii slovar' russkogo iazyka*, 3:131–32.

88. See Molokhovets's recipe for clear fish soup made from perch (and several other species) in Toomre, *Classic Russian Cooking*, 143–44.

89. This lake, known today as "Kieshki," is discussed in Chvanov, *Aksakovskie mesta v Bashkirii*, 33–40. Aksakov refers in his footnote to the mispronunciation of the lake's name as *kishkí* (Russian for "intestines," "gut"). In "Sergeevka," in *Childhood Years of a Bagrov Grandson*, Aksakov's narrator states, "Russians, of course, called the Tatar village, the lake, and the newly settled Russian village of Sergeevka 'Kishkí [Intestines]'—and this name very much suited the lake by indicating its elongated, curving form." Some of the most vivid fishing passages in Aksakov's autobiographical trilogy can be found in "Sergeevka." See note 83.

90. According to Vasmer and Shanskii, *dvoréts* and *dver'* (and hence *dvértsa*) descend from the same root (see Fasmer, *Etimologicheskii slovar' russkogo iazyka*, 1:487, 489; N. M. Shanskii et al., *Kratkii etimologicheskii slovar' russkogo iazyka* [Moscow: Uchpedgiz, 1961], 88). Aksakov's footnote on the wicket first appeared in the second edition of *Notes on Fishing* (1854), 219. Obviously fascinated by these terms, Aksakov had already discussed *dvoréts* and *dvértsy* twice: in a note in "The Migration," *A Family Chronicle* (" 'Wicket' is the name given to a wooden box through which water runs and falls onto the wheels; near Moscow they call it 'palace' [*dvoréts*] ('doors' [*dvérets*]), and 'weirgate' [*skryn'* ]"), and in a note for the coot chapter in the second edition of *Notes of an Orenburg-Province Hunter* (1853): "Wicket: the doors [*dvértsy*] into which water flows along pipes onto waterwheels. Near Moscow they're called a 'palace' [*dvoréts*]—from 'doors' [*dvérets*]?" (*Sobranie sochinenii*, 4:304 n. 2.). Note that *dvérets* is the genitive plural form of *dvértsa*.

91. *Ne liubo ne slushai, a lgat' ne meshai* is also the title of a one-act verse comedy written and published in 1818 by Aksakov's friend, Prince A. A. Shakhovskoi, and first produced, in Saint Petersburg, on 23 September 1818. On Shakhovskoi, see note 77.

92. The town of Karsun (also spelled Korsun) is situated on the Barysh River about fifty miles southwest of Simbirsk.

93. *Acipenser ruthenus;* see Sabaneev, *Ryby Rossii*, 2:483–99, and Berg, *Ryby presnykh vod*, 1:70–76. This relatively small sturgeon of the Black and Caspian Seas is almost extinct today. Highly valued for its yellow roe, the sterlet once provided the fabled "gold" caviar reserved for the table of the Russian royal family.

94. *Esox lucius;* see Sabaneev, *Ryby Rossii*, 1:310–70, and Berg, *Ryby presnykh vod*, 1:458–63.

95. Related terms for *Esox lucius* exist in many Slavic languages. Unlike

Shanskii et al., Vasmer is uncertain about attempts to link *shchúka* with *shchúpat'* (to feel, to touch) and *shchúplyi* (weak, frail, puny); see Fasmer, *Etimologicheskii slovar' russkogo iazyka*, 4:509–10. Given the pike's size, ferocity and robustness, the simple claim that "the fish is so named because of its 'frailness' (*shchúplost'*)" (Shanskii, *Kratkii etimologicheskii slovar' russkogo iazyka*, 387) seems incomprehensible.

96. See Aksakov's full explanation of this alleged phenomenon in Appendix 1, "From New Notes on Sport," and note 149. Aksakov's footnote first appeared in the third edition of *Notes on Fishing* (1856), 259.

97. *Krasnaia ryba* (redfish), as opposed to *bel'* (white). By "sturgeon" (*osëtry*) Aksakov probably intends all members of the genus *Acipenser;* "sevruga" (*sevriúga*) is also called the "stellate sturgeon" (*Acipenser stellatus*); "sheefish" (*belorýbitsa*), also known in North America as "inconnu," refers to *Stenodus leucichthys*. This sense for *krasnaia ryba* is also attested in Aksakov's note for "Orenburg Province" in *A Family Chronicle:* " 'Redfish' refers to beluga, sturgeon, sevruga, ship sturgeon, sheefish, and others." Note that Aksakov also uses the term *krasnaia ryba* later in *Notes on Fishing* (see "Taimen, or Redling") to refer to the Atlantic salmon (*Salmo salar*).

98. From Lëvshin, *A Book for Sportsmen*, 4:486–87. Unfortunately, Aksakov falls short of "perfect exactitude": the title, publication date, and page number are off, and he mistakenly gives "Heilbrock" for Lëvshin's "Heilbronn." I have been unable to identify "Lehmann." The pike's average lifespan is ten years, although rare individuals reach the age of twenty. According to the authoritative *Audobon Society Field Guide to North American Fishes, Whales and Dolphins* (New York: Knopf, 1983), the maximum verified length and weight of North American pike are 52 inches and 46⅛ pounds (402). Berg, however, notes that a Lake Il'men' pike of 75 pounds was reliably reported in 1930, as was a Finnish pike of 56 pounds in 1905; his allusion to reports of pike up to 143 pounds taken from the Lower Dnepr must be viewed with extreme skepticism (Berg, *Ryby presnykh vod*, 1:459). The story of the giant pike at Tsaritsyno is thus a fabrication or the product of a hoax, though it has the ring of historical plausibility: the Tsaritsyno Ponds were created in the late sixteenth century by an impoundment of the Gorodnia River when the surrounding land belonged to Irina Godunova, sister of Tsar Boris Fëdorovich Godunov (r. 1598–1605). Lëvshin then conflates two other famous hoaxes: the nineteen-foot Lake Kaiserwag pike (actually a mounted specimen deceptively reconstructed from the remains of a number of pike; McClane, *McClane's New Standard Fishing Encyclopedia*, 692), and the 267-year-old Mannheim pike, supposedly caught near Heilbronn. This latter story, which is even mentioned by Izaak Walton (Izaak Walton, *The Complete Angler, or The Contemplative Man's Recreation* [London: J. M. Dent, 1993], 99), was first published in Swiss naturalist Conrad Gesner's prefatory letter to Emperor Ferdinand in *Historiae Naturalis Animalium*, book 4, in the 1550s. This specimen, whose alleged bones were kept in Mannheim Cathedral (in Swabia, not

"Swedeland" or Sweden, as Walton and many of his commentators would have us believe; see Walton [1993], 198) was also pieced together from the bodies of many smaller fish (H. G. Seeley, *The Fresh-Water Fishes of Europe* [London: Cassell, 1886], 363). Sabaneev credulously repeats the Mannheim and Tsaritsyno stories as well as accounts of other fraudulent pike (*Ryby Rossii*, 1:312). The Mannheim-pike legend could well have inspired the Tsaritsyno hoaxers, whose tale seems a clever russification of the older German legend. Aksakov's footnote first appeared in the second edition of *Notes on Fishing* (1854), 224–25.

99. See Aksakov's description of what he reckoned to be an even larger specimen in Appendix 1, "Spear-Fishing."

100. See "The Leader."

101. The Voria rises in swampland some sixty-five miles north of Moscow, runs southeast through Abramtsevo (Aksakov's retirement estate), eventually joining the Kliaz'ma River. On the Voria and Abramtsevo, see Appendix 2, "There at last, for all our patience." Aksakov's footnote first appeared in the second edition of *Notes on Fishing* (1854), 227–28.

102. See "Ide."

103. *Aspius aspius;* see Sabaneev, *Ryby Rossii*, 2:415–28, and Berg, *Ryby presnykh vod*, 2:603–6.

104. Vasmer favors a connection between *zhérekh* (used more widely than Aksakov's variant *zhérikh*) and Swedish *gärs* (ruff), though other authorities link the term with the verb *zhrat'* (to eat, to munch); see Fasmer, *Etimologicheskii slovar' russkogo iazyka*, 2:49, and Shanskii, *Kratkii etimologicheskii slovar' russkogo iazyka*, 108. *Sherespër* is usually explained as a combination of *shershávyi* (rough) and *peró* (fin); see Fasmer, 4:430; and Sabaneev, *Ryby Rossii*, 2:416. The application of *kon'* ("steed") to the asp could well have the metaphoric source described by Aksakov. Sabaneev echoes this opinion, and mentions that the asp is also called *kobýla* (mare) in the town of Novaia Ladoga on Lake Ladoga; see *Ryby Rossii*, 2:416.

105. Berg gives the asp's heaviest recorded weight as just over twenty-six pounds (Berg, *Ryby presnykh vod*, 2:603).

106. *Lucioperca lucioperca* (also *Stizostedion lucioperca*); see Sabaneev, *Ryby Rossii*, 1:52–70, and Berg, *Ryby presnykh vod*, 3:1020–28. The originally German term *Zander* (also *Sander*) has supplanted archaic "pike-perch" in modern English-language sources.

107. The zander is not related to the trout, but is instead a very close relative of the North American walleye (*Stizostedion vitreum*) and sauger (*S. canadense*).

108. *Hucho taimen;* see Sabaneev, *Ryby Rossii*, 1:179–89, and Berg, *Ryby presnykh vod*, 1:296–99. Aksakov uses *lokh* (derived from Finnish *lohi*), which in Russian normally denotes the male Atlantic salmon (*Salmo salar*) in spawning colors. A host of details in his description here, however, makes it clear that Aksakov is discussing the taimen (a regional meaning of *lokh*), a species of huchen found from the Kama River drainage eastward through-

out Siberia (Fasmer, *Etimologicheskii slovar' russkogo iazyka*, 2:524; Berg, *Ryby presnykh vod*, 1:205; Ricker, *Russian-English Dictionary*, 133). See also note 38. *Krasúlia*, from *krásnyi* (red), which I render here as "redling," is another regional term for *Hucho taimen*. "During the spawning period," Berg says of the taimen, "almost the entire body becomes copper-red" (*Ryby presnykh vod*, 1:297).

109. Modern taxonomy places the trout (genus *Salmo*) and taimen (genus *Hucho*) together under the family *Salmonidae*. Though members of distinct genera, these two salmonids bear a strong superficial resemblance to one another.

110. See "On Fishing Skill."

111. Rising in Tatarstan near Bugul'ma, the River Zai flows into the Kama River just upstream of where the latter is joined by the Viatka River; the Kama then joins the Volga in what is now the Kuibyshev Reservoir.

112. *Salmo trutta fario*, known in North America as "brown trout"; see Sabaneev, *Ryby Rossii*, 1:194–236, and Berg, *Ryby presnykh vod*, 1:254–58. *Pestrúshka*, which I render as "spottie," derives from Russian *pëstryi* (motley, variegated).

113. The Russian term for trout, *forél'*, is a borrowing of German *Forelle* (see Fasmer, *Etimologicheskii slovar' russkogo iazyka*, 4:203).

114. For a detailed description of spear-fishing for pike from a boat, see Appendix 1, "Spear-Fishing" and "Floodwater and Fishing the Spring Runoff."

115. See "On Fishing Skill."

116. See also Molokhovets's methods for transporting live fish (Toomre, *Classic Russian Cooking*, 534).

117. See "On Fish in General."

118. *Thymallus thymallus;* see Sabaneev, *Ryby Rossii*, 1:237–56, and Berg, *Ryby presnykh vod*, 1:431–35.

119. Sabaneev (*Ryby Rossii*, 1:237) claims that *kutemá* is of Bashkir origin. Modern Chuvash dictionaries have *kutam* (chub) and dialectal *kutan* (gudgeon, ruff), but no similar word for grayling. The standard modern Russian term for grayling is *khárius*, a borrowing from Finnic languages (Fasmer, *Etimologicheskii slovar' russkogo iazyka*, 4:224).

120. Modern taxonomy places the grayling and trout families, *Thymallidae* and *Salmonidae*, under the same suborder (*Salmonoidea*), but these two salmonoids are not as closely related as Aksakov suggests.

121. *Lota lota;* see Sabaneev, *Ryby Rossii*, 1:108–35, and Berg, *Ryby presnykh vod*, 3:943–48.

122. Note that Aksakov chose not to number the chapters on burbot and sheatfish because they are not conventional gamefish, and on crayfish because they are not fish; see the paragraph appended to "Grayling."

123. Molokhovets provided a recipe for burbot soup in the first edition of *Podarok molodym khoziakam* (Toomre, *Classic Russian Cooking*, 588), later added another (625), and gave special notes on using burbot in preparing clear fish soup (143). Like Aksakov, Molokhovets comments on the

tastiness of burbot liver (569). In "A Year in the Country," in *Memoirs,* Aksakov recalls that his family ate so much burbot-liver in winter that they would grow tired of it by Lent.

124. For more details on these and other fish-traps, see Aksakov's comments in Appendix 1, "On Floodwater and Fishing the Spring Runoff."

125. These comments would have instantly reminded Aksakov's readers of his first well-known publication, "The Snowstorm" (1833), which appeared in *Dennitsa na 1834 god* (Moscow: Universitetskaia tipografiia, 1834), 191–207. This semifactual sketch brilliantly described a caravan of grain-haulers caught in a steppe snowstorm (*burán*) outside Orenburg. Aksakov describes the lethal storm's aftermath as follows: "At last, the agitation of the snowy ocean little by little grew quiet, agitation that continues even when the sky sparkles a cloudless blue. Another night passed. The raging wind grew still, and the snows subsided. The steppes looked like a stormy sea that had suddenly turned to ice" (*Sobranie sochinenii,* 2:410). Pushkin's *Kapitanskaia dochka* was influenced by "The Snowstorm"; see Translator's Introduction.

126. Aksakov gives a similarly fond description of burbot-trapping in the Buguruslan River at Christmas in "A Year in the Country," in *Memoirs.*

127. See "Boulters and Trimmers."

128. *Silurus glanis;* see Sabaneev, *Ryby Rossii,* 2:429–59, and Berg, *Ryby presnykh vod,* 2:904–7. This fish is also known in English as "wels," a borrowing from German.

129. Heckel and Kner reported that a poodle and a small boy had been found in the stomach of old sheatfish (Johann Jakob Heckel and Rudolf Kner, *Die Süsswasserfische der ostreichischen Monarchie mit Rücksicht auf die angrenzänder Länder* [Leipzig: 1858], 311).

130. An 1851 letter from Gogol' to Aksakov suggests that the two friends enjoyed eating coulibiac together, and that it was Aksakov's favorite birthday dish; see N. V. Gogol', *Polnoe sobranie sochinenii* (Leningrad: Izdatel'stvo Akademii Nauk SSSR, 1952), 14:250. For Molokhovets's coulibiac, see Toomre, *Classic Russian Cooking,* 280.

131. Small, lobster-like crustaceans of the genus *Astacus.*

132. See "The Bait."

133. See also Sabaneev's detailed discussion of these methods in *Ryby Rossii,* 1:341–44.

134. Aksakov traced his fear of water to a disastrous ferry-crossing on the Kama River while he was on his way back to school in Kazan' in the autumn of 1803: "I'd been frightened down to my very soul, and for the rest of my life was unable to look upon a large river with equanimity, even during calm weather" ("School [Second Period]," in *Memoirs*).

135. First published as the opening piece in Aksakov's *A Sportsman's Stories and Memoirs on Various Kinds of Sport* (Moscow: Tipografiia L. Stepanovoi, 1855), 17–31. The first two paragraphs contain a description that would be used later, in altered form, for an account of the Belaia's thawing in "Winter in Ufa," *Childhood Years of a Bagrov Grandson.*

136. Possibly a reference to Aksakov's "Zamechaniia i nabliudeniia okhotnika brat' griby," first published in *Vestnik estestvennykh nauk*, no. 6 (1856): 162–71. Aksakov had provided the following footnote in "A Year in the Country," in *Memoirs* (written 1853–55): "I never imagined then that mushrooms would be one of the most constant pleasures of my declining years. In gratitude for this I was long ago taken with the idea—and haven't yet given it up—of writing a little book on mushrooms and the pleasure afforded by gathering them."

137. Dal' gives the pole's length as twenty-one feet (Dal', *Tolkovyi slovar'*, 2:1145).

138. In "A Year in the Country," in *Memoirs*, Aksakov had included an account, very similar to the reminiscence given in this paragraph, of springtime fish-trapping below a large mill-dam on the Buguruslan at Aksakovo.

139. First published in *Moskvitianin* 5 (1854), Smes', 159ff., then re-printed as the sixth item in Aksakov's *A Sportsman's Stories and Memoirs on Various Kinds of Sport*, 125–42. For spearing and jack-lighting, see also Sabaneev, *Ryby Rossii*, 2:118–21.

140. See note 134.

141. See note 98.

142. See "On Fish in General."

143. First published in Aksakov's *A Sportsman's Stories and Memoirs on Various Kinds of Sport* as the first item in the section called "Miscellaneous: Little Sporting Stories," 195–208. In *Childhood Years of a Bagrov Grandson*, we learn that Aksakov was exposed to superstitions and omens by his nurse at a very early age ("Successive Recollections"), and that as a boy he firmly believed in premonitions ("The Winter Road to Bagrovo").

144. On the Russian mermaid (*rusálka*), see Linda J. Ivanits, *Russian Folk Belief* (Armonk: M. E. Sharpe, 1989), 75–82, 185–89.

145. First published in Aksakov's *A Sportsman's Stories and Memoirs on Various Kinds of Sport* as the third item in "Miscellaneous: Little Sporting Stories," 214–22.

146. See "On Fishing Skill."

147. The village of Repekhovo is known today as "Repikhovo."

148. First published as the new final item in "Miscellaneous: Little Sporting Stories," in the second edition of Aksakov's *A Sportsman's Stories and Memoirs on Various Kinds of Sport* (Moscow: Tipografiia L. Stepanovoi, 1856), 246–50.

149. See "Pike." Modern research has discredited the widespread belief that pike shed their teeth annually; they instead lose and replace teeth constantly, year-round (see McClane, *McClane's New Standard Fishing Encyclopedia*, 694).

150. N. A. Varpakhovskii (see Translator's Introduction) added the following note on this section: "These 'white butterflies' are probably mayflies (*Ephemeroptera*). I myself have chanced to observe the collection of these insects for angling on the River Sura. The rumor that 'brooms were about'

(this is the local name for these mayflies) gathered a great many fishermen on the riverbanks and here and there they started small bonfires into which the mayflies flew to their deaths in countless numbers" (S. T. Aksakov, *Polnoe sobranie sochinenii* [Saint Petersburg: 1886], 5:195).

151. First published in *Zhurnal okhoty* 1, no. 1 (January 1858): 1–8, as the opening piece in the inaugural issue. "I will not name the contributors," editor Georg Min remarked in the general preface to his new journal, "who have indicated their willingness to supply articles, for the reader will learn of them firsthand as future issues are published. I consider it, however, my grateful obligation to mention S. T. Aksakov, who, thanks to his talent, has deservedly gained the full esteem and sympathy of the public" (vii). For his part, Aksakov published a sparkling review of *Zhurnal okhoty* [Sporting journal] in the important monthly *Russkii vestnik:* "As an old sportsman, and as a person who has written about sport, I consider it my duty to express my full gratitude to Mr. Min. . . . I would be very happy if these words directed the attention of my sporting brethren to Mr. Min's publication and prompted them to participate in *Sporting Journal,* which truly deserves the complete endorsement of all educated readers" (18, [1858], book 1, "Sovremennaia letopis'," 66–69). Aksakov had only two suggestions: "1) that the issues be thicker, and 2) that they consist of articles about mainly Russian sport." In the January 1858 issue of *Sporting Journal,* Aksakov's "A Few Words on Angling in Early Spring and Late Autumn" was immediately followed by his poem, "31 October 1856" (see Appendix 2); another Aksakov poem, "17 October" (see Appendix 2), appeared in the next month's issue (vol. 1, no. 2, pp. 139–40). Aksakov also published two letters to the editor in *Sporting Journal,* one of which, on pike-fishing, appears as the next item in Appendix 1.

152. *Parus ater,* ordinarily known as "coal tit" in English.

153. See note 2.

154. First published in *Zhurnal okhoty* 2, no. 10 (October 1858): 220–21. See note 151.

155. See note 3.

156. In the late 1810s or early 1820s, Aksakov sent this poem, which was never published in this form in his lifetime, from Orenburg Province to his sister Nadezhda Timofeevna in Saint Petersburg. "Our harvest has completely failed," he wrote in the accompanying letter, "and there is even hunger hereabouts, so our place seems all the more sad. I'd intended to write some verses to my homeland, but, when I saw that they were unjust, decided to scrap them." Mashinskii thus suggests that "There is my homeland" is a fragment from a much larger unfinished poem (*Sobranie sochinenii,* 3:771). In the end, Aksakov included a variant of this poem ("Wondrous region, and blest") in the lyrical "Orenburg Province" chapter of *A Family Chronicle.*

157. Among the Romans, a legendary mountain range in the far north, possibly the Urals.

158. See Aksakov's explanation for the genesis of this poem (in "Chub").

"The Fisherman's Woe" is dated 1824, and was published in *Moskovskii vestnik*, part 1 (1829): 149–55. Aksakov's poem is a deliberate tribute to N. I. Gnedich's idyll "The Fishermen" (published in 1822), and imitates its precursor's meter (amphibrachic pentameter), basic structure (conversation between two fishermen), and dramatis personae (Younger Fisherman and Elder Fisherman). As V. E. Vatsuro points out, Aksakov's task in "The Fisherman's Woe" was "to seek out new possibilities for the genre of the idyll in that sphere of sensations and emotions which gives people direct communion with nature—sport, fishing. In other words, he aims not to create an idyllic 'character,' but an idyllic 'situation'" (V. E. Vatsuro, "Russkaia idilliia v epokhu romantizma," in *Russkii romantizm* [Leningrad: Izdatel'stvo Nauka, Leningradskoe otdelenie, 1978], 133). "The Fisherman's Woe," Aksakov's first published piscatory work, is thus an important Romantic experiment in transfusing the details of Russian folk culture—*narodnost'*—into the classical genre of the eclogue.

159. Aksakov refers to the dung-beetle grub known as "eel" near Moscow; see "The Bait."

160. From Aksakov's Moscow album entitled "Semeinye stikhotvoreniia, pisannye na raznye sluchai do 1841 goda" (*Sobranie sochinenii*, 3:775). The poem, unpublished in Aksakov's lifetime, is addressed to his son Grigorii (1820–91), whose nickname in the family was "Grisha."

161. Unpublished in Aksakov's lifetime, this poem describes his search for a new estate in the environs of Moscow in 1843, when the author decided he could no longer make the nearly seven-hundred-mile drive to his Orenburg Province property each year. See the companion poem, "There at last, for all our patience."

162. "Kostia" is Konstantin Sergeevich Aksakov (1817–60), the writer's oldest son. In 1843, when his father wrote this poem, Konstantin was a graduate student at Moscow University working on his master's thesis, "Lomonosov v istorii russkoi literatury i russkogo iazyka"; he was already a widely published critic, poet, and proponent of Slavophilism.

163. Unpublished in Aksakov's lifetime; from the manuscript album "Semeinye stikhi."

164. From "Family Verses"; first published in N. V. Polenova, *Abramtsevo: Vospominaniia* (Moscow: Sabashnikovy, 1922), 6. The poem, which acts as a conclusion to the peevish "Believe me, there's no greater torment," describes Abramtsevo, a beautiful country estate overlooking the River Voria (see note 101) some forty miles northeast of the center of Moscow. It was here that Aksakov wrote his late prose (including *Notes on Fishing*) and spent his final years entertaining the likes of Turgenev and Gogol'. Abramtsevo was purchased in 1870 by industrialist Savva Mamontov (1841–1918), who turned the estate into an important fin-de-siècle colony for Russian artists and musicians. Abramtsevo has been a museum since 1918, and the Voria's lazily flowing ponds still entice wayfaring Muscovite anglers.

165. Abramtsevo has an "Upper Pond" situated above the Voria on the same elevated ground occupied by the manor house.

166. Unpublished in Aksakov's lifetime, this poem is sketched in pencil on the reverse of a draft letter to Gogol' dated 26 July 1847.

167. Mikhail Aleksandrovich Dmitriev (1796–1866): critic, poet, translator, and memoirist; a friend of Aksakov starting in 1824. Dmitriev is remembered today chiefly for his "classicist" attacks on Prince Pëtr Viazemskii and Aleksandr Griboedov in the late 1820s. This poem's complete text was never published during Aksakov's lifetime. The present version, which bears a later date than that of the epigraph for *Notes on Fishing*, is taken from the manuscript album "Semeinye stikhi." Aksakov first tried to publish the last eleven lines as an epigraph for the second edition of his *Notes of an Orenburg-Province Hunter* (Moscow, 1852), but was refused permission by the censor because two lines ("I venture into nature's world, / The world of serenity and freedom") were deemed subversive. Two years later, however, Aksakov was granted permission to use all eleven lines as the epigraph for the second edition of *Notes on Fishing* (Moscow, 1854); see Translator's Introduction.

168. First published in *Zhurnal okhoty* 1, no. 1 (January 1858): 9. See note 151.

169. First published in *Zhurnal okhoty* 1, no. 2 (February 1858): 139–40 (see note 151). Apollon Nikolaevich Maikov (1821–97): a poet and passionate fisherman, famous for his luminous nature lyrics. In 1855, Maikov wrote his 194-line "Fishing," published in *Otechestvennye zapiski*, no. 3 (1856): 287ff. Maikov's poem bore a dedication to some of the most illustrious fishermen-writers in Russian history: "To S. T. Aksakov, N. A. Maikov, A. N. Ostrovskii, I. A. Goncharov, S. S. Dudyshkin, A. I. Khalanskii, and all who understand the subject." In 1857, Aksakov sent "17 October" to Maikov in reply. The following note, in the hand of Aksakov's son Ivan (1823–86), accompanies a manuscript copy of "17 October": "This poem was also written just before he moved from Abramtsevo to Moscow for the winter, but Sergei Timofeevich was never again to return to Abramtsevo. Having fallen ill during the autumn while still in the country, he ailed all winter, and in the summer of 1858 was forced to live in Petrovskii Park in order to be a bit closer to the doctor. On 30 April 1859, he died. These lines are thus a final farewell to his beloved Abramtsevo, a farewell filled with sorrowful forebodings" (*Sobranie sochinenii*, 3:778).

# BIBLIOGRAPHY

Aksakov, Sergei Timofeevich. *A Family Chronicle*. Translated by M. C. Beverley. New York: Dutton, 1961.

———. *Istoriia moego znakomstva s Gogolem* [The story of my acquaintance with Gogol']. Literaturnye pamiatniki. Moscow: Izdatel'stvo Nauka, 1960.

———. *Rasskazy i vospominaniia okhotnika o raznykh okhotakh* [A sportsman's stories and memoirs on various kinds of sport]. Moscow: Tipografiia L. Stepanovoi, 1855.

———. *Rasskazy i vospominaniia okhotnika o raznykh okhotakh* [A sportsman's stories and memoirs on various kinds of sport]. 2d ed. Moscow: Tipografiia L. Stepanovoi, 1856.

———. *A Russian Gentleman* [translation of *Semeinaia khronika*]. Translated by J. D. Duff. The World's Classics. New York: Oxford University Press, 1982.

———. *A Russian Schoolboy* [translation of *Vospominaniia*]. Translated by J. D. Duff. The World's Classics. New York: Oxford University Press, 1983.

———. *Sobranie sochinenii v chetyrëkh tomakh* [Collected works in four volumes]. Edited by S. I. Mashinskii. Moscow: Gosudarstvennoe izdatel'stvo khudozhestvennoi literatury, 1955–56.

———. *Years of Childhood* [translation of *Detskie gody Bagrova-vnuka*]. Translated by J. D. Duff. New York: Longmans, Green, 1916.

———. *Years of Childhood* [translation of *Detskie gody Bagrova-vnuka*]. Translated by Alec Brown. New York: Vintage, 1960.

———. "Zamechaniia i nabliudeniia okhotnika brat' griby" [Remarks and observations of a mushroom-gatherer]. *Vestnik estestvennykh nauk* [Natural sciences herald], no. 6 (1856): 162–71.

———. *Zapiski ob uzhen'e* [Notes on angling]. Moscow: V Tipografii Nikolaia Stepanova, 1847.

———. *Zapiski ob uzhen'e ryby* [Notes on fishing]. 2d ed. Moscow: V Tipografii L. Stepanovoi, 1854.

———. *Zapiski ob uzhen'e ryby* [Notes on fishing]. With engravings, and an afterword by K. F. Rul'e. 3d ed. Moscow: V Universitetskoi Tipografii, 1856.

———. *Zapiski ob uzhen'e ryby* [Notes on fishing]. In *Polnoe sobranie sochinenii* [Complete works], vol. 5. With notes by K. F. Rul'e and N. A. Varpakhovskii, and engravings. Saint Petersburg, 1886.

———. *Zapiski ruzheinogo okhotnika Orenburgskoi gubernii* [Notes of an Orenburg-Province hunter]. Moscow: V Tipografii L. Stepanovoi, 1852.

Ashukin, N. S., and M. G. Ashukina. *Krylatye slova* [Quotations]. 4th ed. Moscow: Khudozhestvennaia literatura, 1988.

Avdeev, M. V. "Dorozhnye zametki: 1854" [Travel notes: 1854]. *Biblioteka dlia chteniia* [Library for reading] 144 (1857).

———. "Poezdka na kumys" [A journey on *Kumiss*]. *Otechestvennye zapiski* [Notes of the fatherland], nos. 10–12 (1852).

Berg, Leo S. *Freshwater Fishes of the U.S.S.R. and Adjacent Countries* [English translation of *Ryby presnykh vod SSSR i sopredel'nykh stran* by Omry Ronen], 3 vols. 4th ed., revised and enlarged. Jerusalem: S. Monson, 1962–65.

———. *Ryby presnykh vod SSSR i sopredel'nykh stran* [Freshwater fishes of the USSR and contiguous countries]. 3 vols. 4th ed., revised and enlarged. Moscow: Izdatel'stvo Akademii Nauk SSSR, 1948–49.

Chernykh, P. Ia. *Istoriko-etimologicheskii slovar' sovremennogo russkogo iazyka* (Historical-etymological dictionary of the modern Russian language]. 2 vols. 2d ed. Moscow: Russkii iazyk, 1994.

Chvanov, Mikhail. *Aksakovskie mesta v Bashkirii* [Aksakov's Bashkiriia]. Ufa: Bashkirskoe knizhnoe izdatel'stvo, 1976.

Dal', V. I. *Tolkovyi slovar' zhivogo velikorusskogo iazyka* [Explanatory dictionary of the living Great-Russian language]. 4 vols. 3d revised and enlarged ed. Saint Petersburg: Tovarishchestvo M. O. Vol'f, 1903–9.

Durkin, Andrew R. *Sergei Aksakov and Russian Pastoral.* New Brunswick: Rutgers University Press, 1983.

Fasmer, M. *Etimologicheskii slovar' russkogo iazyka* [Russian translation of Max Vasmer's *Russisches etymologisches Wörterbuch* by O. N. Trubachëv]. 4 vols. Moscow: Izdatel'stvo Progress, 1964–73.

Gogol', N. V. *Polnoe sobranie sochinenii* [Complete works]. 14 vols. Leningrad: Izdatel'stvo Akademii Nauk SSSR, 1938–52.

———. *Vechera na khutore bliz Dikan'ki* [Evenings on a farm near Dikan'ka]. Vol. 1. Saint Petersburg: Tipografiia Departamenta narodnogo prosveshcheniia, 1831.

Gornfel'd, A. G. "Okhotnich'i sochineniia S. T. Aksakova" [Aksakov's sporting works]. In *Sobranie sochinenii* [Collected works], by S. T. Aksakov, 5:3–10. Saint Petersburg: Tipolitografiia Tovarishchestva Prosveshchenie, 1910.

Hawker, Peter. *Instructions to Young Sportsmen.* 11th ed. London: Longman, Brown, Green, Longmans and Roberts, 1859.

Heckel, Johann Jakob, and Rudolf Kner. *Die Süsswasserfische der ostreichischen Monarchie mit Rücksicht auf die angrenzänder Länder.* Leipzig: W. Englmann, 1858.

Ivanits, Linda J. *Russian Folk Belief.* Armonk, N.Y.: M. E. Sharpe, 1989.

Khomiakov, A. S. "Sergei Timofeevich Aksakov." First published in *Russkaia beseda* [Russian conversation], no. 3 (1859): i–viii. Quoted from A. S. Khomiakov, *O starom i o novom: Stat'i i ocherki* [On old and new: articles and essays]. Biblioteka "Liubiteliam rossiiskoi slovesnosti": Iz literaturnogo naslediia. Moscow: Sovremennik, 1988.

Koval', N. "Pisateli-rybolovy: A. N. Maikov i ego druz'ia" [Fishermen-writers: A. N. Maikov and his friends]. *Rybovodstvo i rybolovstvo* [Fish culture and fishing], no. 3 (May–June 1961): 51–53.

Lëvshin, V. A., trans. and adapter. *Kniga dlia okhotnikov do zverinoi i ptichei lovli, takzhe do ruzheinoi strel'by i soderzhaniia pevchikh ptits* [A book for sportsmen interested in animals and other game, as well as in shooting and the keeping of songbirds]. Vol. 4. Moscow: V Tipografii S. Selivanovskogo, 1819.

———. "O prudakh, sazhelkakh, rvakh, zavedenii ryby, torgovle ryboiu i proch" [On ponds, pens, ditches, raising fish, trading in fish, and so forth]. In *Vseobshchee i polnoe domovodstvo* [The universal and complete art of housekeeping]. Vol. 4. Moscow: V Universitetskoi Tipografii, 1795.

———. "O rybnoi lovle" [On fishing]. In *Vseobshchee i polnoe domovodstvo* [The universal and complete art of housekeeping]. Vol. 4. Moscow: V Universitetskoi Tipografii, 1795.

———. *Sovershennyi eger', ili Znanie o vsekh prinadlezhashchikh k ruzheinoi i prochei okhote* [The perfect huntsman, or knowledge of all the appurtenances of field sport with guns and other means]. Saint Petersburg, 1779.

Liger, Louis. *La nouvelle maison rustique, ou Économie rurale, pratique et générale de tous les biens de campagne.* 11th ed. Vol. 2. Paris: Chez les Libraires Associés, 1790.

*The Lubok: Russian Folk Pictures (17th to 19th Century).* Edited by Alla Sytova. Leningrad: Aurora Art Publishers, 1984.

*McClane's New Standard Fishing Encyclopedia and International Angling Guide.* Edited by A. J. McClane. Enlarged and revised ed. New York: Holt, Rinehart and Winston, 1974.

*Medieval Russia's Epics, Chronicles and Tales.* Edited by Serge A. Zenkovsky. Rev. ed. New York: Dutton, 1974.

Paustovskii, K. G. *Sobranie sochinenii v shesti tomakh* [Collected works in six volumes]. Vol. 6. Moscow: Gosudarstvennoe izdatel'stvo khudozhestvennoi literatury, 1968.

Pokrovskii, V. I., ed. *Sergei Timofeevich Aksakov: Ego zhizn' i tvorchestvo* [Sergei Timofeevich Aksakov: His life and work]. 2d ed. Moscow: Sklad v knizhnom magazine V. Spiridonova i A. Mikhailova, 1912.

Pushkin, A. S. *Kapitanskaia dochka* [The captain's daughter]. Literaturnye pamiatniki. Leningrad: Izdatel'stvo Nauka, Leningradskoe otdelenie, 1985.

Ransome, Arthur. "Aksakov on Fishing." In *Rod and Line.* London: Jonathan Cape, 1929.

Ricker, W. E. *Russian-English Dictionary for Students of Fisheries and Aquatic Biology* (Bulletin 183 of the Fisheries Research Board of Canada). Ottawa: Fisheries Research Board of Canada, 1973.

Rovinskii, D. A. *Russkie narodnye kartinki* [Russian folk pictures]. 5 vols. Saint Petersburg: Tipografiia Imperatorskoi Akademii Nauk, 1881.

Sabaneev, L. P. *Rybolovnyi kalendar'*, *Trudy po rybolovstvu* [The fisherman's calendar, works on fishing]. Moscow: Terra, 1992.

———. *Ryby Rossii: Zhizn' i lovlia (uzhen'e) nashikh presnovodnykh ryb* [Fishes of Russia: the life and capture (angling) of our freshwater fishes]. 2 vols. Moscow: Terra, 1992.

Shanskii, N. M., V. V. Ivanov, and T. V. Shanskaia. *Kratkii etimologicheskii slovar' russkogo iazyka* [A short etymological dictionary of the Russian language]. Moscow: Uchpedgiz, 1961.

Shklovskii, Viktor. *Chulkov i Lëvshin* [Chulkov and Lëvshin]. Leningrad: Izdatel'stvo pisatelei v Leningrade, 1933.

*Sobranie pisem Tsaria Alekseia Mikhailovicha, s prilozheniem ulozheniia o sokol'nichem puti* [Collected letters of Tsar Aleksei Mikhailovich, with rule of the falconer's way]. Edited by P. I. Bartenev. Moscow: Pëtr Bartenev, 1856.

Seeley, H. G. *The Fresh-Water Fishes of Europe*. London: Cassell, 1886.

Soloukhin, Vladimir. "Chistaia kliuchevaia voda" [Clear springwater]. In *Volshebnaia palochka* [The magic wand]. Moscow: Moskovskii rabochii, 1983.

T'iunkin, K., ed. *F. M. Dostoevskii v vospominaniiakh sovremennikov* [F. M. Dostoevskii in the memoirs of contemporaries]. 2 vols. Moscow: Khudozhestvennaia literatura, 1990.

Toomre, Joyce. *Classic Russian Cooking: Elena Molokhovets' A Gift to Young Housewives*. Bloomington: Indiana University Press, 1992.

Turgenev. I. S. *Polnoe sobranie sochinenii i pisem v dvadtsati vos'mi tomakh: Sochineniia* [Complete works and letters in twenty-eight volumes: works]. 15 vols. Moscow: Izdatel'stvo Nauka, 1960–68.

Vengerov, S. A. "Sergei Timofeevich Aksakov." In *Kritiko-biograficheskii slovar' russkikh pisatelei i uchënykh (ot nachala russkoi obrazovannosti do nashikh dnei)* [Critical-biographical dictionary of Russian writers and scholars (from the beginning of education in Russia to the present)], vol. 1, nos. 1–21. Saint Petersburg: Semënovskaia Tipolitografiia I. Efrona, 1889.

Vinogradov, V. V. *Istoriia slov* [The history of words]. Moscow: Tolk, 1994.

Walton, Izaak. *The Complete Angler, or The Contemplative Man's Recreation*. Edited and with an Introduction by Jonquil Bevan. London: J. M. Dent, 1993.

Walton, Izaak, and Charles Cotton. *The Compleat Angler*. Edited by John Buxton. With an Introduction by John Buchan. The World's Classics. Oxford: Oxford University Press, 1982.